Discovering
Aberdeenshire

Discovering
Aberdeenshire

ROBERT SMITH

JOHN DONALD PUBLISHERS LTD
EDINBURGH

To Rachel, Daniel, Hannah, Katy and Robb, so
that they may one day discover their roots

ISBN 0 85976 229 7

Phototypesetting by Newtext Composition Ltd., Glasgow
Printed in Great Britain by Bell & Bain Ltd., Glasgow

Acknowledgements

A great many people have helped in the making of this book. Among them are the North-east folk whose lives are mirrored in these pages. My thanks are due to them for sharing their stories and their memories.

I am grateful to the staff of the Local History Department of Aberdeen Central Library, who have been unfailingly courteous and helpful. The Central Library provided a number of historic photographs.

Invaluable assistance was also given by the North East Scotland Library Service at Oldmeldrum and by the local section of Aberdeen University Library.

Finally, a word of thanks to my wife Sheila, whose encouragement and criticism kept me on the right course during my journey of discovery through Aberdeenshire.

Contents

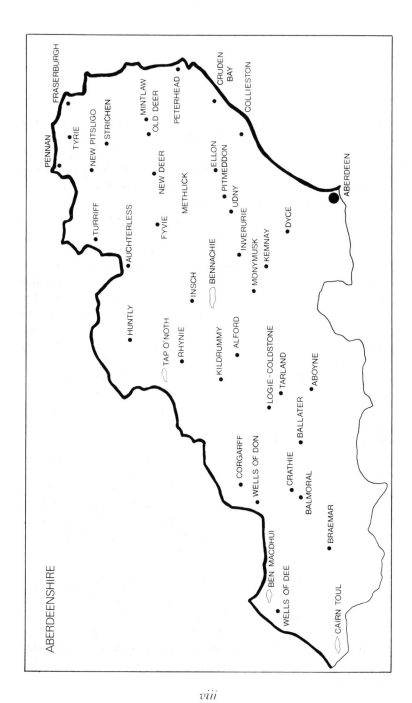

ABERDEENSHIRE

Introduction

Aberdeenshire was swallowed up by Grampion Region in 1975 and split into a series of hybrid districts with unfamiliar names like Banff-Buchan and Kincardine-Deeside. Despite the reorganisation of local government, however, this great elbow of land covering more than a million and a quarter acres of North-east Scotland is still known to most people by the old names – Deeside, Donside, and Buchan, with the city of Aberdeen as the base.

These are the areas into which this book is divided. It begins in the Silver City, sweeps up Royal Deeside, explores the hidden valleys of the Don, and takes a look at Buchan, the 'land o' plenty'. It is a book about people as well as places, for before you begin to know an area you must know the folk who live in it. Their story is told in the light of oil-boom developments, through their music and literature, and against the background of a rich and often turbulent history.

You can walk the grey granite corridors of Aberdeen, meet the Bard of Corgarff, explore the old smuggling villages along the Aberdeenshire coast, climb the Garioch's favourite mountain and ask 'Foo aul's Bennachie?' and tap your feet to the music of the fiddles of Buchan.

The coming of North Sea oil wrought great changes to Aberdeenshire, not outwardly, but in terms of progress and prosperity. Almost overnight, Aberdeen became the oil capital of Europe; thousands of new jobs were created and colonies of American and Dutch oilmen settled in the city. Distance became irrelevant; a modern, expanding airport put the North-east within easy reach of London and Europe, and Dyce became a major helicopter base.

But some say that the North-east has changed little in the past two decades . . . that Aberdeen is still a big 'village', where everybody knows everybody else; that the broad North-east tongue is still very much alive, despite dire warnings that it is in its death throes (there are more people writing in Doric to-day than ever before), and that the folk are as canny, friendly, couthy and wise as they ever were.

The oil industry has gone through a period of decline in recent years, but indications are that the upturn is on its way. One thing is certain – oil will be with us for a long time to come. That means that more and more people will be drawn to Aberdeenshire, not only to work, but to spend their leisure-time, to ski and walk in the hills, to enjoy the beauty of the Dee and Don valleys, and to wander through towns and villages that have an unmistakeable character of their own.

This book is not a tourist guide, but it will be a useful guide to the many people, visitors and local folk alike, who want to discover Aberdeenshire. It would be impossible in a work of this kind to mention every community, so the aim has been to give a broad picture of an area that is fascinatingly diverse, a land that has been described as self-contained and self-sufficient, but never inward-looking or insular.

ABERDEEN

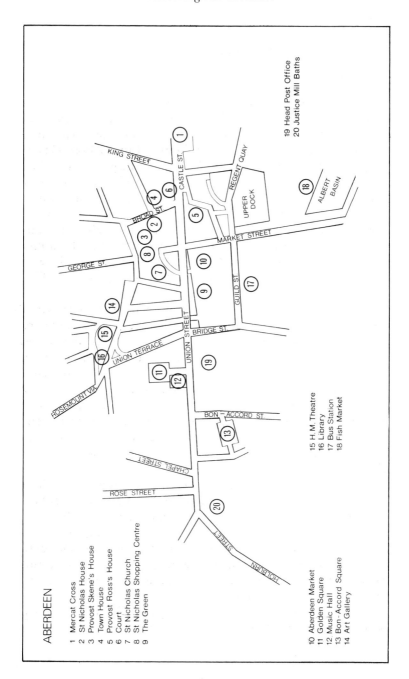

ABERDEEN

1 Mercat Cross
2 St Nicholas House
3 Provost Skene's House
4 Town House
5 Provost Ross's House
6 Court
7 St Nicholas Church
8 St Nicholas Shopping Centre
9 The Green

10 Aberdeen Market
11 Golden Square
12 Music Hall
13 Bon-Accord Square
14 Art Gallery

15 H.M. Theatre
16 Library
17 Bus Station
18 Fish Market

19 Head Post Office
20 Justice Mill Baths

Chapter 1
Granite and Roses

Aberdeen is a city of granite and roses. The granite has always been there, but it is only in recent years that the city has enhanced its image by sticking a rose in its lapel. The man behind the metamorphosis from Granite City to Rose City is David Welch, the director of leisure and recreation, who has smothered almost every acre of waste ground in the city with flowers. The British Association of Rose Growers dubbed him the Rose Crusader. Under his guidance, Aberdeen won so many Britain in Bloom competitions that it was debarred from taking part in the contest, but it sneaked back into the arena and in 1987 carried off the trophy for the tenth time. Now it has started up a Floral Trail and is promoting itself as 'The Flower of Scotland'.

It is claimed, with some justification, that Aberdeen's parks are among the most beautiful in Britain. Roses predominate. The Duthie Park, whose Winter Gardens are world famous, is well-known for its 'Mountain of Roses', a colourful array of over 100,000 bushes. Hazlehead, the largest park in the city, has a rose garden, and it is an odd coincidence that before the policies were bought by Aberdeen Town Council they were owned by the Roses of Hazlehead. The Roses were prominent ship-owners in Aberdeen and the founder of the family, William Rose, lived in the mansion house at Hazlehead from 1775 to 1834.

The old tag of Silver City by the Sea has been pushed into the background by this explosion of rose petals, not to mention a rainbow trail of daffodils and crocuses as you enter Aberdeen from the south in the springtime. Here, sweeping down the broad carriageway to the Bridge of Dee, the city suddenly opens up in front of you, grey and glittering, but it is the daffodils that catch your eye. In summer, a ribbon of roses leads you up Anderson Drive, the ring-road, which was the perimeter of the city until it was engulfed by new housing estates, creeping westwards.

About two miles north of the Bridge of Dee, in the Stocket lands gifted to Aberdeen by Robert the Bruce, there is a spot still shown on Ordnance Survey maps as the Hill of Rubislaw. It would make better sense if they re-named it the Hole of Rubislaw, for it has been described as 'the biggest granite hole in Europe'. Two centuries have passed since workmen began to chop off the top of the hill and dig downwards. Now, all that remains of it is a yawning 500ft. chasm. It was from this granite womb that Aberdeen emerged. From it came the stones that gave the city its storeyed tenements, its mansion houses, its kirks and cathedrals, its granite statues – and even its tombstones.

The thought of grey granite from birth to death appalled Lewis Grassic Gibbon. He walked through Allenvale Cemetery, 'where the dead of Aberdeen lie in serried lines under immense granitic monuments', and was moved to 'wondering horror'. 'Granite, grey granite', he wrote, 'in birth, in puberty, adolescence, grey granite encasing the bridal room, grey granite the rooms of blear-eyed old age . . . and even in death they are not divided'.

He would have been fascinated by the current rash of roses, as well as by the Aberdeen Tourist Board's attempts to turn the city into a national 'Flower' centre. I wonder what he would have thought of the assertion that Nellfield Cemetery is probably the finest rose garden in Britain. In recent years, there has been a good deal of discussion over what should happen to Union Terrace Gardens, which were laid out in 1877. Some people would like to see them raised to the level of the adjoining streets, with car parking facilities provided for hard-pressed motorists, but traditionalists have manned the barriers against such vandalism.

In one of its publicity hand-outs, the Tourist Board describes Union Terrace Gardens as 'a splendid green oasis in Aberdeen city centre'. It draws attention to the floral clock in the garden, the city crest laid out in flowers, and the tall trees 'waving idly in the gentle breeze'. Lewis Grassic Gibbon certainly never quenched his aesthetic thirst at this oasis. He wrote disparagingly about Union Terrace and 'an attempt at a public Garden'. 'The flowers', he said, 'come up and take one glance at the lour of solicitors' offices which man Union Terrace, and

Where the flowers always bloom in the Rose City ... an attendant arranges a display inside the Winter Gardens in the Duthie Park. The Winter Gardens was Scotland's top visitor attraction in 1987, marking up a total of 1,130,000 visitors.

scramble back into the earth again, seeking the Antipodes'. Gibbon wasn't alone in chipping at Aberdeen's granite image, for it is a chameleon stone that comes from the Hill of Rubislaw. It is at the mercy of the weather, dour and depressing one moment, bright and sparkling the next, and always at its best when warmed by the sun after a shower of rain.

It was once said cynically that it was only suitable for banks and tombs, yet it is known throughout the world. The streets of London may not be paved with gold, but at one time they were paved with granite setts or 'cassies' from Aberdeen. There were 600 sett-makers in the city at the end of the eighteenth century and many of them went out into the world to teach their craft to others. That was the start of it. Later, granite from Rubislaw, as well as from other North-east quarries (see Chapter 6), began to shape the Granite City, as well as bridges and buildings in other major cities.

One Aberdeen granite merchant, however, left more than a legacy of stone to the city. His name was Alexander Macdonald and he bequeathed to Aberdeen Art Gallery an important collection of nineteenth-century paintings – the Macdonald Collection – which still hangs in the gallery today, more than eighty years later, showing what a wealthy 'artisan' did for Art in Aberdeen. Interestingly, it was one of Macdonald's friends, John Forbes White, a local meal miller and a well-known patron of the arts, who said that he found 'more real taste and discrimination and feeling for Art among artisans than among any of the better classes'.

Macdonald began collecting in the 1860s and '70s and was encouraged by White, who was the driving force behind the development of Aberdeen Art Gallery and its Sculpture Gallery. His father, Alexander Macdonald, senior, had already made his mark, but in a different way. He began life as a stonemason in Perthshire, but when he set up in business as a mason in Aberdeen he became one of the pioneers of the granite trade. He supplied granite for the building of the Imperial Opera House in Paris and the Town Hall in Brisbane. He invented machinery for the dressing and polishing of granite, built up a flourishing business, and when he died in 1860 left his fortune to his art-loving son.

Rubislaw stopped producing granite in 1971, when it was no longer commercially viable. Today, the quarry is encased in a Berlin Wall of wire, a high barrier with huge DANGER signs spaced at intervals around it. At various points along the wire you can catch a glimpse of the rock face. It is a far cry from the days when people were able to stand on a shaky wooden platform on top of the quarry and peer down into Rubislaw's murky depths. Even accepting that there are dangers (and the owners may be haunted by the memory of a student crossing the quarry on a blondin wire as a charities week stunt), it seems sad that Aberdeen has been shut off from its granite roots in this fashion.

The question, of course, is what to do with a 500ft hole. There have been plenty of suggestions, one being to use it as a rubbish dump, another to build a viewing platform and a restaurant and turn the quarry into a tourist attraction. Consultants commissioned by Aberdeen Construction Group, owners of the land, suggested using laser beams or holograms to project a laser image of the city on to the floor of the quarry.

This would be a neat piece of symbolism ... Aberdeen rising from the depths of Rubislaw. Less spectacular, but more likely to appeal to citizens who suffer from vertigo, is a proposal to reconstruct an old-style granite yard and a museum where granite souvenirs could be sold to visitors. It is, to say the least, surprising that Aberdeen has a maritime museum but no granite museum.

Back in the Thirties, when people came out from the city to look at the quarry, they ended up strolling down the leafy dens of Rubislaw to see how the other half lived. The city's top people had their homes there, and still do, cocooned from the rest of the world by wealth and status, their large, dignified mansion houses a showcase for the stone hewn from the quarry on their doorsteps. A. Alvarez, who wrote *Offshore*, the story of North Sea oil, spoke to Sir Maitland Mackie, former Lord Lieutenant of Aberdeenshire, about prosperity and granite. Mike Mackie, whose broad North-east tongue has been little affected by commercial and social success, said that there must have been plenty of money in Aberdeen long before the oil boom, otherwise 'they couldna' hae built these nice granite houses'. He himself lived in a 'nice granite house' in Rubislaw Den North before moving to Banchory.

There was a Glenburnie Distillery in Rubislaw at one time, not far from the toll house, which is now a shop fronting Queen's Road, and a house in Rubislaw Den North carries the name Glenburnie. When the distillery went out of existence in 1857, the buildings were used by Aberdeen's pioneering photographer, George Washington Wilson. Near here was a croft with the odd name of Hirpletillim. William Carnie, a local poet, wrote about 'Daavit Drain o' Hirpletillim', who lived 'near Robslaw quarries':

> Storm nor stour ne'er dang could kill him,
> Up wi' the lark – fae morn till dark
> Was heard the soun' o' Hirpletillim.

The original heart of the granite industry in Aberdeen was not at Rubislaw, but in the Rosemount district, where tall tenements began to poke their smoky lums to the skies at the end of the nineteenth century. One of the earliest quarries was the Loanhead quarry, which was opened in 1730, a decade before quarrying began at Rubislaw. There is a topographical mix-up here for the hamlet of Loanhead lay half a mile away from the Loanhead Terrace that Aberdonians know today. The houses stood at the top of what is now Craigie Loanings. Loanhead, according to a visitor in 1780, was 'wholly possessed by labourers who wrought in the adjacent quarries, or was the occasional residence of beggars, who were not permitted to settle in town'.

New luxury flats have gone up in Craigie Loanings in recent years, and opposite them are the tenements of Wallfield Place and Crescent, which, along with the more exclusive Rubislaw, were immortalised in lines sung by Aberdeen's home-bred comedian, Harry Gordon:

> Fittie folk, Kitty folk, country folk
> and city folk,
> Folk fae Constitution Street an' folk
> fae Rubislaw Den,
> Wallfield, Nellfield, Manofield an'
> Cattofield,
> List' tae local stories that professors
> dinna ken.

Wallfield Place was where I was born and brought up. There were shared lavatories on the landings of the three-storeyed tenement, guttering gaslight on the stairs, a living room with a kitchen sink looking out on to the back-green, and a parlour that was used only on Sundays and holidays. As well as being a drying-green, the 'backie' was a stage for itinerant musicians and one-man bands. We used to throw pennies to them from the top-floor window, hurling them down in the hope that one would strike its target.

At the corner of Skene Terrace and Rosemount Viaduct a tenement block has cloaked itself in spurious grandeur by adopting an unusual conical roof. The building of this block in 1897 was an attempt to emulate the style of the mansion blocks of flats springing up in London and other cities. The Skene Terrace building was in some ways before its time, for now there are no tenements, or very few of them. They are all flats,

Coffee and culture in Aberdeen's Art Gallery. Ian Mackenzie Smith, Director of Aberdeen Art Gallery and Museums, has turned the gallery in Schoolhill into a modern cultural centre that draws hundreds of visitors and local people to its doors.

smart, modern, boasting every mod. con; bathroom suites instead of zinc baths. Something has been lost, for the tenement was the spiritual home of the Aberdonian. His allegiance to the work ethic, his humour, his thrift, his loyalty to the family . . . they were all nurtured in these grey canyons of stone. When the tenements began to disappear, many of these virtues disappeared with them.

The Rosemount area east of Loanhead was the heart of tenement land, yet at one time the houses there were in the suburbs of the city. Rosemount Square, with its sculpted figures on horseback representing Wind and Rain (familiar elements in this windy North-east city) was started in 1938 and completed after the war. It was the last of the granite tenement blocks to be built in Aberdeen and it contrasts oddly with Strachan's Mill Court, a recently-built block of modern retirement flats opposite the square. The flats are at the top of Jack's Brae, which takes its name from John Jack, who was a farmer at Gilcomston in 1750. Down at the bottom of Baker

Street are the Gilcomston Steps, but you would look in vain for
any steps. They were there in the eighteenth century, leading
to what was known as Nether Gilcomston. Only the street name
remains.

There is an interesting painting above the door of the
Gilcomston Bar at 5 Gilcomston Steps, showing a setttlement
surrounded by a moat, with a circle of standing stones nearby.
Ron Milne, buildings manager for Scottish Brewers, researched
the history of the area and had a special painting made of
'Gillecolaim's Toun'. The trees in the background represent the
Stocket Forest. The standing stones were two monoliths which
formed part of a Bronze Age circle crowning the hill which
gave Hill Street its name. Before being absorbed by the city,
Gilcomston had a population of 2000. Most of its inhabitants
worked at the Craigie Loanings quarries, at a lint mill
operating between Jack's Brae and Leadside Road, and at the
meal mill.

It is a fascinating area, for it was from Gilcomston that the
early settlers moved to the Green, where the burgh of
Aberdeen took roots and flourished. Not far away is
Woolmanhill, which was often spelt Womanhill, but it had
nothing to do with the female sex – 'woo' meant wool, and
Woolmanhill was where a wool market was held. Generations
of Aberdonians knew Woolmanhill because the city's main
hospital was there before the building of the Royal Infirmary at
Foresterhill. Woolmanhill mended broken bones, but a few
hundred yards away there were other things to be considered –
the trinity of buildings known as Education, Salvation and
Damnation. These were represented by the Central Library, St
Mark's Church and His Majesty's Theatre.

Education should have included Robert Gordon's College
and, no less important, the Institute of Technology at
Gordon's, which has played a vital role in oil development in
the past decade. The 'damnation' inflicted on the city by H.M.
Theatre goes back to 1906, when the theatre was opened by
Robert Arthur, who owned Her Majesty's Theatre in Guild
Street, later renamed the Tivoli. The Donald family, who have
had a finger in many of the city's entertainment pies, took over
the theatre in 1933 and have remained closely involved with it
ever since, even today, when it is owned by the district council.

It is run for the council by Jimmy and Peter Donald, grandsons of James F. Donald, who bought the theatre more than half a century ago.

Ivor Novello, Gracie Fields, Ellen Terry, Sybil Thorndike, Vivien Leigh, Robert Donat, Anna Neagle . . . these are only a few of the stars who trod the boards at His Majesty's between the two wars. A complete tally would add up to a long and ghostly roll-call. Harry Lauder was there with his tammy and crooked stick, and there was another Harry who held a firm place in the affections of Aberdeen audiences. Like Lauder, Harry Gordon cut his entertainer's teeth on 'mean Aberdonian' stories in the days when comics got their best laughs by poking fun at Scottish thrift. Lauder said that the 'Scotch' joke was 'a lie we have never taken the trouble to kill because it has been fine free publicity for us as a nation'.

The 'mean Aberdonian' story ceased to have a place in the Scotsman's sporran when Aberdeen became the oil-boom capital of Europe, but it was recently revived in a more venomous form by author Paul Theroux, who enraged the city by attacking its stinginess in his book, *Kingdom by the Sea*. He hated Aberdeen and said so. He thought it was the most prosperous city on the British coast, yet it had 'the sort of tight-fistedness that made me think of the average Aberdonian as a person who would gladly pick a halfpenny out of a dunghill with his teeth'.

Aberdonians have little inclination to defend themselves against accusations of meanness. The hoary old jokes about empty streets on a flag day, or streets crowded with people during house-to-house collections, have long since run their course, but if statistical proof were needed it could be found in the minutes of the local council's licensing committee, which approved a programme of forty-nine flag days for 1988 and threw in thirty-two house-to-house collections for good measure.

What probably upset most people about the Theroux attack was the fact that he was capital
alising on a myth that Aberdonians had themselves created. The belief that people in the Granite City were 'canny' was carefully nurtured in the thrifty Twenties. During this period there was an avalanche of books about Aberdeen stinginess. They had titles like *Canny*

Tales fae Aberdeen, Hoots! and *The Aberdeen Jew*. They even invented a character called Isaac Levi, who wanted to know why no one turned up to hear a lecture on 'How to treat the Jews'. That sort of humour, innocent though it may have been, disappeared for all time on the outbreak of the Second World War.

Although Lauder was given a knighthood, Harry Gordon never reached such elevated heights, although he had a title of sorts. Born in 1893, he was known as the Laird of Inversnecky. The whereabouts of Inversnecky always remained a mystery (some people actually believed that it existed), but it must have been somewhere near the Beach Pavilion, on Aberdeen's sea front, where he joked and sang his way into the hearts of his audiences. 'Mean Aberdonian' stories were part of his stock-in-trade, but his humour went well beyond that. He poked fun at people and places they knew . . . the 'fowk fae Rubislaw Den', the Inversnecky fireman, the Woodside girl with a kiss as big as a wagonload of hay, and Inversnecky's 'picture hoose and public hoose'. His songs had titles like 'The Auldest Aiberdonian', 'The Beadle o' the Kirk' and 'The Bells of' Inversnecky'.

The Laird of Inversnecky has drifted into local folklore, and later generations of Scots comics are going the same way. The public appetite for tartan humour has become jaded. Billy Connolly's raw Glasgow humour was a reaction to the years of tartan tammies and thumbs-in-the-gallusses nostalgia. Audiences no longer wanted to keep right on to the end of the road; they had already arrived there. The recently-restored interior of His Majesty's Theatre, which one architect described as 'a banquet of Edwardian exuberance', is no longer the Mecca of Scotland's stand-up comics.

Yet the link is not completely broken. The inheritors of the Inversnecky tradition are three Aberdeen men who gave up professional posts to become entertainers under the mocking banner of 'Scotland the What?' Buff Hardie, a graduate of Aberdeen and Cambridge, was secretary of Grampian Health Board; Steve Robertson was a local solicitor; and George Donald was assistant rector of Perth Academy. The fourth offstage member of the team is Jimmy Logan, who manfully hides his irritation at being confused with his Glasgow

The towering figure of William Wallace, arm outstretched as if pointing to the entrance to H.M. Theatre, The statue, which was originally intended for the Duthie Park, was built in 1888 in Rosemount Viaduct, overlooking Union Terrace Gardens.

namesake. There is not the slightest trace of tartan when they take the stage. Their attitude to the pseudo-patriotism of songs like 'The Scottish Soldier' is there for all to see in their rendering of 'The Scottish Plumber' – 'There was a plumber, a Scottish plumber, no finer plumber than he, to mend your WC . . .'

They 'take-off' everyone from the Pope to Dolly Parton, but they mostly have their sights fixed firmly on local targets. They are seldom far from Auchterturra, which is to a modern generation of Aberdonians what Inversnecky was to their grandfathers. Just as Harry Gordon did fifty or sixty years ago, they have learned that the citizens of Aberdeen like to laugh at themselves. They have successfully exported their Aberdeen humour to 'foreign' places like Glasgow and Edinburgh. They have even been to London, where Sandy Thomson, who features in one of their sketches, isn't above phoning up Buckingham Palace with the friendly greeting, 'Is that you, Beldy?' He has been known to ask her Majesty to bring 'a bilin' o' jam' with her for the bring-and-buy sale when she comes north on her holidays.

There are still, it has to be said, a lot of Sandy Thomsons about. Beneath the veneer of sophistication brought to the city by the oil boom, there are unflinching ranks of honest-to-God Aberdonians struggling to get out. They may dine at Gerard's, with its carefully cultivated Gallic flavour, or eat hot dishes at the latest Tandoori restaurant, but they secretly long for a poke of chips at Kenny's fish bar or a plate of mince and tatties. They still say 'Fit like?' and drop 'Ayes' into their conversation, and they tackle complex business problems with mental tackety-boots, having little or no time for subtleties. 'Ca'in' a spade a spade' is a local virtue.

No one exemplified this more than the late Bob Farquhar, who cashed in on the oil boom by building mobile homes and prefabricated office buildings all over the North-east for the oil companies. When Bob was demobbed from the Royal Navy after the war, he bought a horse and cart and sold bags of firewood around the countryside. Later, with a second-hand truck, he graduated to building and selling henhouses, sheds, garages and greenhouses. He also built portable loos for the oil industry and he would say, with great relish, that he started his working life 'sellin' sheds, chalets an' shitehooses'.

Bob Farquhar's homely brogue was as thick as porridge, and Sir Maitland Mackie always thought he 'put it on a little'. I have sometimes had a sneaking suspicion that Sir Maitland himself is careful not to over-anglicise his vowels. The nearer you get to the top, the harder you hang on to your roots.

Both were in the tradition of a former Lord Provost of Aberdeen, Sir Thomas Mitchell, who was known to everybody as Tommy. Tommy, a master baker to trade, never addressed people in the affected speech once known as 'pan loaf' (pan loaf because it was more expensive than plain loaf). It was probably his most endearing quality, and one that made him a great favourite with the Royal Family. The story is told that during one Royal visit, when Princess Elizabeth and Princess Margaret were present, he leaned over to the Queen (now the Queen Mother) and whispered, 'Div the quinies need the lavie?' Councillor Alex Collie, a more recent holder of the Lord Provost's office, is cast in the same mould. When he was representing the city at an oil conference in Houston, Texas, he turned up at a reception in his carpet slippers. These sound like situations that Buff Hardie and his colleagues would dream up for their show, but they actually happened, and it is this kind of unconscious Aberdeen humour that is grist for the 'Scotland the What?' mill.

So the ghost of Harry Gordon still haunts the stage of H.M. Theatre, where he first appeared in 1923, and maybe even Inversnecky, down at the beach. There is not much to remind you of Harry on Aberdeen's sea-front nowadays. The Beach Pavilion has long since gone. The Aberdeen comedian's links with it ended in 1940, but it continued for a decade after that with a summer show featuring Scots entertainers like Dave Willis, the wee man with the Chaplin moustache, and others from over the Border, including Morecambe and Wise, Dick Emery, and the Beverley Sisters.

Various other enterprises moved into the Beach Pavilion over the years, including a night club, but now a modern restaurant, the Cafe Continental, stands on the site. Next door is the Inversnecky Cafe, which offers an alien dish, the 'Inversnecky carry-out'. Beyond it is a cafe called The Pavilion. The straggle of ice-cream parlours and cafes gives way to Codonna's Amusement Arcade, a brightly-coloured building housing an astonishing array of video games and one-armed bandits. On the Links behind it is the Funfair.

The past has been buried or wiped out on Aberdeen's promenade. There is a curiously lumpy area of grass, with a few decorative boulders strewn over it, on the opposite side of the road from the Amusement Arcade. A large, ugly red-brick building with towers, turrets and a tall chimney once stood on the site – the Beach Baths, or the Bathing Station, as it was called when it opened in 1896. The inside of the Beach Baths was as Victorian as the outside. It was like descending into some Mephistophelean pit. The heat came up in waves and the smell of chlorine stung and smarted the eyes. Nothing is left of the old Beach Baths; the boulders on top of the grass sit on it like tombstones.

The Shelter near the Beach Baths was demolished recently. It was built largely of glass and people sat in it, safe from the snell winds blowing along the prom, and read their papers or gazed out to sea. Now they sit in their cars. The Shelter was topped by a magnificent clock, so that people on the sands or strolling on the prom always knew the time. The building was allowed to slip into such a state of disrepair that it had to go. Nevertheless, it could have been saved, and there was a feeling of resentment and irritation at its disappearance, for Aberdeen folk were fond of their Shelter. It touched chords of nostalgia for them. The old bandstand has also disappeared from the scene. Photographs from the 1930s show hundreds of people standing round the bandstand listening to the brass bands.

Behind the Beach Ballroom is the Broad Hill, once known as Cunningar Hill, a name that means 'rabbity'. It is a pygmy hill, and not much to boast about as a holiday attraction, but it was always a good place to roll your Easter eggs, and the view is interesting. The whole sweep of Aberdeen Bay lies to the east. Behind, citywards, it is less impressive . . . a glimpse of dreaming spires before the high-rise flats come into view; a panorama of tombstones in St Peter's cemetery; and the dispiriting sight of the city's old gasometer on Gallowhill. As far back as 1949, planning consultants W. Dobson Chapman and Partners pointed out that the gasometer stood 'ungracefully conspicuous between the Queen's Links and beach and the spires of the city'.

It was often said that the trouble with Aberdeen Beach wasn't the seafront, it was the backdrop on the edge of the city, behind the Links . . . a clutter of yards, workshops, factories, and a gas-holder with a capacity of 3¾ million cubic feet. For good measure, throw in the Gas Works. 'The site of the Gas Works', said Dobson Chapman, 'together with that of the adjacent Sandilands Chemical Works, is, to say the least, unfortunate, lying as they do immediately behind the Queen's Links, where they form very conspicuous features which obtrude on the views from the greater part of the seafront'.

The Gas Works, happily, are no longer there. The death knell of that piece of rusting industrial archaeology was sounded in the late 1970s when natural gas arrived. The works have vanished – and the pong with them – and now the smart, modern offices of British Gas Scotland stand on the site at Links Road. Sandilands, next door, remains, and the planning consultants' comments forty years ago are no less relevant today than they were then.

MAK' IT SAXPENCE.

Lady to beggar: "I'll give you a penny, my man, not because you deserve it, but because it pleases me." Beggar: "Thank ye kindly, ma'am, but mak' it a saxpence and thoroughly enjoy yersel'."

Aberdonians made money out of their alleged tightfistedness when the 'mean Aberdonian' myth flourished more than half a century ago. They sold postcards showing Aberdeen on a flag day, with Union Street deserted. There was another postcard showing Union Street crowded with people – on a house-to-house collection day.

The gas-holder on Gallowhill is what is known as a three-lift holder, going up and down as the city's housewives switched their cookers on and off. It has been out of commission for a number of years, but I found to my surprise that it could still be brought back into operation if necessary. With gas streaming in from the Frigg gas field to St Fergus its services are not likely to be required. Some day it will disappear and the last chapter will have been written in a story going back to 1824, when the first Gas-Light Company was started in Aberdeen.

Gallows, gas and goals . . . the three come together on a hill where the chained bodies of criminals swung from a creaking gibbet as a warning to other wrongdoers. The gas-holder overlooks Pittodrie Park, home of Aberdeen Football Club, whose fortunes in the past eighty-five years have gone up and down with the regularity of the three-lift gas tank. The present club was founded in 1903 by the amalgamation of three smaller clubs, one of them also carrying the name of Aberdeen F.C. That first Aberdeen F.C., set up in 1881, played on the Links and other grounds until it was given land on the Gallows Marsh.

Before it became a football pitch the Marsh was a dunghill for the city's police horses, and the name Pittodrie is said to be a Celtic place-name meaning 'the place of manure'. If that is true, it opens up potent opportunities for disgruntled supporters on the terracing. Dons fans hurl their verbal shafts with deadly effect. In the early days, one of the Aberdeen players was young Dick Donald, who at that time was in charge of the Cinema House in Skene Terrace, now a bingo hall. Dick was having a bad game and another well-known player, W. K. Jackson, called out 'Hard luck, Dick!' Quick as a flash came a roar from the terracing, 'Hard luck, my arse! Ye're jist wantin' a free ticket for the pictures!' Dick Donald was a member of the family who ran H.M. Theatre, as well as a chain of cinemas, an ice-rink and a dancing academy. Today he is chairman of Aberdeen F.C. Quietly spoken, reticent about his own part in the club's affairs, he is a man who likes to stay out of the limelight, yet he has done more than most people to put the club on top and to turn Pittodrie, the old Gallows Marsh, into one of the most modern football stadiums in the country.

The players originally wore white strips and were known as 'the Whites', but a new black and gold strip won them the nickname of 'the Wasps'. Today, the colour is Red – and a boisterous, chanting Red Army follows the Dons wherever they go at home and abroad. It followed them to Gothenburg in 1983, the year of their greatest triumph, when they not only won the Scottish Cup but took home from Gothenburg the European Cup-Winners' Cup – the first time a European honour had come to Pittodrie. Some 20,000 people turned up at Pittodrie to acclaim their heroes.

People were kicking a ball on the Links long before the Dons appeared on the scene. James Gordon, Parson of Rothiemay, said it was played on 'the fair plaine called the Queens Lynks' in 1661. 'Heer the inhabitants recreat themselves with several kynds of exercises, such as football, goffe, bowling and archerie', he wrote. 'Heer lykewayes they walk for their health.' Bowling is still played, as well as 'goffe'. An eighteen-hole golf course stretches north over the Links to the mouth of the Don, and across the bay at Balnagask there is another municipal course. Aberdeen is well served with municipal golf courses, as well as private ones.

If you had been walking on the Links for your health in 1639, you would have found it a little overcrowded. In March of that year, nine thousand Covenanters, with the Earl of Montrose at their head, were camped there, covering part of what is now the Beach Ballroom. The troops were told to go to breakfast either 'in the lyynkis or in the toun'. Only a small number went into town for their breakfast, and they soon returned to camp grumbling that they 'payit deir for sic as they gat', a complaint that is still being hurled at landladies and shopkeepers three centuries later.

Although sport is well catered for on the Links, there has always been a feeling that larger development is needed at Aberdeen Beach. It is a subject that has been debated endlessly by the local council. Grandiose plans have been drawn up, scrapped, and drawn up again, but God's mills and Aberdeen councillors' minds grind slowly. Nothing has happened. The Links act as an almost invisible barrier between the city and the sea. It is less than half a mile from the Castlegate to the beach, yet it has always seemed longer. Like Montrose's Covenanters, you are cut off from the centre of the town.

Unlike some coastal resorts, Aberdeen has never had houses on its seafront. If this type of development had taken place, things might have been different. It would have been the missing piece of the jigsaw, bringing the promenade and the east end of the town closer together. The nearest anyone ever got to it was a proposal to build a luxury hotel on the front, but nothing ever came of it, largely because it was felt that a hotel would be too cut off from the city centre. Winter yawned bleakly in the minds of the planners, conjuring up pictures of guests staring out at a rain-sodden promenade, and the blueprints were pigeon-holed, along with other plans for the Beach.

In winter, the Beach Ballroom is almost isolated. On the face of it, there is no reason why it should not be a success, but for

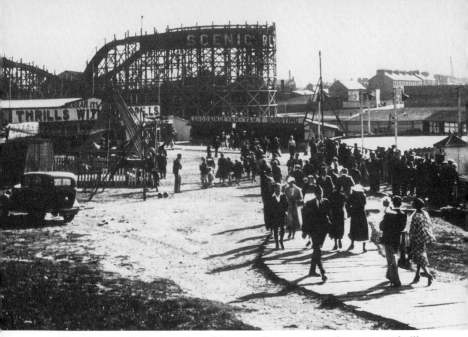

The Scenic Railway ... a fairground attraction that gave 'thrills without spills' to thousands of local people and visitors in the days when Aberdeen's beach was crowded with trippers. This picture of the city's pleasure park, better known locally as the Beach Carnival, was taken in 1935. Picture by courtesy of Aberdeen City Libraries.

years it has struggled to hold its head above water, frenetically swinging from pop concerts to old-time dancing and big-band events for a generation put in the mood by Glen Miller. The problem is that people have a psychological reluctance to go 'down to the Beach' for their indoor entertainment, particularly in midwinter.

Arguments have swung backwards and forwards over the future of the Beach Ballroom, but the wider question is the future of the whole beach area. There are still people who nurse the dream that Aberdeen can win back its pre-war standing as a seaside holiday resort. The Aberdeen Beyond 2000 group, set up to plan for next century, set out as one of its aims the establishment of a major all-weather family water fun centre. In the autumn of 1987, work began on a new Leisure Centre adjoining the Beach Ballroom. Its major attraction is a modern swimming pool – the Bathing Station is back again! The past lies buried in that grassy mound near the site of the old Shelter, the future lies across the promenade in the shadow of Cunningar Hill.

Chapter 2
Offshore and Onshore

Aberdeen has never outwardly flaunted its status as the oil capital of Europe. There have been as many as six thousand Americans in the city, but a ten-gallon Stetson hat in Union Street is a rare sight. The city centre, apart from its smart new restaurants and modern shopping developments, looks much the same as it always did. It is down in the bustling harbour area, or out in the bay, that the ebb and flow of the battle for oil is best seen . . . in the oil supply vessels pushing their way up the navigation channel, in the rigs that lie offshore, and on the busy quays where the old familiar pattern of trawler masts has given way to towering cranes and storage tanks.

Helicopters clatter overhead on their daily run to the oil fields. From Aberdeen Heliport, the busiest heliport in the world, the 'choppers' fly something like 50,000 flights a year to a vast network of oil platforms with names like Tern and Eider, Thistle and Deveron, Ninian and Murchison. A minimum of ten flights each week are made to Murchison, while supply boats run up 200 trips to the platform each year. The 263 men on board get through 21 tons of food a week, including 2 tons of meat and fish, 40 gallons of ice-cream, 1800 pints of milk, and 45lbs of instant coffee.

The main deck of the Murchison platform covers the same area as Pittodrie football pitch, but this intriguing statistic means little to the men offshore, who are separated from the fortunes of Aberdeen Football Club by endless miles of grey North Sea. Still, they talk a lot about the Dons, the pubs and the discos, about what is happening 'back on the beach'. By that they mean their onshore bases, or their homes, or the city itself, where they can find short-lived relief from the noise and monotony of life on a production platform. The 'beach' is the oil man's 'Blighty'. In the summer of 1986, when there were signs of a downturn in the oil business, things 'back on the beach' looked bad.

From the beach – the real beach – idle rigs could be seen lying out in Aberdeen Bay. They were the dinosaurs of the oil age, squat and ugly, looking as if they had slipped into a long hibernation. No one knew when the 'hibernation' would end, or even if those sleeping giants would finally be hauled off to the breakers' yards, but during the summer of 1986 their numbers grew. They were the signposts of slump, markers of a downturn in oil prices that sent a shiver of apprehension through the industry. After more than a decade of prosperity, it looked as if the oil boom was coming to an end.

From the oil giants Shell UK Exploration and Production, whose modern glass and concrete headquarters on Tullos Hill seemed like an affirmation of faith in the future of the oil industry, there came an announcement in late 1987 that they were to undertake a far-reaching organisational review. The company spoke of 'adjusting to the business environment of the next decade', and of total oil production falling as the older, larger fields declined.

The drop in production as well as oil prices made the review inevitable, they said, and there would be job losses. They were 'preparing for the long-term challenges of the 1990s'. The announcement came less than six months after Grampian Regional Council, in its eighth 'Oil and Gas Prospects' report, said that in addition to the thirty-six fields already in production and a further eight under development, there were about sixty more fields likely to be developed over the next twenty-five years. Half the new fields developed in the next ten years would be small extensions of existing fields. The Shell UK announcement came as no surprise. Belt-tightening and pruning had been going on for some time, and it was felt that the industry would emerge leaner and fitter, ready for the century ahead.

As the months rolled on into 1988, the number of rigs in the Bay diminished, hopeful sign of a slow recovery in the oil game. Meanwhile, the service vessels continued to deliver their weekly shopping lists to the oil fields . . . to Beryl and Mabel and Joanne and Josephine. They came thrusting up the channel, their ungainly prows dipping in salute as they passed the Round House, sending long crescents of water curving up the wall of the North Pier. On the jetty below the Round House (officially known as the Harbourmaster's Station) a stone can be seen with the inscription on it. 'Jno Abercrombie Provost 1789'.

Before the oil . . . the steam drifter *Eveline Nutten,* owned by E.C. and H.E. Nutten, passes the Round House on her way up the navigation channel at Aberdeen Harbour as she sets sail for the fishing grounds. Behind the Round House are the rooftops of Fittie. Picture by courtesy of Aberdeen City Libraries.

It is barely readable, and to study it you have to risk falling into the icy waters of the channel. It is an unlikely spot to commemorate a Lord Provost of Aberdeen.

The explanation is that this is Abercrombie Jetty, named after Provost John Abercrombie, the surveyor who supervised its construction. It was originally called Smeaton's Jetty after John Smeaton, the harbour engineer who planned the North Pier to prevent sand being thrown into the harbour entrance by north-east winds. He later went on to design the jetty, setting the seal on a harbour entrance that for the next two hundred years was to welcome a salty cavalcade of whalers, herring boats, seine-net boats, pilot boats, cargo and passenger boats and, in the 1970s, a vessel that was to become as well-known as the once-familiar trawler – the oil boat.

There should be a stone at the other end of the North Pier commemorating the fact that John Smeaton's masterpiece was used by generations of anglers, who sat on its walls and fished for saithe. They were mostly old men and young boys. Saithe was never a popular dish. The fish fed from the sewers which disgorged the city's waste into the channel and they were known locally as 'Shittie Sadies'. Nobody ate them, but they were fun to catch.

The Harbour Board closed off the North Pier a number of years ago, much to the annoyance of people who liked to stroll along it and watch the boats go by. It was opened up again recently, but fishing is now banned – even for saithe. Most of the Aberdeen harbour area is fenced off – the North Pier mentality all over again. Perhaps a more enlightened harbour board will tear down the fence and let it be integrated with the city, as it was at one time.

The Aberdeen Beyond 2000 Committee put forward a proposal for establishing a Fisherman's Wharf at the harbour, with fish sales and a sea-food restaurant, but Bert Allen, the city's director of town planning, pointed out that, unlike other British cities, Aberdeen did not use much of its waterfront for tourist-related activities, partly because there was little 'redundant' wharfage. He made it clear that he was all in favour of greater 'visitor use' of the harbour, pointing out that, although the port penetrated to the heart of the city, it was largely cordoned off.

There are no fences at Footdee, the old-world community lying between the Beach promenade and the North Pier. Footdee has its back to the shore, as if it had turned away from the sea's stormy petulance, but on a rough day the spray still comes spattering over its rooftops. The real name of the village is Futty, which sounds like a corruption of Footdee but isn't. The name appears to have been 'corrected' by well-meaning folk who probably thought that Footdee had something to do with the foot of the Dee. Although it is still shown on maps as Footdee, everyone calls it Fittie, which seems to be a reasonable Aberdeen compromise. There are no longer any fishers there, but Fittie still supplies men for the pilot boats. The lifeboat was always manned by Fittie men, but now there is only one Fittie man in the crew. The rest come from all over the city, from a variety of occupations.

Fittie folk always tended to keep themselves to themselves, having nothing to do with the townspeople to the west. There is still a little of that in their make-up, and I was told that most of the 'strangers' who come from outside to live in Fittie are concentrated in one street. The community is made up of three squares, North Square, South Square and Pilot Square, but there is a fourth square stuck in the middle and, logically, it has been named Middle Row. It has its own church in the centre of North Square, and each house has a kind of backyard bothy. They were once tumbledown wooden sheds where the fishers kept their nets, but now they have been modernised.

James Gordon, the Parson of Rothiemay, said that 'Futtie' was '500 walking passes' from the Weigh-house. A 'pass' is a pace, or step, and at first I thought he must have had a long stride, but the Parson was talking about Fittie on its original site, where St Clement's Church is now. The old Weigh-house was demolished at the end of last century, but Weigh-house Square, at the west end of Regent Quay, is still there, and it was from the 'square' that I tested Parson Gordon's 500 walking passes. The route was as near to the seventeenth-century road as possible and it took me almost to the gate of St Clement's Kirk. In James Gordon's day, the road to Fittie was so soft and grassy that it was known as the Carpet Walk. Courting couples 'walked the carpet', and set the pattern for the modern custom of Walking the Mat in Union Street.

If you follow Parson Gordon's method of calculating distance, it is about 400 walking passes from Weigh-house Square along busy South Market Street to Jamieson's Quay, where visitors can finally get behind the Harbour Board's fence. Here, at Victoria Dock and the Albert Basin, you get a whiff of history. At Victoria Dock is the terminal for the Orkney and Shetland services of P. & O. Ferries, successors to the old 'North Boats', upholding a tradition going back to the days when sailing ships plied between Aberdeen and the Baltic, and across the water from Blaikie's Quay are the shipbuilding yards where a century and a half ago the famous Aberdeen Clippers were built. Now the last of the big yards, Hall, Russell and Company, struggles to keep alive.

It is in the Albert Basin that Aberdeen clings most fiercely to its fishing past. Up almost till the end of last century, King Herring reigned supreme. Between 1875 and 1896, Point Law was crowded with curing yards and kippering sheds, and in

1896 more than 3000 men and women were working in the curing yards. But in the late 1880s the emphasis began to change as the city's trawling industry expanded, and by 1900 Aberdeen found itself caught up in a trawling boom. Albert Basin became the home of the city's trawling fleet. A fish market was built in 1889 and in twenty years the number of trawlers had risen to over 200.

It took seventy years before another boom hit the harbour, and this time it was oil. The decline of the Aberdeen trawling fleet coincided with the advent of oil, and was partly accelerated by it. Between 1981 and 1984 the number of vessels in the fleet fell by nearly half. The majority of the port's fleet of large vessels is now operated by two companies, compared with about ten in the 1970s, when the first impact of oil was felt.

Oil wasn't the only reason for the downturn in trawling. An ageing fleet and the extension of national fishing limits to 200 miles were other factors. The restrictions of the National Dock Labour Scheme also meant that Aberdeen lost out to other non-scheme ports, although it remained a major centre for processing and marketing. But the impression you get as you walk around the harbour is that fishing is suffocated by oil. The trawler fleet, or what is left of it, is the cinderella of the port. The trawlers seem puny alongside the supply vessels crowding Blaikie's Quay, seagoing giants with names like *British Forties, Icelander* and *Northern Fortune*. They come from Leith and Liverpool, Aalesund and Oslo.

Oil has also taken over across the River Dee in Old Torry, which, ironically, climbed to prosperity on the back of the trawling boom at the turn of the century. It was to Torry that fisher folk from the coastal villages came for the trawling, so that its population – only 370 in 1843 – began to mushroom. The opening of the Victoria Bridge in 1881 added impetus to the growth. It took a major tragedy to speed up the building of the bridge, which had been talked about for a number of years. Previously, a ferry operated between Point Law and Torry. On April 5th, 1876; a local holiday, it was kept busy carrying Aberdeen people to and from Torry, and on one of its trips to the south side of the Dee it was badly overloaded, carrying about sixty people, more than double its normal load. The

One of the many oil supply vessels that daily come and go from
Aberdeen Harbour nowadays on trips to the North Sea oilfields, 'their
ungainly prows dipping in salute' as they pass the Round House on
their way up the navigation channel.

ferry boat's wire rope broke and the boat capsized. Thirty-
three passengers were drowned.

There is little left to remind you of Aul' Torry. Much of it
disappeared when the area north of Sinclair Road was cleared
to make way for oil installations. The leading lights which
guided ships up the navigation channel still turn an unblinking
red eye (green when the channel is closed) towards the North
Pier, but these mini-lighthouses on Sinclair Road seem almost
incongruous against the oil background. This corner of Old
Torry is dominated by oil supply vessels, whose movements in
1984 totalled nearly 5000. The casing, drilling muds and
chemicals which they carry to the rigs and platform are loaded
from service bases like the Shell base at Old Torry. Charming
closes and quaint old-fashioned fishermen's homes vanished
when the redevelopment took place.

Texaco, Shell, Total and the Wood Group all have bases in
Sinclair Road. The name Wood seems to pop up wherever you
go in the harbour area. At one time, it was associated with
trawling, but since oil came to the North-east of Scotland the

company has moved into a variety of industrial enterprises. Ian Wood, head of the John Wood Group, is chairman and one of the founder members of Aberdeen Beyond 2000, an organisation set up by local business leaders to stimulate action to develop the city's economic base activities.

Greyhope Road takes over where Sinclair Road leaves off, climbing up Balnagask brae above the navigation channel to the Torry Battery and swinging round past Girdleness Lighthouse to the Bay of Nigg, mecca of city picknickers before the last war. There is a car park beside the Battery where you can look out over Aberdeen Bay, across the channel to Fittie and the North Pier, and down over the docks and basins of the harbour. Behind stretch the blue-grey roofs of Aberdeen, reaching out to the Grampian hills.

Standing there, I watched a procession of curious-looking craft come chugging up the channel and head towards the harbour. They were enclosed lifeboats, five of them in line, and they were from the Offshore Survival Centre on North Esplanade East, run by Robert Gordon's Institute of Technology. They were coming home from a training session in the bay. Thousands of North Sea oilmen have gone there to learn how to cope with emergencies in one of the world's most hostile environments.

I wondered if the thought of the *Oscar* had haunted them as they passed Greyhope Bay, for it was on the rocks there, behind the breakwater, that the whaling ship *Oscar* was driven ashore in April, 1813, on a day when the gale was so fierce and the snow so thick that few people were able to stand on their feet. Only two of the crew survived. A Captain Richard Jamson, who was in the crowd watching from the shore, saw an object floating in the boiling surf and, reaching out with his stick, pulled it towards him. It was his nephew, John Jamson, the first mate. The other survivor was a seaman called James Venus. Forty-two men lost their lives. There were no liferafts or 'offshore survival' training in those days.

Something like £25m is expected to be spent on wide-ranging improvements to Aberdeen Harbour in the next ten years. The Aberdeen Beyond 2000 group anticipates that with increased efficiency there will be a fall in the size of the fleet and that Aberdeen's recovery as a fishing port is dependent on

Tall-masted sailing ships ride at anchor in Aberdeen Harbour . . . a scene that has long since vanished from the port. The picture was taken in 1875. In the background is the Post Office in Market Street, then under construction, now closed. Picture by courtesy of Aberdeen City Libraries.

the removal of National Dock Labour Scheme restrictions. As for North Sea oil and gas, its view is that they will remain the most important sources of employment into the next century.

Today, the port has nine offshore support bases, two ferry terminals and major deepwater cargo-handling facilities, as well as its fishing. It has come a long way since an eighteenth-century merchant called John Ross sat in his house in the Shiprow and watched his ships in the harbour. Ross was Provost of Aberdeen in 1710-11. His house, which stood in one of the oldest streets in Aberdeen, is one of the city's oldest surviving buildings. Today it is the home of the Aberdeen Maritime Museum. The story of the port . . . its days as Scotland's premier whaling port, the excitement of the sailing ships, the great line fishing and the fisher girls, the 'North Boats' and the 'London Boats', the early days of diving and the coming of oil . . . are all recalled in vivid detail in the museum.

But history lies on its doorstep, as well as inside Provost Ross's House, for a rich slice of the city's past can be traced to this cobbled street. Another famous citizen who had his home in the Shiprow, or Ship Raw as it was called, was Aberdeen's hero provost, Robert Davidson, who marched with his burghers to the Battle of Harlaw – 'gude Sir Robert Davidson, wha Provost was of Aberdeen'. Provost Davidson, who had a tavern in the Shiprow, fell at Harlaw. His body – the body of 'a man brave and bold, who prospered in all things' – was carried to the city and interred in St Nicholas Church.

Not far from Provost Ross's House, across Union Street and up Broad Street, is another house which was owned by a Provost who made his money from shipping. He also lived in a 'Row', a street haunted by ghosts and weighed down by the memory of 'Butcher' Cumberland. It stood in the Guestrow and was the town house of Sir George Skene of Rubislaw, a wealthy merchant, who was Provost from 1676 to 1684. Folk who lived in the Guestrow, or Ghaist Raw, were supposed to have seen ghosts walking in nearby St Nicholas Churchyard. The Duke of Cumberland – 'Butcher' Cumberland – stayed there for a few weeks in 1746, and the house, which became a model lodging house, was known for a long time as Cumberland House, a name it tried to shrug off when it was restored and turned into a period domestic museum. Its future was in doubt when St Nicholas House was built virtually on the same site, but bureaucracy embraced it, perhaps a little unwillingly, so that now it is hidden away in the courtyard of this fourteen-storey office building.

It would take more than a municipal skyscraper to hide the Gothic magnificence of Marischal College, opposite Provost Skene's House. Not everyone loves Marischal (it was once described as a wedding cake in indigestible grey icing), but no one can ignore it. The late Dr Cuthbert Graham described it as 'highfalutin'. He thought that it was in keeping with the Aberdeen temperament, which was normally plodding and pedestrian but at times had high flights of passion. The college was founded in 1593, almost a century after King's College, and the two were unified in 1860.

In 1842, before the two universities united, Lord Cockburn, in his *Circuit Journeys*, said that to maintain two universities in

When Aberdeen's municipal offices in Broad Street were planned, controversy raged over what to do with Provost Skene's House, which stood on the site. The city council's answer was to build around it and this seventeenth century building now sits in the arms of bureaucracy, hemmed in by St Nicholas House. It is used as a period museum.

such a place was absurd. He declared that they should give up the one in the town, Marischal, and retain 'the old, venerable well placed academic looking King's College'. Nearly a century and a half later, Lord Cockburn's proposal again took wings when Aberdeen University, faced with a threatened £2,500,000 cash cutback in its funding, looked around for ways of dealing with what was a major financial crisis. With its costs under attack from the University Grants Committee, it had to come to terms with the inevitability of severe cost-cutting and internal restructuring.

Before drawing up a strategic plan to put to the University Grants Committee – a plan envisaging the closing of six departments and the loss of nearly 250 jobs – the possibility of selling off Marischal College was given serious consideration. In the detailed report that was drawn up it was clear that the proceeds from the sale of the building would be substantial. But there was one major snag; the cost of converting it would be so prohibitive that no one would want to buy it. The idea was abandoned – Marischal was saved.

The late John R. Allan had his roots in the Aulton and studied at King's College. Writing some years ago about the transfer of Marischal College departments to Old Aberdeen, he said he hoped that the old would 'not be overlaid by the new'. There is little doubt that in recent years the emphasis has swung away from Marischal towards the 'venerable, well-placed' college in Old Aberdeen. More and more students have been taking the traditional route 'over the Spital Brae' to the Aulton – up the Gallowgate, Mounthooly and the Spital to King's. At one time, the theory was that everything would move to King's College, but with the downturn in oil and the realisation that the Broad Street college could not be sold the University took a decision to expand at Marischal.

What bothered John R. Allan even more was the thought that the University might possess all the Aulton, that the time would come when there would be 'none left in it but the professors and lecturers and a few shopkeepers'. He saw it as a loss if the day ever arrived 'when the professor no longer lived next door to the scavenger' and all that you heard in the Aulton were 'accents veneered over by Oxford and Cambridge'. Despite promises made a number of years ago that this would never happen, it looked in recent years as if links with the local community were weakening. While there may have been pockets of non-academic dwellers in the Aulton (there may even have *been* a 'scaffie' living next door to a professor), the impression you got was that it was rapidly becoming a university precinct.

Today, there is less likelihood of this happening. The University at one time bought up every building that came on the market in Old Aberdeen; now, because of its financial problems, it has actually been selling off property. Houses west of St Machar Drive have been sold and even property in the Chanonry has been put on the market. The policy is to retain houses in the immediate vicinity of King's College.

As you climb over the Spital Brae and drop down into the academic calm of the Aulton, with its ancient buildings and streets steeped in centuries of history, there is a tendency to think that little here is relevant to the industrial changes that

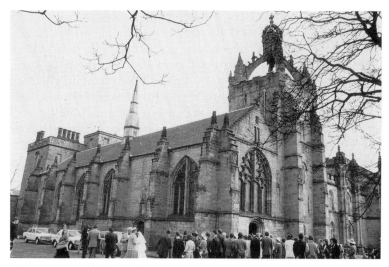

The tower of King's College, topped by its Imperial Crown, is a familiar setting for the marriages of Aberdeen University graduates. The tower and college chapel, on the east side of College Bounds, were built in the early years of the sixteenth century.

have taken place in Aberdeen. Nothing could be further from the truth. For a start, the university has made considerable expenditure in oil-related research, particularly in the marine, medical and environmental areas, and one small indication of how it has adapted to commercial needs can be seen in a small office in College Bounds. Outside it are the initials AURIS. They stand for Aberdeen University Research and Industrial Services Ltd., which is the holding company for the University's commercial interests. Set up in 1981, it now employs forty-four people and has a turnover of £1m.

Interestingly, its address recalls an earlier Aulton enterprise – the Old Brewery. The Aulton Brewery, which closed in the 1920s, was one of three major breweries in Aberdeen. The others were the Devanha Brewery on the River Dee and a brewery at Gilcomston, which was opened in 1768. The beer brewed in the Aulton was said to have been of a very fine quality, but the authorities ensured that it was not over-appreciated. They laid down that no drink was to be sold after 9 p.m.

Past and present sit unprotestingly together on the edge of

the Aulton. On the west side of College Bounds there is a massive wall which, on the face of it, seems ready for the demolition squad. This is not surprising, for it has been standing there for centuries. There are a number of these ancient walls in the Aulton. In the seventeenth and eighteenth centuries they were built around the old burgh and now they are 'protected'. What makes the College Bounds wall particularly interesting is the filled-in archway in the middle of it, surmounted by the coat of arms of Bishop William Elphinstone, Chancellor of Scotland and founder of the University.

The archway is thought to have led originally to the romantically-named Snow Kirkyard. The entrance today is by the gateway to the Crombie and Johnstone halls of residence, but as far as the kirkyard is concerned it might also be blocked up, for there is nothing to indicate that it even exists. Yet the story of how Bishop Elphinstone gave it its name is a fascinating one. The Snow Kirk (*St Mary ad Nives*) was founded in 1497. Bishop Elphinstone was intrigued by a legend connected with the founding of S. Maria Maggiore in Rome. The Pope of the time had a dream in which St Mary appeared to him and indicated that a church should be built and dedicated to her on a site which would be marked out by snow. Next day, despite the intense summer heat in Rome, snow fell on the exact spot. S. Maria Maggiore was built there.

So the new church in the Aulton became St Mary ad Nives, the Snow Kirk. It stood until 1640, but all that remains of it is its kirkyard. The inscriptions on the tombstones are mostly written in Latin and the only one of any particular importance is a large stone dated 1669 and carrying the name of Gilbert Menzies of Pitfodels. This tiny piece of Aulton history, hemmed in by a brick wall, seems lost and out of place against the background of modern buildings that loom over it to the west of College Bounds and the High Street. These teaching blocks, built to accommodate a rapidly growing student population, stand on the former market lands of Old Aberdeen, which was merged with the city in 1891. Clean-lined and functional, they nevertheless fit in comfortably with the early architecture.

Further down College Bounds there is a curious touch of

The attractive entrance to St Machar's Cathedral in Old Aberdeen. The cathedral, with its twin spires, overlooks Seaton Park, where the River Don winds its way seawards under the Brig o' Balgownie.

Eastern promise in the minarets adorning the huge Powis Lodge Gate, one of the entrances to Crombie Hall. There is another minaret on Powis Lodge itself. The lodge was built in 1697 by Alexander Fraser, Sub-principal of King's College, and another Alexander Fraser, an architect, designed the minarets for John Leslie, a young laird of Powis, who was an admirer of Lord Byron. The minaretted gateway was Leslie's tribute to the poet.

From here it is only a short distance to the High Street and King's College, the crowning glory of the Aulton. There has been enough written about King's to fill half the shelves in its magnificent library, but for those who stroll the length of the High Street, from the Chapel to the Old Town House, there are other delights to be discovered. Not least among them are the narrow streets and lanes that branch off the main thoroughfare ... Thom's Court and Thom's Place, Duncan's Place and Douglas Place, Grant's Place and Wrights' and Coopers' Place.

The High Street and Don Street beyond it throw up an interesting mixture of patterns and styles. There are cobbled closes and pavestoned lanes, wrought-iron gateways and circular staircases. Tenements and old town houses contrast with quaint cottages and elegant professors' houses. Times have changed a good deal since J. B. Bulloch, a graduate of 1888, who became a well-known journalist and author, wrote about the city's home-grown 'Profs':

> In the good old days we love to praise
> Our Profs were a home-grown lot,
> With homely ways and a Doric phrase,
> For each was a sturdy Scot.

To take a mental leap back into the early eighteenth century all you have to do is walk up Grant's Place, whose one-storey pantiled cottages were restored in 1965. They date back to the 1720s. On the lintel of No. 2 are the initials AL and IMD, separated by a heart and with the year 1732 divided on either side of the letters. Who, I wonder, were these young lovers of two and a half centuries ago?

Grant's Place and Wrights' and Coopers' Place were restored with money from the MacRobert Trust. At the end of Wrights' and Coopers' Place is a small pond with a carved metal sundial in it, commemorating Lady MacRobert and her sons Alasdair, Roderic and Iain, who were killed while flying with the R.A.F. between 1938 and 1941.

The stately Chanonry sits aloof from the bustle of the High Street. It runs down by the Cruickshank Botanic Gardens and loops past the main gates of St Machar's Cathedral to meet up with Don Street. Chanonry Lodge, opposite the entrance to the

Cathedral, is the official residence of the Principal of the University. Round the corner at No. 9 is the Mitchell Hospital, old almshouses restored and converted to cottages. They were built in 1801 to house 'five widows and five unmarried daughters of merchant and trade burgesses of Old Abedeen'. In Don Street is the Dower House, a three-storey house built on the site of the house of the Cathedral's Treasurer.

On St Machar's Drive, just round the corner from the north end of High Street, there is a cottage called Cluny's Port. Back in the fifteenth century, the ground occupied by St Machar's Cathedral was surrounded by a high wall which had four gates or ports. The main entrance was Cluny's Port. James Gordon's map of Old Aberdeen in 1661 shows 'Cluyns Garden' between the Cathedral and the now-vanished 'Loch of Aberdon'. Cluny's Port was the gate house to Cluny's Garden, which is today the Cruickshank Botanic Gardens. Laid out in 1898, they have become increasingly popular with both local people and visitors in recent years. The aim of the founder, Anne Cruickshank, was that the 11-acre gardens should serve the needs of teaching, research and botany, as well as giving pleasure to the public, and that is exactly what has happened.

Have a look for gulls circling and squawking over your head the next time you walk down St Machar Drive. If there aren't any, there may be trouble ahead. John Spalding, who wrote *Memorialls of the Trubles* during Covenanting times, regarded it as a portent in 1641 when no mawes (gulls) were seen in the Lochs of New or Old Aberdeen after the soldiers came to town. Before that they had 'flokkit and clekkit (bred) in so gyrte aboundans that it wes plesour to behold them fleing aboue our heidis'.

Spalding said that 'some maid use of their eggis and burdis', and, in fact, black-headed gulls which 'clekkit' on the Loch were protected because they were a source of food. Young gulls, which were regarded as a tasty dish, were plucked and salted for future use. Some estates kept gull ponds and regarded black-headed gulls as domestic birds. Near Cluny's Port, the Old Town House stands guard at the junction of St Machar Drive and the High Street. It was built in 1788, but the burgh's coat of arms, seen above the doorway, dates from the previous building of 1721. There was a time when the 'road' from the Town House to King Street was a lane so narrow it was called the Needle's-e'e Road.

Across from the Town House, on the east side of the High Street, is Market Lane, recalling the weekly Market Day and the old-time fairs. There were two annual fairs in the Aulton in former years, one on Skeir Thursday (the day before Good Friday) and the other on St Luke's Day. The St Luke's Fair, or Aulton Market, lasted for eight days. There are moves afoot to revive it in time for the 500th anniversary celebrations in 1989 of the granting of free burgh status to Old Aberdeen. The aim would be 'to bind the Old Aberdeen community' by involving the whole of the Aulton and the surrounding areas. One of the aims would be to provide a focus for crafts and local industrial enterprise.

The revived St Luke's Fair will be held in Seaton Park, under the twin spires of St Machar. They will be trying to recapture the atmosphere that Katherine Trail, wife of the Professor of Botany at the University, wrote about when she set down her memories more than half a century ago. St Luke's Market had virtually died out by the early Thirties, but Mrs Trail never forgot the excitement of the fair, the caravans, the whirling merry-go-rounds, the coconut shies and the rifle ranges. It was, she said, 'the most ardently looked-forward-to day of the year by all the Old Aberdeen children'.

Some things, of course, will never come back. There were what Mrs Trail called 'wonderful prodigies of Nature' – human and animal freaks. 'The most wonderful exhibits were to be seen in the shows', said Mrs Trail, 'fat women, calves with two heads, calves with no heads, and other freaks of nature'. You can almost picture it all, the noise, the swings, the blare of music, the colour. Roll up, roll up, gaze in wonder at the two-headed boy, see the one-and-only fat lady, marvel at the boneless man . . . the fun of the fair, said Mrs Trail, was fast and furious. No doubt it will be again.

Chapter 3
The Duke tae Babbie Law

A round yellow plaque hangs on a wall near Peacock's Close in Aberdeen's Castlegate. It reminds passers-by that this dingy alley once led to the house where Francis Peacock, the city's official dancing master, lived and worked more than two centuries ago. 'I can min' fin there wis peacocks doon in Peacock's Close', sang Harry Gordon. There never were any peacocks there, only Mr Peacock himself, strutting about his ballroom as he taught his pupils the *Pas seul* and the *Pas de Trois*. He was the kind of man who thought that a well-set head and 'an expressive modesty of eye' were more conducive to an elegant performance than twinkling feet. 'The jigging part and the figures of the dances', he said, 'I count that little or nothing.'

He was twenty-four when he came to Aberdeen from his native Edinburgh in 1747 and he was still dancing the night away when he died in 1807 at the age of eighty-four. His dances started at four o'clock in the afternoon and often finished at four o'clock next morning. The town's top people attended his public balls. When he wrote a book on the theory and practice of dancing in 1805, the town council bought twenty copies. The thought of Aberdeen's civic fathers reeling and hooching under Mr Peacock's watchful eye made a local versifier reach for his pen:

> God prosper long our Lord Provost,
> Town Clerk, an' Bailies a';
> An' grant that in their reelin' fits,
> Doup-scud* they winna fa.

> Ere twa three bouts, their win' will fag,
> An' puffin' come instead;
> Nae wonder they'll be soon dane out,
> For dancin's nae their trade.

> * *doup-scud:* heavily on the backside

41

Mr Peacock was also a member of the Aberdeen Musical Society, which had the cream of North-east society in its ranks. He often wrote the music for local events, including an anthem for celebrations marking the Coronation of George III. The magistrates and councillors, accompanied by 'noblemen and gentlemen of distinction' and led by the drums, fifes and French horns of the Musical Society, marched from Marischal College to a theatre set up at the Market Cross, where they drank his Majesty's health.

For years now, the Castlegate has been little more than a bus terminal and a clutter of pedestrian crossings, the old Mercat Cross adrift in a sea of traffic. The area around the Castlegate was at one time a warren of courts and closes – Smith's Court, Shuttle Lane, Burnett's Close, 'Shelly' Close (a landlord who owned some of the houses in the close decorated them with shells) and Skipper Scott's Close, now known as Chapel Court.

The Castlegate is a storehouse of famous names. James Francis Edward Stuart, the Old Pretender, dined in Skipper Scott's tavern in 1715. The artist James Cassie had a studio in the Castlegate and there is a yellow plaque on the south side marking the spot where Robert the Bruce's biographer, John Barbour, Archdeacon of Aberdeen, was born. Another poet, the future Lord Byron, whose mother had a house in Broad Street, nursed a small boy's passion for his little cousin, Mary Duff, who lived near the Plainstanes in the Castlegate. Edward Raban, Aberdeen's first printer, set up his printing press there in 1622. But, although the Castlegate was the heart of the city, disease and poverty gnawed at its bones, for behind the black closes were the slums.

The Castlehill area had a seedy reputation up until comparatively recent times. Drunkenness and prostitution were rife. John R. Allan wrote about 'the dragons of Peacock's Close and Shuttle Lane'. He recalled how, as a bairn, an old harridan with whisky on her breath lifted him up into her 'bosie' and told him about the chamber pots they emptied on policemen's heads in Shuttle Lane. Long before that, in 1850, a petition was raised by feuars and proprietors in the Castlegate to have the name of Peacock's Close changed. It said that it had 'fallen into such disrepute that the very name is sufficient to deter parties from taking houses in the area'. Happily, the petition was

The Castlegate of half a century ago, when regular markets were held around the old Market Cross. This picture was taken in 1934, when the last Timmer Market was held in the Castlegate. It later moved to a stance in Justice Street. Picture by courtesy of Aberdeen City Libraries.

rejected – and now Peacock's Close is coming into its own again.

If Harry Gordon had been around today, he could truthfully have claimed that 'there wis peacocks doon in Peacock's Close' – or at least one peacock. It flutters its fine feathers above the entrance to Peacock Printmakers. The organisation was founded in 1974 to provide facilities for artists to make prints. There are monthly exhibitions in three galleries, and across Smith's Court are the Artspace Galleries, whose exhibitions include work of national and international importance. Mr Peacock would have approved. In addition to his dancing and musical talents, he was an accomplished painter of miniatures. There is also a print museum, almost on the spot where Edward Raban produced his first *Aberdeen Almanac*. The almanacs proved so popular that other printers stepped in and copied them.

The Printmakers are not actually in Peacock Close, but in the close next to it, and the yellow plaque recording that 'the Father of Scottish country dancing' lived and worked there is also well away from it. It is a shabby pend, as are most of its neighbours. Peacock bought a piece of ground running along the back of Skipper Scott's tavern. He built several houses on it and established his home and dancing school there. If the council purchased the property in the neglected area behind the Castlegate closes and opened up enterprises similar to the Printmakers' project, this corner of the city could have a new lease of life.

A new city square is expected to arise Phoenix-like from the dereliction of the Castlegate, but some take the view that the area should be left to history and a new square developed elsewhere. The possibility of turning Broad Street into a square, with Marischal College as its background, was raised when plans were being drawn up for St Nicholas House, but the skyscraper protagonists won the day, raising a concrete and mosaic tile monument to 'modern' architecture, while building the ground floor of granite as a gesture to tradition. The Aberdeen Beyond 2000 group would like to see Union Terrace Gardens turned into a city square, for there it would 'fully reflect the grandeur of Aberdeen's architectural heritage'.

That architectural heritage has been badly misused by post-war planners. It has been said that the early nineteenth-century architects, men like Archibald Simpson and John Smith, added grace and dignity to the city. Whether future generations will say the same of late twentieth-century planners remains to be seen. Simpson and Smith left their imprint mainly on the centre of Aberdeen, and the Castlegate is a natural starting point for a stroll into the city's architectural past – 'fae the Duke tae Babbie Law'. The phrase once measured the length of Union Street, but no longer, for the Duke and Babbie have both moved on. The Duke was George, 5th Duke of Gordon, whose statue was erected in the Castlegate in 1842 and removed to Golden Square in 1952. Babbie Law ran a shop at Holburn Junction.

With pedestrianisation of the Castlegate and the revival of the old open-air markets near the Mercat Cross, the area will regain some of its old glory. The markets go back to the days

Aberdeen's Union Street is to the Granite City what Princes Street is to Edinburgh. This view along the mile-long thoroughfare was taken from the top of the Salvation Army Citadel in the Castlegate. On the right is the Clydesdale Bank, with its familiar coloured terracotta figure of Ceres, the Goddess of Plenty. Behind it is the Old Tolbooth, while west of it is the Town House.

when there were hucksters' booths in the Castlegate, and the
Timmer Market, now a pale shadow of its former self in its
Justice Street setting, was also held there. The Mercat Cross has
been shuffled around like a pawn on a chess board, for it stood
at one time opposite the entrance to Lodge Walk. The 'Mannie
in the Green', now in the Castlegate, has also been pushed
around a bit, and some people think his rightful place is in the
Green. This curious little statue on top of a stone well-house
dates back to 1708. It stood in the Green for over a century,
but its original stance was in the Castlegate, where it
ornamented the Castlegate well. It was simply known as the
'Mannie o' the Well'. It was taken down when the Mercat Cross
was moved in 1841 and erected in the Green in 1852.
Alexander Robb, a local tailor and deacon of the Tailor
Corporation, who had a reputation as a poet, wrote 'The
Mannie o' the Well's Lamentation' when the statue was
uprooted from his Castlegate stance:

> Whare's a' my frien's in Aberdeen?
> Why am I flittit to the Green? –
> 'Mang carls and carlines I've never seen
>   Why am I set?
> When 'mang my frien's I sud hae been.
>   In Castlegate

Towards the end of last century, the Aberdeen historian
William Robbie, commenting on the fact that the arches of the
Mercat Cross had once been boarded up so that the Cross
could be used as a Post Office, said: 'Men seemed to be utterly
blind to anything like architectural beauty'. He added smugly,
'We are now more aesthetic in our tastes'. That was in 1893,
when work had just begun on the building of the Salvation
Army Citadel (or Barracks, as it was called then), which was to
dominate the east end of Union Street. It looked over the head
of the Duke of Gordon to the North of Scotland Bank (now the
Clydesdale), the work of Archibald Simpson, and to Simpson's
Union Buildings on the opposite side of the street, and beyond
them along the shining length of Union Street.

Now we can look back and ask ourselves if we are any more
aesthetic in our tastes another century on. The late Fenton

Wyness, an architect by profession and a local historian of considerable note, wrote in 1971 that when the generation then starting school had grown up the face of the city would be completely altered. That generation has now reached maturity, and Wyness's fears have already been justified. He thought that the Granite City was being replaced by architectural forms which broke with tradition both in expression and materials, and he warned that if the city continued to follow the trend it would fall from architectural grace.

As Aberdeen moves into the last decade of the twentieth century on the back of the most ambitious redevelopment scheme in its history, there have been complaints about bland and ill-considered shopping centres and Philistines converting the entire city into concrete boxes. This is the age of pedestrian precincts and shopping malls, although Aberdeen calls them 'Centres', not malls. These bright, soulless arcades of consumerism have sounded the deathknell of many independent stores in the city centre. The Trinity Centre was built on the site of Trinity Hall, home of the Seven Incorporated Trades until it moved to Holburn Street. The St Nicholas Centre was, in effect, spawned by the Marks and Spencers development. It virtually wiped out St Nicholas Street, changed the whole character of this corner of Union Street, and presented a frontage that did little for the architectural beauty of the area, but a great deal for 'Markies'.

Morrison's Economic Stores once stood on the site. An older generation of people remembered the days when 'Raggie' Morrison was king and when the old tramcars came rattling and swaying down George Street. They spoke nostalgically of 'the Queen', the statue of Queen Victoria, where courting couples met, and they thought of how Victoria had twice been banished from St Nicholas Street. The first time was in 1888, when her statue was moved to the vestibule of the Town House because the marble was decaying, the second was in 1964, when she was banished to Queen's Cross to gaze forlornly westwards towards Balmoral. Dukes, queens and Babbie Law, all had to give way to progress . . . the sort of 'progress' that made Fenton Wyness raise a questioning eyebrow.

On the north side of the St Nicholas Centre, where Schoolhill dips down to meet the Upperkirkgate, you are on the edge of

Aberdeen's St Nicholas Street as people knew it before the First World War, with tramcars rattling up the street and Queen Victoria surveying the scene from her pedestal near Union Street. The site where Marks and Spencer now stands was known as Queen's Corner.

another massive development – the Bon-Accord Centre. Climb the fourteen storeys of St Nicholas House and look down on it from above Provost Skene's House and you become aware of the vast space it occupies. Moreover, you realise that Aberdeen will never be quite the same again. The heart has been torn out of it.

In the early days of the development, when bulldozers were churning up the land between the Upperkirkgate and St Andrew Street, I looked across the dust and rubble towards the Gallowgate, whose demolition, along with that of the Guestrow, was described by Fenton Wyness as 'a major disaster', although what took place there was slum clearance, not commercial redevelopment. I was thinking of an arcade far removed from the glass and glitter of the modern shopping mall. This was the Arcade in the Northern Co-operative Society's office block, between Loch Street and the Gallowgate, where generations of

48

Aberdonians collected their twice-yearly dividend – the 'divi'. 'Divi' day was as important as Hogmanay or the Trades holiday. Housewives cashed their 'Co-opy checks' and went into the Arcade to spend their money. It was a unique and architecturally fascinating shopping precinct and its destruction was little short of vandalism.

Standing out in the wasteland east of George Street was the Northern Co-operative store, built in the late Sixties, a four-storey building whose ribbed concrete walls, symptomatic of the 'new' architecture, were universally detested by Aberdonians. Rising almost incongruously next to it was a small granite building which once housed the Aberdeen Soup Kitchen, where, back in the early nineteenth century, Willie Godsman sipped his broth.

Willie was a beggar who earned a few pennies by selling ballads. One of the ballads he unsuspectingly peddled was a satirical take-off of the town council's efforts to overcome the city's financial difficulties, with the result that the magistrates banned him from the soup kitchen. Our old friend Deacon Alexander Robb wrote a poem about it and Willie hawked it through the street, earning himself the princely sum of £9, enough to buy his own broth for weeks to come:

> Then buy my lamentations, frien's,
> Your penny pieces draw,
> An' Willie aye will bless the day
> His broth was ta'en awa'.

Of all the new shopping centres, the most interesting to come up for consideration in 1987 was the St Nicholas Triangle, which, as the city's department of planning recognised, lay at the historic and commercial heart of Aberdeen. Upper and lower level malls were planned for the Triangle, which was bounded by Union Street, St Nicholas Street and Correction Wynd. 'Sympathetic restoration' was what the planners had in mind for this development. Correction Wynd got its name from a House of Correction which stood there in the seventeenth century. The steps that lead to it from Union Street are adjacent to the colonnade fronting the churchyard of the Mither Kirk of St Nicholas, which was the work of John

Smith, Aberdeen's first city architect, known to most people as 'Tudor Johnnie'.

This facade was erected in 1829, and for ten years before that a stretch of waste land separated Union Street from the churchyard. Visiting circuses and menageries used it, including Wombwell's, who put on performances for Queen Victoria at Balmoral when they came north. The wild beast shows were popular – Wombwell's had thirteen lions and lionesses. No one would expect clowns and lions in St Nicholas kirkyard today, but the Aberdeen magazine *Leopard,* looking at proposals for the redevelopment of the city, pointed to the immense opportunities for greater use of the church complex for secular as well as religious projects. At present, folk sit about the churchyard eating their lunch-time sandwiches, although some years back there were complaints that they were desecrating the graveyard by sunbathing on the slabs.

The Mither Kirk has never really capitalised on its main attraction. St Nicholas churchyard is Aberdeen's miniature Père-Lachaise. This is the French cemetery where Paris buries its famous dead, and it has become as popular a tourist haunt as the Champs Elysées. The names in St Nicholas may not be internationally known, as in Père-Lachaise, but they are famous enough to Aberdeen folk. There are authors and artists, soldiers and musicians, provosts and poets. 'Tudor Johnnie' lies not far from his granite screen, and Archibald Simpson is buried under a simple granite stone in the shadow of the East Church of St Nicholas, which he restored in 1835-37. The artist William Dyce is buried there, and the printer Edward Raban, as well as two other notable printers, James Chalmers, who produced the first *Aberdeen Journal* in 1748, and John Forbes, who was involved in the publication of the city's first newspaper in 1657.

Behind the gloomy tombstones, many of them green with mould, lurk mystery and magic. John Anderson, the great illusionist, who was born in Kincardine O'Neil in 1814, is buried in St Nicholas. He was known as the Wizard of the North, an apt title for a man who could catch bullets between his teeth. Anderson lies in the same grave as his mother, Mary Robertson, who died in 1830 at the age of forty. Below her name are the lines:

The St Nicholas Street that generations of Aberdonians knew has gone, shut off from Union Street by the St Nicholas Centre and a Marks and Spencer store development. The street, or what remains of it, is now linked to George Street by a shopping mall.

> Yes! She had friends when fortune smil'd,
> It frown'd, they knew her not,
> She died, the Orphans weep but liv'd to
>   mark this Hallow'd Spot.

What story lay behind this bitter little verse? Anderson, who must have been one of the orphans who wept for Mary Robertson, died a pauper seventeen years after her death. Below his name on the tombstone are the words, WIZARD OF THE NORTH.

Near Anderson's grave are the Drowned Soldiers, four young soldiers of the Royal Highlanders who lost their lives while bathing at Aberdeen Beach in 1864. Dr Thomas Livingstone, the 'miracle physician'; Gavin Turreff, a local historian who was said to look like 'a cultured Micawber'; Catherine Symes, the Princess of Benevento ... the list is endless. The city's department of leisure and recreation produced a booklet with a map of the kirkyard. It would be useful if a larger version of the map was displayed in the churchyard, or some sort of information board put alongside the more interesting stones. Whether they would last is another matter, for both kirk and kirkyard have suffered at the hands of the grafitti merchants.

Down the Correction Wynd steps the road leads under Union Street to the Green, which, after going through a period of decay and neglect, now looks forward to 'conservation-led' redevelopment. At the east end of the Green is the unattractive gable-end of the Aberdeen Market, all that is left of the New Market. In 1971 it became part of the British Home Stores and was confined to two lower floors. There is nothing there now that has any real link with the glory days of the building designed by Archibald Simpson. It was built in 1842, burned out in 1882, and immediately rebuilt almost in its original form.

It was, I suppose, the forerunner of the modern shopping mall, with everything under one roof, a huge arcade with galleries running round the whole length of the building and a basement floor leading into the Green, while the magnificent main entrance was on Market Street. It had character, a soul if you like, which is more than can be said of the present New Market. It smelt of salty fish, raw meat and market candy. There were, I seem to remember, a proliferation of butchers' shops. The sharp Aberdeen tongue mixed with the accents of Buchan and the Mearns, and from all around the hall a babel of noise drifted up into the vast glass and wrought-iron ceiling.

At the end of the corridor leading from Union Street to the main hall there was a slot machine which provided heart-stopping drama for the price of a penny. When you put a coin into the machine it creaked into motion to show a fireman rescuing a damsel in distress from the first-floor window of a burning house. I often wondered what happened to that machine; it would be worth a fortune today.

The hall and the basement provided food for the stomach; upstairs was food for the mind. There was an Aladdin's Cave of second-hand books in the galleries, row upon row of them, piled high on stands that groaned under such intellectual weight . . . Greek and Latin classics, romances, books on law, architecture, and mathematics, anything and everything the bookworm would want. For those who were less literary-minded there were other attractions. You could get your arm tattooed or have your palm read by a fortune-teller. Did they look into their crystal balls and foresee the day when the New Market would disappear down the throat of a monolithic superstore?

Up on Union Street, fourteen cats were sitting staring at me. They are called Kelly's Cats, but they are actually leopards. They got their nickname from Dr William Kelly, who used them as *filials* when he designed new parapets for the Union Bridge. In 1964 the cats on the south side disappeared and the cats on the north side found themselves gazing across Union Street at a glossy row of shops. The gap had been filled in. Today, Kelly's Cats – and Aberdonians – have an uninterrupted view of a fashion shop, a Pizza Hut, a shoe shop and a Tie Rack . . . all this in place of a striking panorama looking south to Torry and Tullos Hill. William Robbie, who thought that men were blind to beauty a century and a half ago, might have had something to say about this piece of visual blasphemy.

Happily, the skyline to the north, including the Central Library, the South Church and H.M. Theatre ('Education, Salvation and Damnation'), will remain inviolate, for the iniquities of earlier civic fathers are not likely to be visited on present-day planners, who talk about the valley of the Denburn, including Union Terrace Gardens, as 'the most significant landmark feature in the centre of the city'. The introduction of a dual carriageway on the Denburn is an important factor in the development of the area, but the idea of raising Union Terrace Gardens to street level or turning it into a car park has never really gained much support.

Looking down on the Denburn from Union Bridge, I tried to imagine how it had looked in the days when the old Bow Brig spanned the burn. The burn itself disappeared underground when the railway came in the 1860s. Below, where the road vanishes into the gloomy cavern created by the Trinity Centre, stone steps take you from the Green to Windmill Brae, where the brig crossed the Denburn on the route of the old highway into the city from the south. Up the

Horse-drawn tramcars and cabs . . . and Union Bridge with a view on
both sides. When this picture was taken about 1880, a statue of Albert,
the Prince Consort, stood at the corner of Union Street and Union
Terrace. In 1911, when the bridge was widened, it was moved to the east
end of Union Terrace and replaced by a statue of King Edward VII.

Denburn to the north was the Mutton Brae, which ran down
from Schoolhill. People coming down the Brae could get to
Union Terrace by crossing the Denburn on a footbridge. No
such link exists today, but the question of access to the Gardens
from the Denburn has featured largely in the city planning
department's proposals for the area.

Mutton Brae was the haunt of some of the many odd
characters who lived in the centre of Aberdeen a century ago.
In Mutton Brae there were Feel Peter and Feel Jamie, while up
in the Castlegate you would find Feel Roddie, Turkey Willie
and Piddlie Guyan. No one seems to know how Mutton Brae
got its name, but it can be found in different parts of
Aberdeenshire as well as in the city. It is a pity that these old
names were lost when the streets disappeared . . . names like
Dubbie Raw, which vanished when St Nicholas Street was built,
or Aberdeen's own Rotten Row, a continuation of the Shiprow.

Some, of course, are best forgotten. Skene Lane, off Skene Street, was known as Swine's Close, and, according to G.M. Fraser, whose 'Aberdeen Street Names' was recently republished, the reason for its name was pungently obvious.

The Doocot Brae is also gone. No one would recognise it by that name, yet it was known to generations of Aberdonians . . . as the Monkeyhouse. Officially, it is the Commercial Union Assurance building at the junction of Union Terrace and Union Street, but thousands of couples still call it the Monkeyhouse – 'Meet me at the Monkeyhouse' – undeterred by the fact that the Doric porch where they wait has been shut off by an unromantic management. Now they stand on the steps in the rain.

The Assurance building, where a dovecot once stood, was originally a private house, but in 1854 it was leased to the Northern Club, and from its window in 1863 Victoria unveiled the statue of her beloved Albert at the corner of the Union Bridge. Albert was moved to Rosemount Viaduct in 1914 to make way for King Edward VII. They seemed to make a habit of shunting Royalty about in those days.

The Doocot was where two thousand soldiers led by Sir John Cope camped in 1745 after ordering the town to give up its arms. From here to Schoolhill, not counting the cast-iron leopards on Union Bridge, five statues survey the scene – the massive granite and bronze sculpture of Edward VII, Robert Burns with his daisy, the seated figure of the Prince Consort, Sir William Wallace with his outstretched arm pointing the way to the parterre stalls in H.M. Theatre, and, outside Gordon's College, the statue of General Gordon of Khartoum. For my money, Rabbie and the Prince have the best view, for they look on to what is one of the most elegant streets in the city.

West of Union Terrace you run into a pocket of streets named after precious stones – Diamond Street, Silver Street, Ruby Lane, Golden Square and, on the other side of Union Street, Crown Street. Why they were called that is a mystery. Diamond Street was where they danced away the war to the music of Archie Alexander and his band at the Palais de Danse. Golden Square became the home of that ducal escapee from the Castlegate, George Gordon. The Duke has a perfect right to be there, for back in the early years of last century he headed a committee formed to raise money for the building of the Assembly Rooms, to which the Music Hall was added in 1858. The block backs on to Golden Square and South Silver Street. The familiar Union Street frontage was the result of a competition run by the Duke's committee to find a suitable design for the Assembly Rooms – the winner was Archibald Simpson.

The Duke of Gordon has become a parking attendant. He looks down on a nightmare of traffic. At one time there was a lovely lawn in the centre of the Square; now there are cars, cars, cars, all circling desperately in the hope of finding a vacant place. It has been one of the major problems facing city planners. The complaints have rumbled on over the years, but there has been little action. Now, enhancing and restoring the character of the Square has moved up the priority list, one idea being to clear parking so that there is an unobstructed view from Union Street. The Duke would come into his own again.

The same problem exists in nearby Bon-Accord Square. Unlike Golden Square, Bon-Accord Square does have a small garden area. A simple block of grey granite stands in the middle of it – a memorial to Archibald Simpson, who designed both the Square and Crescent. Simpson lived for a time in Bon-Accord Square and died in 1857 at No. 1 East Craibstone Street, one of the short streets which funnel traffic into the Square from either end. Craibstone is really Crab's-toun. John Crab, a Flemish immigrant who settled in Aberdeen, owned Crab's-toun (or Craibstone) at Bucksburn and was also the owner of Crabstone Croft in the town's inner marches. The Crab Stane at the corner of Langstane Place and Bon-Accord Terrace was the old boundary stone.

Both the city council and the Aberdeen Beyond 2000 group look upon the west end of Union Street as being ripe for development as an upmarket shopping area. The council points to Thistle Street, Rose Street and Chapel Street as streets which might have a 'speciality shopping role'. Chapel Street has already moved a long way towards that goal. Thistle Street and Rose Street were said by G.M. Fraser to be in a 'region of fanciful names'. One of them, Henry Street, which ran to the wall of the old Bridewell prison at the end of Rose Street, has long since vanished. It was named after George Henry, Provost of Aberdeen in 1850-53, who was said to be 'a very quaint personage'. He was the last person in Aberdeen to wear powdered hair.

The Capitol Cinema has been a prominent landmark in the Union Street scene for more than half a century. Before that the Electric Theatre stood there. It was the city's first cinema, opened in 1910. You could get a seat, a cup of tea and a cake for sixpence (threepence without refreshment), and the tradition of catering for the inner needs of cinemagoers is still maintained in the Capitol Restaurant. It was also the first cinema in the North-east to introduce a cinema organ. Its neighbour, the Playhouse, has disappeared, as has the Majestic and the old Poole's Palace in Bridge Place.

The only other cinema remaining in Union Street is the ABC at the Shiprow. The Cosmo in Diamond Street, the Belmont in Belmont Street, and the Queen's Cinema at the corner of Back Wynd have all gone, along with other smaller cinemas off Union Street . . . fleapits like the Starrie (Star) in Park Street and the Globie (Globe) in Nelson Street. They said there were so many hungry fleas in them that you went in with 'langers' (long trousers) and came out with shorts.

The Queen's building was originally the Advocates' Hall, designed by John Smith in 1836. When the Society of Advocates quit their Back Wynd premises in the middle of last century they moved to Concert Court, off Broad Street, where in 1987 the city's legal brethren cautiously opened their doors to the public to celebrate the bicentenary of the Advocates' Library. There are 10,000 volumes in the library, providing a fascinating insight into how Aberdeen's lawyers have helped to advance and record the city's history.

Union Street begins and ends with a benediction. At the Castlegate there is the Salvation Army Citadel and at Holburn Junction there is Christ's College. The college, with its familiar square tower and battlemented turret, was built in 1850 to train ministers for the Free Church. Babbie Law's 'bit shoppie' at No. 8 Wellington Place (now a part of Holburn Street) was a favourite haunt of the Free Kirk students, as it was with farmers heading home after the Friday markets. They found it a 'shoppie weel stocket, door seldom locket'.

C

Babbie's shop, which closed in 1885, was licensed, which made it popular with carters coming down from Rubislaw with granite setts from the quarry. So we are back where we started, with the stone that made Aberdeen what it is today, a Granite City. In one of the reports prepared by Bert Allen, the city's director of planning, he makes an interesting comment on how Aberdeen should present an environment attractive to tourists. 'It is important', he declared, 'to complement the city's 'Britain-in-Bloom' image with an equally vigorous promotion of the architectural heritage of our unique 'Granite City.' In other words, Aberdeen – a city of granite and roses.

DEESIDE

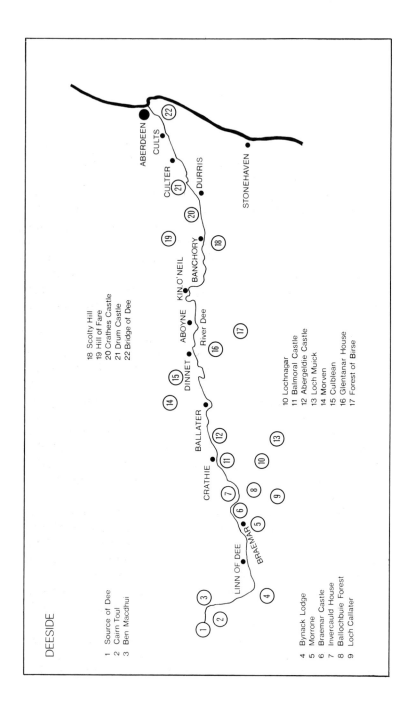

DEESIDE

1 Source of Dee
2 Cairn Toul
3 Ben Macdhui

18 Scolty Hill
19 Hill of Fare
20 Crathes Castle
21 Drum Castle
22 Bridge of Dee

4 Bynack Lodge
5 Morrone
6 Braemar Castle
7 Invercauld House
8 Ballochbuie Forest
9 Loch Callater

10 Lochnagar
11 Balmoral Castle
12 Abergeldie Castle
13 Loch Muick
14 Morven
15 Culblean
16 Glentanar House
17 Forest of Birse

Chapter 4
A Queen's Paradise

Aberdeen's main street was lined with 80,000 people – more than the city's total population at the time – when Queen Victoria landed at Waterloo Quay from the Royal yacht *Victoria and Albert* on Friday, September 8, 1848. People had come from far and wide for the great day – it was the first visit by Royalty in nearly 200 years. Once outside the city, the Queen's open carriage passed through twenty-three triumphal arches on its journey up Deeside to Balmoral. There were receptions at Banchory and Aboyne, and at Ballater a 21-gun salute was fired from the rocky summit of Craigendarroch, where a huge flag fluttered over the scene. 'We arrived at Balmoral at a quarter to three', the Queen noted precisely in her *Journal.*

In the century and a half since Queen Victoria made that journey from Aberdeen to Balmoral, countless thousands have taken the Royal road up Deeside. The first trickle of tourists became a flood when the Deeside Railway was opened in 1853 and the Queen travelled to Balmoral by train. She was a poor railway traveller. On one occasion, an irate John Brown stamped along the station platform to convey to the driver her Majesty's displeasure. The train, he said, was 'shakin' like the very devil'. Nevertheless, the *Aberdeen Journal* predicted that the line was 'likely to become the high-road to the Royal residences'.

The final boost came in 1868 when the Queen wrote about her 'dear Paradise' in her *Journal of our Life in the Highlands*. Long before that, some early travellers had set down their thoughts on Deeside. Among them was John Taylor, the Thames Waterman known both as the Water Poet and the Penniless Pilgrim, who came over the hills in 1618 to hunt with the Mar gentry, admiring their 'Tartane' hose and their plaids ('a mantle of divers colours'), and, in 1769, Thomas Pennant, the naturalist, gazing in awe at the 'vast theatre' of the mountains, their naked summits topped with 'perpetual snow'. As Dr Joseph Robertson, the Aberdeen historian and journalist, pointed out more than a century ago, the writers praising Deeside included 'Pennant, Cordiner, Sutherland, Taylor, Mrs Grant, Robson, Skene Keith, Sir Thomas Dick Lauder, and a whole string of et ceteras'.

The tourist trek to Deeside was gathering momentum before Queen Victoria put her Royal stamp on it, and not everyone welcomed the possibility, as Robertson put it, that Deeside was about to be 'desolated by cockneys and other horrible reptiles'. With his tongue in his cheek, he advocated the forming of anti-cockney unions in every village, and, parodying Byron, he pictured a lisping Cockney sitting on his portable three-legged stool on the summit of Lochnagar, admiring the 'vite summits' of the mountains and sighing 'for the wallies of da'k Loff ne Gar'. His fears about what a tourist invasion might do to Deeside were to prove remarkably prophetic.

Deeside became the sporting playground of Royalty, and in a book on King Edward VII as a sportsman Captain Blair Oliphant, of Ardblair Castle, Blairgowrie, wrote about its great peaks and little hills, its solitude and its storms, and what he called 'the laughter of a thousand streams'. In the middle of all this, he said, the river was the soul of the land. The River Dee rises high in the Cairngorms, bubbling into life on the great gravelly plateau of Braeriach and plunging down towards the long gash of the Lairig Ghru. It passes through some of the loveliest country in Britain, fed on its 85-mile journey to the sea by tributaries like the Clunie, the Gairn, the Muick, the Tanar and the Feugh.

The Feugh is the last major tributary to join the Dee as it rolls on through Banchory to Aberdeen. It featured in David Grant's poem about the great spate of 1829, 'the like o' which, sin' Noah's flood, the warl' never saw'. Rampaging through the Forest of Birse, the spate carried all before it − 'harrows, barrows, cairts an' pleughs, an' neep machines and sleds, skeps o' bees an' sowen sieves, an' skulls an' tattie creels'. The farms mentioned in Grant's epic poem can still be seen by those who explore this quiet backwater south of Banchory . . . Dalsack, Clinter Mill, Dalbreck, Bogendreep and Ennochie. It was at Ennochie that a 'cluckin' (hatching) hen' was seen sitting on a chest in the middle of the river, causing Grant to speculate:

Gin she were carri't to the sea,
Afore her ark gaed wrang,
An' may be spairt by Davie Jones
To bring her cleckin' oot,
Gin she wad rear them like a hen
Or like a water coot?

Hundreds of picknickers laze on the banks of the Feugh during the summer, but in winter the narrow road through the Forest of Birse traces a cold and lonely finger far into the Firmounth hills. There was a time when anyone walking in the Birse woods in winter was liable to come upon a curious portable wooden shed with a glass frontage. Inside the hut was a figure in a fur-lined coat, with his legs and feet wrapped against the cold, busily painting the snowy scene. The artist was Joseph Farquharson, the laird of Finzean, whose winter landscapes became known the world over.

Because of his liking for snow scenes with sheep in them, his fellow Academicians nicknamed him 'Frozen Mutton', but Farquharson – or his ghost – has had the last laugh. Half a century after his death in 1935 his pictures are back in vogue, on show at Aberdeen Art Gallery and selling briskly as prints and Christmas cards. He was one of a number of prominent nineteenth-century painters who made Deeside their canvas, many of them, like Edwin Landseer, winning the patronage of Queen Victoria. Among the local painters who found favour with the Queen was James Giles, the Aberdeen artist, whose watercolour sketches of Balmoral helped Victoria and Albert make up their minds that their Scottish home would be on Deeside.

The Feugh tumbles into the Dee below the Brig o' Feugh at Banchory, where spectacular salmon leaps have become a tourist attraction. They have even laid out a small car park so that people can stop and watch the fish jumping. Before local government reorganisation, Banchory was the only Deeside community of any size that lay outside the Aberdeenshire net. It belonged to Kincardine, where it now remains under Kincardine and Deeside District Council but it was mentally annexed by Aberdeen a long time ago and the physical take-over came when it grew into a commuter bedroom for the sprawling city. It is still a popular spot for Aberdonians out on

James Scott Skinner, the Strathspey King. His father was a gardener at Banchory-Ternan and Skinner was influenced by Peter Milne, of Tarland, whom he regarded as one of Scotland's 'grandest Strathspey players'. There is a memorial tablet to Skinner in Banchory's High Street.

their traditional 'Sunday run', or visiting Crathes Castle, two miles away, which has become one of the most popular castles in the Dee valley. They drive into Banchory for their cakes and coffee, and there are times when the High Street is a motorist's nightmare.

One of the places they stop for a meal is Scott Skinner's Restaurant, which, much more than the barely noticeable plaque in the High Street, is a reminder that Banchory was the home of the Strathspey king, although the great man would have twitched his waxed moustache in disapproval at the caricature of a Highlander with a fiddle outside the building. There is a lounge inside called 'The Laird of Drumblair' after one of James Scott Skinner's compositions. He once recalled that the tune came to him, 'pat and complete', in the middle of the night, and he jumped out of bed and wrote it down on the only paper he could find – a piece of soap paper. There is a set of bagpipes as well as a fiddle in the lounge, recognising, consciously or otherwise, the affinity that once existed between the two instruments.

Deeside produced many famous pipers, but it was no less noted for its fiddlers in the nineteenth century. There were men like John Cameron, of Crathie, a 'celebrated performer' who for forty years went over the Mounth every winter to entertain the folk in the remote upper reaches of Glenesk; Willie Blair, Queen Victoria's official fiddler; Duncan Cumming and John Sivewright at Braemar Castle; and Alexander Troup, a fiddler and dancing master at Ballater. In the Square at Tarland there is a memorial to Peter Milne, who gave Scott Skinner his first fiddle lessons and was regarded by Skinner as a genius. Milne became an opium addict and ended up busking for pennies.

Skinner was born at Banchory-Ternan in 1843 and died in 1927 – the last of the great fiddler-composers. His best-known tune was 'The Miller o' Hirn'. Hirn is three and a half miles north-east of Banchory and Skinner's composition was named after his friend, James Johnston, who was miller there. It is a forlorn, neglected place now. Looking at it, I had a mental picture of the bewhiskered Skinner sitting there, bow scraping, fingers dancing, 'shakin' his fit' as John Brown had told him to do at a ball at Balmoral. Skinner first played before Queen Victoria when he was still in his teens, appearing at Balmoral as a member of a juvenile musical group known as 'Dr Mark's Little Men'. The 'little man' grew up and was invited to teach the tenantry on the Royal estate. The fact that he had more than a hundred pupils is a clear indication of the widespread interest in fiddling. Skinner was on friendly terms with John Brown, and it was at a ball attended by Victoria that Brown shoved him towards the Queen and said in a loud voice, 'Noo,

Skinner, ye're in the richt quarter noo! Shak' yer fit, man!
Shak' yer fit!'

Eight miles west of Banchory is Kincardine O'Neil, the oldest
village on Deeside, which was by-passed by the Deeside Railway
in 1857. Now, with a peculiar kind of irony, the railway has
disappeared and the village wilts under an endless stream of
traffic rumbling through on its way to Aboyne and Ballater.
The ruined medieval church in the centre of the village was
once a hospice serving travellers going south by the Cairn a'
Mounth, a route regularly taken by Alexander Ross, a native of
Kincardine O'Neill, who taught at Loch Lee in Glen Esk. This
dominie-poet, who was described by Robert Burns as a 'wild
warlock', wrote a pastoral tale called *Helenore* which made him
famous. He was still crossing the hills from Loch Lee to
Deeside when he was in his eighties. He died in 1784 in his
eighty-sixth year.

The village of Aboyne is too far from Balmoral to bask in its
reflected glory, which is probably why it was regarded at one
time as 'a dull, half-way house'. It began to change in the mid
nineteenth-century, when George Walker, an Aberdeen book-
seller, was touring Deeside with Aberdeen's pioneer photographer, George Washington Wilson. Walker, one of GWW's
closest friends, often went with him on his photographic
expeditons and became Boswell to Wilson's Johnson,
chronicling their travels in a 17-volume manuscript journal.
In 1859, he saw Aboyne becoming a 'lodging-house village'.
The visitors were sportsmen 'with gay knickerbockers of a loud
pattern and Turkish caps', and, like Joseph Robertson, Walker
looked at the future with an uneasy eye. 'We began to fear for
Deeside', he wrote.

Aboyne is still a 'lodging-house village', but not to the same
extent as neighbouring Ballater, and, like Banchory, it has a
large commuter population. A survey in 1978 showed that 64%
of its working population travelled to work in Aberdeen. Not
much, according to the planners, is likely to change in Aboyne,
but it can happily rest on its laurels, for it has a modern
community school and centre with a swimming pool, games
rooms and cafeteria. Its once-grand railway station, which lay
in a ruinous condition for many years, is now a smart shopping
centre. It has an excellent golf course and a large village Green

The setting for the Ballater Games at the foot of Craigendarroch, the Crag of the Oaks. Ballater sits between two hills, Craigendarroch and Craig Colillich, the Hill of the Old Women, which is used as the course in the Games' annual hill race.

in which kilted Deesiders doff their caps to the Laird at the annual Aboyne Games. The Games were at one time held in the middle of the same week as the Braemar Gathering, but when attendances began to slump they were moved to a Saturday.

Just outside the village, gliders dip and swoop over the Deeside hills, watched by sightseers from a picnic lay-by specially laid out to cash in on this high-flying sport, and across the River Dee is the estate of Glentanar, part of which is a national nature reserve. It was opened up to the public some years ago through the Glentanar Charitable Trust, set up by the present owner, the Hon. Jean Bruce. When you walk through its woods and over its hills you find the initials 'WCB' stamped on stones, wells and monuments. They can be seen, for instance, on the Rest and Be Thankful, a place where walkers can sit and admire the view after puffing up the Fungle hill.

The Rest and Be Thankful was laid out by WCB – Sir William Cunliffe Brooks, an eccentric laird who, among other things, built the beautiful Chapel of St Lesmo in Glentanar. It stands on the ruins of Braeloine House, where there was once a thriving community catering for the passing trade on the old Firmounth road to the south. I once saw a photograph of the redoubtable Sir William standing outside Glentanar House with a party of house-guests. The picture was taken by a local photographer whose work, although it stood comparison with that of George Washington Wilson, never received the recognition it deserved, either locally or nationally. His name was Robert Milne. He took over where Wilson left off and became one of Queen Victoria's favourite photographers. He had studios in both Aboyne and Ballater and in 1896 was appointed Photographer to Her Majesty in Ballater.

Two years ago, I came upon a unique collection of Milne's photographs, now in posession of his grand-daughter, Mrs Margaret Mair, in Aberdeen. Two old albums were packed with pictures, not only of Queen Victoria and the Royal Family, but of life on Deeside at the end of the last century. Sadly, his negatives were all destroyed in a fire in the studio in Ballater, which may have at least partly explained why the spotlight shone so brightly on GWW and never on the Deeside photographer.

Visitors exploring the paths and tracks in Glentanar seldom wander into Wilcebe Road. It is not one of the offical walks. It stands on a back road on Belrorie Hill and as you puzzle over the name the penny begins to drop . . . Wilcebe . . . Will C.B. . . . William Cunliffe Brooks. Sir William named the road after himself. There are about half a dozen wells along Wilcebe Road, each inscribed with a message from the laird. One, a play on the word 'well', tells you that you are 'Well to know when you are well off', another is a reminder of the whisky smuggling that went on in Glentanar – 'The worm of the still is the deadliest snake in the hill'. You leave Wilcebe Road with this WCB homily ringing in your ears – 'Drink, Thank, Think'.

The road from Aboyne runs on to Dinnett and the twin lochs of Kinord and Davan, also a nature reserve, lying at the foot of Culblean and its big sister Morven – Byron's 'Morven of Snows', which Queen Victoria climbed on her fat little pony (it 'panted dreadfully', she said) and, looking out from the summit, marvelled at 'such seas of mountains'. Below Culblean is the great rocky bowl of the Burn o' Vat, where the outlaw

Gilderoy had his hiding place. To the south, the River Dee loops round to meet the main Deeside road at Camus (or Camas) o' May, the bend of the plain. There was also a Camas na Ciste there, but it has disappeared from Ordnance Survey maps. The name meant the bend of the coffin, so presumably it had some connection with the old kirkyard at Tullich.

Tullich looks across the Dee to the inn on the slopes of Pannanich Hill. Both lie in the land of lost dreams. Tullich, which once had a market, a post office and an inn known as the Change-house at the Stile of Tullich, suffered from the boom which followed the discovery of 'miracle' waters on Pannanich. The old ferry across the Dee was unable to cope with the hordes of sick and ailing people who flocked to Pannanich Inn, which was built for the miracle-seeking pilgrims, and the new village of Ballater began to take shape. Tullich's days were numbered, but Pannanich's reign as a great spa was even more transitory. There are no more miracle cures at Pannanich, the wells are neglected and unused, and the inn has to compete with a huddle of hostelries in the village it helped to create. In recent years, it had been closed for long periods, its shuttered windows facing over the Dee to the ruins of Tullich kirk, but in 1988 it opened its doors again.

Ballater's future was assured, and Tullich's doom sealed, when Queen Victoria opened a new bridge over the Dee in 1885. It was one of the successors to the first bridge that carried traffic away from Tullich. The Royal link has been maintained, for Ballater acts as butcher, baker and candlestick-maker to Balmoral. There are more Royal coats of arms per square foot in Ballater's Bridge Street than in any other town in Scotland. Some show appointments to the Queen, the Queen Mother and the Prince of Wales. It is one of the most popular tourist towns on Deeside, with the largest number of hotels, boarding houses and B&B establishments. A recent major development was the setting up of a time-sharing complex at the Craigendarroch Hotel.

Ballater, nestling snugly between Craigendarroch and Craig Coillich and set against the distant backdrop of Lochnagar, has had a fairly stable population over the last decade or so, running at about 1200 in 1986 and expected to rise to 1325 by 1991, but the figures are dramatically swollen by summer

The Braemar Gathering in 1849, when it was held in front of Braemar Castle. A year earlier, Queen Victoria saw her first Gathering at Invercauld House.

visitors, who come for its scenery, its 18-hole golf course, its walks – and its Royal connection. Yet this lovely little town, built around a village green which has Glenmuick Church as its centrepiece, has remained relatively unspoiled by tourism, partly, perhaps, because most of its notable buildings are listed, including the Royal bridge over the River Dee. The Victoria Barracks are among the listed buildings. The barracks look as if they had been built for the great British Raj, their design more in keeping with the plains of India than with Deeside. There is a highly improbable story that plans were mixed up and that Ballater ended up with barracks intended for India.

In the Deeside Survey, Kincardine and Deeside District Council pointed out with a faint air of surprise that one building *not* listed was Ballater Station, 'scene of much Royal patronage in the past'. There is a plaque on the station wall commemorating the rebuilding of the station in 1886 and the opening of a Royal Waiting Room for Queen Victoria. Across the Station Square are the Victoria and Albert Halls, with a large stone slab on the wall reminding passers-by that the Prince Consort was regarded by his adoring subjects as 'Albert the Good'.

The station stands at the end of the Deeside line (Victoria wouldn't allow it to extend any further), but there is nothing to show that the trains that came puffing into it unloaded more history on Ballater's doorstep than any other village of its size was ever likely to see. When King George VI arrived at the station he always made a brisk dash towards the Royal car, anxious to get away from crowds and cameras, but the Queen (now the Queen Mother) invariably tugged at his sleeve and held him back until the photographers got their shots.

The Shah of Persia was one VIP who passed through the station porch on his way to Balmoral to visit Queen Victoria. He was a villainous-looking man, surrounded by grim-looking bodyguards with drooping moustaches and long coats. The Princess Royal complained that he always had a roasted lamb in his room and pulled it to pieces with his fingers. When Nicholas II, Tsar of Russia, arrived in September, 1896, a hundred men of the Black Watch stood in the station square in the pouring rain as he set off to Balmoral in a torchlight procession of five Imperial carriages and an escort of Scots Greys.

Visitors can walk back through history by strolling along a walkway laid out on the disused line from the Station Square to Cambus o' May. There has been a good deal of talk about creating a long-distance footpath on the old Deeside Railway, but they may have left it too late. I have walked the line from the Duthie Park in Aberdeen to Ballater and much of it is impassable. Farmers have bought sections of the line and fenced it off; at other points the line is overgrown and impenetrable.

The hills close in on you as you move up Deeside, becoming more majestic, sometimes more threatening, opening up tantalising glimpses of the corries of Lochnagar. Beyond the Dee a huge stone pyramid rises about Easter Balmoral. This was the cairn built by Queen Victoria after the death of her beloved Albert. It looks down on a track running up Glen Gelder to a building standing in an isolated woodland on the approaches to Lochnagar. Above the door an inscription tells you that this is 'Ruigh nan Bhan Righ' – the Queen's Shiel – which has been a Royal picnic spot since Queen Victoria had afternoon tea there with Empress Eugénie of France.

Looking up the Clunie Water to Morrone, which overlooks Braemar. This was the view shown in a photograph by George Washington Wilson. John Duff, who is restoring the old Mill of Auchendryne, seen on right, has a Wilson print of the mill on his wall.

Nowadays the Royal picknickers do their own barbecues.

Two miles beyond Crathie is the old coaching inn at Inver. From Inver a track runs north up by the Fearder Burn to Aberarder. There was a farm called Auchnagymlinn at the top of the glen, but it was destroyed in the Muckle Spate of 1829. They say a giant is buried there, the last of his race, and if you want to find his burial place you will have to search for a grave 20 ft. long. The highest farm is now Auchtavan, where the Queen Mother has a shiel, although it is seldom used nowadays. It is a lonely place, with magnificent views over Ballochbuie Forest to Lochnagar. West of Auchtavan is the Bealach Dearg, the red pass, an old route from Deeside to Speyside by Loch Builg, Inchrory and Tomintoul.

The Bealach cuts through Invercauld estate, whose laird, Capt. A.A.C. Farquharson, owns vast acres of Upper Deeside. In 1874 it was estimated that the estate extended to 87,700 acres, and today it is not far short of that. It may even be more, for lairds are coy about spelling out how much land they own. What is certain is that Captain Alwyne Arthur Compton

72

Farquharson is the biggest landowner in Aberdeenshire.

The estate employs twenty-seven people, seven of them keepers and three of them ghillies. With the drop in the number of grouse, the sporting emphasis has swung to deer-stalking, as it has on the Mar Estate, farther up the Dee. Both estates turn a wary eye on hill-walkers and other 'intruders'. Invercauld has put up a 'Keep Out' sign on a lovely walk along the banks of the Dee from Invercauld to Allanquoich when, in fact, it is, or was, a public road. A.I. McConnochie, author of *Deeside,* one of the classic books on the area, wrote in 1900 about 'a right-of-way westward along the north bank of the river.' It was obviously used at one time for vehicular traffic, for McConnochie pointed out that 'this public road has been allowed to become somewhat impracticable for carriages'. The local community council claims the road as a right of way and it is surprising that no one has taken it further. Kincardine and Deeside District Council say it is 'unfortunate' that the estate has put a 'no entry' notice on this 'attractive route'.

There is another road where a proliferation of 'Private' signs has caused concern. It runs close to the rear of Invercauld House and leads through Gleann an t-Slugain to Beinn a' Bhuird. Invercauld House is sometimes called Invercauld Castle, which is not surprising, for it is no less castle-like than its Braemar neighbour, also owned by the Farquharsons. In fact, Braemar Castle has been described as a sham and its pepper-pot ↱ turrets criticised as 'unsightly English-style crenellations'.

Be that as it may, they are romantic enough to draw a steady stream of paying visitors. Invercauld, on the other hand, is not open to the public, which is the public's loss, for there is probably as much history inside its walls as there is at the Braemar fortalice. The laird's lady, American-born Frances Strickland Lovell Oldham of Seattle, Washington, has been a flamboyant figure on the Upper Deeside social scene over the years, responsible, among other things, for setting up Invercauld Galleries.

Invercauld was very much at the centre of Deeside life in Victoria's time. The Braemar Gathering was held at Invercauld House in 1848, when the Queen and the Royal Family made their first appearance at the games. A marquee capable of

The Linn of Dee, where the road ends and the wilderness begins. It can be a dangerous spot. Byron slipped and almost fell into its deep pools when he visited the Linn.

holding 800 people was erected in the grounds. The following year the gathering took place at Braemar Castle, and in 1859 it was held at Balmoral, which was the venue on four other occasions. It went to Cluny Park, Invercauld, in 1903, when King Edward turned up with his two eldest sons; he jokingly called them 'The Duke o' York's twa loons'.

The games were also held at Mar Lodge, where the great Donald Dinnie took part. When the Prince of Wales (later King Edward VII) turned up late at Mar Lodge, Dinnie was asked to go out and throw the hammer and caber. 'Ay,' said Donald, 'I'll gang oot, but I want twa pound.' When he was told it was an honour to throw before the Prince, Dinnie said, 'I dinna gie a damn'. Later, when other competitors failed to toss the caber, Donald went on to the field and showed them how.

The Royal link with the Braemar Gathering goes back to the time when King Kenneth II (971-95) held a race on the hill which carries his name, Craig Choinich. That, at any rate, is what they say, and it is a nice touristy story. What *is* certain is that the Gathering, with its Royal patronage, has put this curiously Victorian village on the international map.

Braemar was originally two villages, linked by the bridge over the River Clunie. On the east side was Castleton, on the west Auchendryne. When I stood on the bridge and looked up the Clunie, I was gazing through the lens of George Washington Wilson's camera. It was from there in 1870 that he took a photograph of the old Mill of Auchendryne against the background of Morrone. A copy of the picture hangs on the wall of John Duff's house – inside the mill.

John, a retired police officer, became known far and wide as the leader of the first Braemar mountain rescue team. Now he spends his time renovating the old mill, which was a ruin when he took it over on his retirement. The original mill wheel is still intact. The Granary, as he calls it, is now his home, and he has brought life back to a building that has been a landmark in Braemar for almost 200 years. Some time ago he discovered an entry in an eighteenth-century diary kept by the Earl of Fife which read, 'This day examined the new mill on the Clunie'. The date was July, 1790.

From Braemar one road– the highest public motor road in the country – chases the Clunie south over the Cairnwell to Glenshee, while another follows the Dee west to the mouth of the Cairngorms. For veteran drivers, the Cairnwell revives memories of cars spluttering up the Devil's Elbow with boiling radiators. People still talk about going over the Devil's Elbow, although only a few isolated stretches of the old military road are left. I have always thought that the double-turn of the Elbow should have been retained alongside its modern successor, perhaps as a picnic area. It would have been as much a tourist attraction as the falls at the Linn of Dee.

Still, there is no shortage of visitors at the Cairnwell. Glenshee is a major skiing area, second only to Glenmore on Speyside. Its main problem at peak periods is congestion at chairlifts and ski tows, not to mention car parks. It has a car-park space for nearly 1500 vehicles and its uplift capacity in 1988 was 16,000, double what it was five years earlier. The Deeside Survey, carried out by Kincardine and District Deeside Council, said there was potential for more residential accommodation not only in Braemar but in the glens. There is constant pressure for new ski runs – and a never-ending battle

The Cairnwell, just outside Braemar, draws thousands of visitors to the ski slopes in winter. Here, Mike Grant, a Braemar ski instructor, teaches youngsters on the nursery slopes.

over conservation. The National Planning Guidelines, produced by the Scottish Development Department in 1984, identified areas suitable for skiing but ruled out for other reasons. The Beinn a' Bhuird area was said to be 'undesirable' because of its outstanding scenic attraction, and the Deeside Survey recalled proposals in the 1960s to introduce skiing in this area.

The great Mar Lodge fiasco is likely to make developers think twice about repeating the Beinn a' Bhuird experience. When the estate was bought from Capt. Alexander Ramsay by Swiss brothers Gerald and John Panchaud, from Lausanne, in 1961 the plan was to turn it into a major ski centre, with a ski tow behind the lodge, a restaurant, a cafeteria, a huge car park, a ski school and a children's crèche. There were also to be lunches and tea dances in Mar Lodge's historic ballroom. Just in case there was a shortage of snow, a snow-making machine which would cover an area of twenty acres was brought in.

In December, the Aberdeen *Press and Journal* confidently predicted 'plenty of snow', and for the first few weeks heavy falls covered the slopes. The start of the New Year saw 'abnormal conditions' – no snow. Artificial snow was pumped over the hillside, but it turned to slush and finally into rock-hard ice. The Mar Lodge company also flirted with the idea of bulldozing a track 3700ft. up Beinn a' Bhuird to give access to new ski slopes, but nothing came of it. In the end, the project was abandoned and the estate returned to its original aim of catering for game and fishing sportsmen. Today, wealthy guests, many from the Continent, pay fat fees to shoot grouse, stag and ptarmigan.

Mar Lodge, with its half-timbered gables and red-tiled roof, looks as if it would be more at home in Gerald Panchaud's native Switzerland, but it is less exotic than its predecessor. New Mar Lodge, which had stags' heads decorating the roof of the building. When this building was destroyed by fire in 1895, the Duke of Fife's first thought was, 'Save the stags' heads!'

There have been three Mar Lodges. New Mar Lodge stood on the south side of the Dee at Corriemulzie, while the first lodge was behind the present building. New Mar Lodge must have been a lively place. In September, 1852, Queen Victoria danced at an open-air torchlight ball at Mar Lodge, and five years later 'the ladies' in the Royal party returned from the Lodge at five o'clock in the morning and set out with the Queen four hours later to open the new bridge at the Linn of Dee.

The Victoria Bridge spans the River Dee at Mar Lodge and the road from there to the Linn passes through some of the most picturesque scenery on Deeside. Only a short distance west of the Victoria Bridge is the little hamlet of Inverey, where the famous Maggie Gruer played host in her homely cottage to hundreds of hill-walkers and climbers. At the far end of the village is a new shooting lodge built by Captain Ramsay, who is a good deal less popular with hill-goers. He enraged hill-walkers, conservationists and the local authority by bulldozing a massively ugly track well into the glen, Kincardine and Deeside District Council took steps to have it put right, but it is unlikely that it will ever return to anything remotely resembling its original appearance. The Linn of Dee, where the river boils and gushes spectacularly through a narrow rocky channel, is the end of the line for most people, although a road runs along the north side of the river, behind Mar Lodge, to the Linn of Quoich, where Jacobite toasts were drunk at another watery rock formation, the Earl of Mar's Punch Bowl, when the Standard was raised in 1715.

The Linn of Dee is a popular tourist spot, but it can be a dangerous place. The poet Byron is said to have almost lost his life there when his lame foot caught in the heather and he stumbled and fell. An attendant caught him before he went over the edge. There was a wooden bridge over the Linn from about 1830, but before that the only way to get across was by a precarious plank – or by jumping. Aberdeen's pet poet, Deacon Alexander Robb, told of one man who attempted this 'grand gymnastic feat' while on an outing to 'the roaring rumblin' linn' before there was a bridge. He was with a party which set off from Ballater in a horse-drawn coach and dog-cart. Robb wrote a poem about it called 'A Deeside Jaunt', and in it he described what happened when one of the travellers, 'puff'd up with self-conceit', decided to leap the gap. He got over all right, but when he turned to jump back his face was 'white as drifted snow'.

> O, when I saw his look o' wild despair,
> I turned me roun', and I could glower nae mair.

A piper with the party ran and got two boards, which they were able to throw across 'the frightful span'. They helped the unhappy athlete back over the planks to the other side, where everyone 'curs'd him with a hearty curse'. When they got back to Ballater, the Deacon slipped away to have a dram or two. His epic poem ended with the lines:

> I declare
> I got oblivious and mind naething mair.

Chapter 5

Royal Hunters

The Linn of Dee sits on the edge of the wilderness some six miles west of Braemar. From the Linn a track runs west up Glen Dee to the White Bridge, where it forks north and south, one route going through Glen Tilt to Blair Atholl, the other turning up by the Chest of Dee to the Lairig Ghru. Beyond the Linn to the east is the entrance to Glen Lui, the most popular Deeside gateway to the Cairngorms. Up at Derry Lodge, two famous passes lead to Speyside, one by the Lairig an Laoigh, the other by Lairig Ghru.

The Cairngorms have always seemed to belong to Speyside, with Deeside as the back door, but few people realise how far the old Aberdeenshire boundary pushes into this mountain terrain. The greater part of the Cairngorm range is in Aberdeenshire, including Ben Macdhui (4296 feet), the highest summit, and Cairntoul (4241 feet). Braeriach (4248 feet), where the infant Dee springs into life, has the county boundary with Banffshire running across its summit ridge.

Cairngorm itself (4048 feet) is claimed by Inverness-shire. It is the focal point of development in the Spey Valley, the magnet that draws an ever-increasing number of skiers, climbers, hill-walkers, and holidaymakers to the area. The storm over conservation is heard more loudly on Speyside, but echoes of it rumble through the valleys to where the Dee spins its silver thread eastwards.

Deeside has been described as one of the most important mountain and wildlife areas in Scotland. It has one of the greatest concentrations of nature conservation sites in the country, for, as well as a number of Sites of Special Scientific Interest, it can boast five national nature reserves. The largest, Cairngorm, is partly in the Highland region, while another, Caenlochan, is shared with Tayside. The smallest, and probably the least well-known, is the oakwood at Dinnet, between Ballater and Aboyne. The Muir of Dinnet is also a nature reserve and is becoming increasingly popular with members of the public.

This vast, beautiful land is no longer the exclusive preserve of the lairds. Some estates, like Glen Tanar, have taken steps to cater for the inrush of visitors; others play King Canute, discouraging the public, ignoring rights of way, and showing unbending hostility to climbers and hill-walkers. 'Landowners are generally reluctant to recognise any but the most significant rights of way over their land,' stated the Deeside Survey produced by Kincardine and Deeside District Council.

Upper Deeside, the scene of many historic rights of way battles, has always been the playground of the wealthy. Salmon fishing and deer-stalking were status sports a century ago, made even more so by the arrival of Royalty on Deeside. Today, cash goes hand-in-hand with status. The letting of shooting rights brings in a considerable income, as does the sale of venison. Yet the same sort of thing was happening in a more gentlemanly way at the beginning of the last century. In 1800, Sir John Maxwell formed a sporting consortium to take a ten-year lease of Abergeldie estate and in the next twenty or thirty years the number of advertised deer forests trebled.

There are still crumbling monuments to these bygone days in some of the remote Deeside glens ... old, ruined shooting lodges lying at the head of the Slugan Glen on the Invercauld estate; by the banks of the Geldie Burn on the way to Glen Feshie; and at Bachnagairn above Loch Muick. Hill-walkers pushing through Glen Dee to the Lairig Ghru pass a rickle of stones on the edge of a burn tumbling down from a rocky hill called Sgor Mor. This is Reenacula, whose dead stones are a reminder of the day when a Company of Sportsmen

> Resolv'd to march, be't fair or foul, a'
> From Buchan to Reenacula.

That was in 1816 and the sportsmen were the last of the free-ranging hunters, roaming the moors at will, shooting wherever they saw game. It was the kind of practice that came to an end when profit-conscious lairds began to let out their deer forests for hunting.

They set off from Auchry in Buchan. With them was an Aberdeenshire gamekeeper-poet called Jamie Christie, who recorded their exploits in 600 lines of poetry that owed something to Burns and a lot to McGonagall. His hilarious verse itemised an impressive 'bag' at the end of the day:

> Twenty-one braces and two hunder
> Of grouse, besides nine 'tarmigan,
> Thirteen score fowls they sure brought in,
> Besides six deer were kill'd anon.

As the happy poet summed it up, 'Who would have thought to kill so many, all in six days, part of them rainy'.

South of Reenacula, on the road to Glen Tilt, lie the ruins of Bynack Lodge, where Queen Victoria stopped to drink the health of the Duke of Atholl on her way home to Balmoral from Blair Atholl. In 1987 I met a sprightly octogenarian called Nell Bynack, who got her by-name from having spent her childhood at Bynack. Her real name was Helen Macdonald, but nobody ever called her that.

Nell is probably the last of the legendary Cairngorm figures, taking her place alongside the famous Maggie Gruer at Inverey. Her father was gamekeeper at Bynack and she told me with a chuckle, 'I'm hill-run'. She had been to the top of Ben Macdhui twenty-two times as an unofficial guide to hotel guests and she knew the hills like the back of her hand. One of her friends was Seton Gordon, the naturalist, who often stayed with her when she moved to Luibeg, near Derry Lodge. He always carried a spyglass which the Prince of Wales had given to him when they were at Cambridge together.

There are other reminders of the old deer-stalking days seldom seen by the public. Whatever you think of Mar Lodge from the outside (its style was once described as 'suburban Tudor'), there can be few complaints about its interior, with its paintings and works of art, and its chapel containing memorials to members of the Royal Family. When the earlier New Mar Lodge was destroyed by fire and the Duke of Fife cried 'Save the stags' heads', his plea must have been answered, for the ceiling of the ballroom at the present Lodge is decorated with hundreds of stags' heads. It is a pity that it isn't opened up to the public during the off-season like its near-neighbour at Balmoral.

Stags' heads are still very much in demand, particularly by

Deer on the track to Loch Muick. In winter they come down to feed at the Spittal of Glen Muick. The narrow path climbing up from the far end of the loch is one of two routes to the Broad Cairn, where a track goes by Bachnagairn to Glen Clova.

the German hunters who come to Mar Lodge. Willie Forbes, who was head stalker on Mar Lodge estate, helped his shooting guests to track and kill some of the 5000 red deer that roam the 77,500 acres of the estate – then he 'stuffed' them. He is a skilled taxidermist, as well as an accomplished artist, and his work is on show in a sporting store in Ballater's Bridge Street. He has 'stuffed' all sorts of birds – capercaillies, swans, geese and waterfowl, and he has also 'set up' sea trout and salmon. One of his best-known paintings is called 'The Drookit', set against the background of Ben Macdhui and Derry Cairngorm. Rain slants down over the hills as a drenched ('drookit') ponyman splashes through a stream with a dead deer slung over the back of his pony.

Willie's biggest 'catch' was the President of the United States. When President Gerald Ford was staying at Inverary Castle he caught his first salmon, and Willie was asked to 'stuff' it. It was only a six-pounder, but it found its way to the White House. He has also done a lot of work for Balmoral, and his most interesting job was 'stuffing' a pair of blood pheasants sent to him by an Army major who had been in the Himalayas.

Like most stalkers, he has a great love of the hills. He spoke about being out on the moors, of seeing eagles in flight and hearing stags in rut, of watching a sudden change of light in the hills, and of how nature gave him inspiration for his work as an artist. Stalkers have a curiously sensitive relationship with the animals they hunt. Jimmy Oswald, head keeper of the Glen Tanar estate at Aboyne, once told me of how he had been winter feeding a herd of deer when a party of hill-walkers came in sight. The deer were instantly alert, nervous and ready for flight, but they looked at him as if they wanted him to go with them. They moved away, hesitated, looked back as if urging him to follow them. Finally, when the walkers came too close for comfort, they fled.

I was with Jimmy in the ballroom of Glen Tanar House, looking at another ceiling studded with antlers and stags' heads. There were over 500 sets of antlers on the roof, dating from the 1800s through to the 1970s. Some carried the letter 'G' for Glen Tanar and others had the familiar 'WCB' initials of William Cunliffe Brooks. There was a row of six skulls inscribed with the words 'We killed Seven'. A shield in the middle explained that the missing seventh had been taken away by a Gustavus Schwabe, who took part in the stalk.

We were looking for the skull of the Haunted Stag. On Duchery Beg, high above the Water of Tanar, there are two pillars on the moor, each with a huge stone ball perched on a pyramid, standing 267 yards apart. The faded inscriptions tell how on 9th October, 1877, Cunliffe Brooks shot a deer from a distance of 267 yards, which was no means feat a century ago. These monuments to Victorian marksmanship can easily be found by following one of the tracks above the Water of Tanar. What happened to the Haunted Stag's antlers no one knows. We never found them.

The major deer forests on Deeside take in five estates – Abergeldie, Invercauld, Mar, Mar Lodge and Balmoral. Although deer shooting is commerically important to the estates, grouse shooting is less so. The Glorious Twelfth is not as glorious as it once was, for the number of birds has declined and shooting is regarded by some as no longer economic.

Hunting has always been a popular sport at Balmoral. Prince Albert was an enthusiastic deer hunter, but a bad marksman. Our picture shows St Hubert, the patron saint of hunters, on a bas-relief on the walls of Balmoral Castle. The sculptor was John Thomas.

There is a wide variation in the amount of shooting. On Balmoral there is shooting nearly every day of the week from August to December.

On one of the walls of Balmoral Castle there is a relief sculpture showing St Hubert, the patron saint of hunters. There should be another alongside it of Prince Albert, for it was the Prince Consort's enthusiasm for the gun that put the Royal seal of approval on the sport on Deeside. By all accounts, he was a bad shot and an even worse sportsman. He blazed away at anything he could see, sometimes hitting a deer he wasn't aiming at. He even shot a tame stag from the dining-room window of Blair Castle.

When you walk up Glen Gelder from Easter Balmoral and look west across the Gelder Burn you can see a long dark line running across the moor towards the Ballochbuie woods, below Ripe Hill. This is The Ditch, a trench four or five feet deep and nearly a mile long. Prince Albert had it dug out of the heather so that he could cross the open moor out of sight of the deer. That, at any rate, is the official explanation. The truth is that Albert disliked crawling about on his stomach when out shooting. The Ditch allowed him to stay on his feet, popping up periodically to take pot-shots at his quarry.

I have often wondered if Prince Charles has ever inspected The Ditch, or even walked along it, although its walls are beginning to crumble. He often goes horse-riding in the area. Not far from The Ditch there is a hitching-post near a path which leads to the Prince's Stone, a huge boulder on the edge of the Feith an Laoigh. On it there is an inscription, almost unreadable, which says that Prince Albert spent a night there when out shooting. But there was no question of Albert roughing it, for two wooden bothies were built, one for the Prince Consort, the other for the servants. Queen Victoria visited them, later recording in her journal, 'We lunched in the little 'housie' at the open door'.

Glen Gelder, lying in the shadow of the great corrie of Lochnagar, was a favourite haunt of the future Edward VII when he was Prince of Wales. It was there on Conachcraig that he killed his first stag in September, 1858, at the age of sixteen. Another Prince of Wales, Edward VIII (the Duke of Windsor), was also sixteen when he shot his first stag in 1910. It was a six-pointer weighing 13 stone 11 pounds. Edward was introduced to the sport by beating for his father, George V, for two shillings a day. 'I love shooting more than anything else,' he once wrote to the King.

Another member of the Royal Family who was 'blooded' while still a teenager was the present Queen, who often went stalking with her father, King George VI, at Balmoral. Princess Elizabeth, as she was then, also killed her first stag when she was sixteen. A silver tablemat gifted to King George marked a special day at Balmoral in September, 1945, when it was decided to try for as many species as possible. The bag included seventeen grouse, twelve partridges, six ptarmigan, three rabbits and one mountain hare. Only one stag was shot. It was duly listed on the tablemat – 'Lilibet (stag)'.

The Queen no longer shoots and the future Queen, Princess Diana, has only a limited interest in the sport. Prince Charles however, has inherited the Royal passion for stalking and both he and his father come north for a weekend on the Deeside moors long after the Balmoral season is over. I was once climbing the Capel Mount track from the Spittal of Glen Muick to Glen Clova when I was stopped by two soldiers, who were leading ponies and carrying walkie-talkies. They told me I would have to turn back because Prince Charles was shooting on the hill. I resisted the temptation to tell them that I was on an ancient right of way.

It was probably in the same area that the Duke of Edinburgh had an unusual confrontation with two walkers. After carefully stalking a stag, he was taking aim when it suddenly lifted its head in alarm and fled. The Duke, surprised, looked up and saw two young walkers heading in his direction. Despite the fact that they were on the Royal estate, there was no law to prevent them crossing the hill, but the Duke went down to ask what they were doing there. The apologetic answer was that they were taking part in the Duke of Edinburgh's award scheme and were out training for their gold medal.

There was a certain irony in the situation, for the Duke of Edinburgh's scheme is one of many which have encouraged young people to go out into the hills, yet incidents like these hold the seeds of conflict between landowners and hill-walkers. The landowners have formed themselves into a body called the East Grampian Deer Management Group, which has published a leaflet giving advice to walkers. It is insufficiently detailed, and not many walkers see it. Even if they did, it is more than likely that they would regard it as a restriction on their right to walk where they please in the hills.

The North-east Mountain Trust and other similar groups take the view that walking, mountaineering and cross-country ski-ing are legitimate economic land-uses. 'It is notable', said the Trust's sardonic response to the Deeside Survey, 'that the Survey omits to comment that stalking and shooting could be a problem for hill-walkers.' There is no easy answer. With the number of walkers increasing each year, the question of rights-of-way, skiing development, deer disturbance, and erosion is not likely to go away.

Whatever the importance of deer and grouse shooting to the Deeside economy, the salmon is still king, although, like grouse, there has been a significant decline in its numbers. The causes are said to be over-fishing in the feeding grounds and over-fishing off the coast. Nevertheless, as the Deeside Survey points out, the Dee Valley is still one of the best salmon rivers in the country, attracting fishermen from all over the world and making a significant contribution to the economy. As far back as 1898, Sir Herbert Maxwell, an authority on the subject, was saying the same thing. 'The Dee has become the very best angling river in the whole kingdom', he declared.

Dee salmon are small on average, but big fish are there for the taking, forty-pounders mostly, but few fifty-pounders. A forty-two-pounder caught at Birkhall (now the Queen Mother's estate) in June, 1926, can be seen in the tackle shop in Ballater's main street. Records show that a fifty-six-pounder was caught on the Ardoe water in October, 1886, and a fifty-two pounder at Park in 1918.

Royal historians have said little about Prince Albert's skill with the rod, preferring to stick to his deer-shooting escapades, but the Prince Consort certainly fished, and on one occasion took part in the ancient sport of leistering (spearing fish) at Balmoral. Queen Victoria, in her *Journal,* described how one hundred men waded through the river, 'some in kilts with poles and spears, all very much excited'. Albert, she reported sadly, stood on a stone but 'caught nothing'.

Unlike shooting, fishing was regarded as an acceptable sport for Royal ladies. Queen Alexandra fished for trout when staying at Abergeldie Castle, and her daughters, the Princesses Victoria, Louise and Maud, fished the pools below Birkhall, now the Queen Mother's home on Deeside. The Queen Mother was, and still is, an ardent fisher. From the Old Line, a wooded walk by the Dee from the outskirts of Ballater to the Bridge of Gairn, you can look across the river to a fishing lodge which the Queen Mother's closest friends gave to her as an 80th birthday present. The Old Line, incidentally, was the route which was to carry the Deeside railway from Ballater to Braemar, but Queen Victoria put a stop to the extension.

Back in 1967, the Queen Mother created a panic when she went fishing on the Dee near Birkhall. She had to wait for the pools to fill up after a long period of low water and at six o'clock in the evening her ghillie told her that there was now enough water to fish. When she failed to return by dusk a search party was organised. Armed with torches and hurricane lamps, they were about to set off when the Queen Mother

The Glas-allt-Shiel, the Royal lodge built by Queen Victoria on the edge of Loch Muick. 'The scenery is beautiful here,' she wrote, 'so wild and grand.'

arrived back. Unconcerned at all the fuss, she held up a twenty-two pound salmon and said, 'This is what kept me late!' The Queen Mother, who has always been very close to Prince Charles, her eldest grandson, taught him to fish by casting on the lawn at Birkhall.

There was a time when members of the Royal Family fished on Loch Muick (Prince Philip had a speedboat in the boat-house there), but that has become a thing of the past. There are two reasons for this: the absence of fish and the presence of crowds. Lock Muick gave good trout fishing in earlier years. Old paintings and photographs show fish being hauled in by net, and Queen Victoria wrote about rowing on the Muich, as she called it, with 'the boat, the net and the people in their kilts in the water'. Mabel Gordon, who was housekeeper at Birkhall, once showed me a photograph of her father helping King George V to haul in a net on Loch Muick. Mabel's grandfather, Geordie Gordon, was one of Queen Victoria's ghillies.

Colin Gibson, in *Highland Deer Stalker*, the story of a Balmoral stalker called Allan Cameron, wrote about house parties from the castle fishing on Loch Muick in King Edward VII's time. 'Balmoral had two boats – a heavy one, six-oared, and used for transport along the three miles of the loch, and a flat-bottomed coble for angling. Glenmuick had one boat, housed down at the Spittal end. These fishing parties were good fun, but nobody took the fishing very seriously. A few rowed over to the islet, while the majority walked round to the head of the loch and fished from the bank. The trout were small.'

Nowadays, the Royal fishers would have a gallery of hundreds. Glen Muick provides a jarring reminder of how much pressure is placed on Deeside by public hunger for the great outdoors. The Wildlife Reserve there is managed by Balmoral estate with the agreement of the Scottish Wildlife Trust and the backing of the Countryside Commission. In 1968, some 30,000 people passed through the Spittal of Muick, and in 1982 the figure rose to 50,000. It is still rising.

Thirty years ago there was no car park at the Spittal, only an unofficial lay-by where climbers left their cars when they went off to climb Lochnagar. Now there is a proper car park owned by Kincardine and Deeside District Council and at busy weekends it is packed with vehicles, with an overflow spilling along the road and on to the moor. The problem facing the council is whether to expand the car park; if they do, more visitors will be attracted to the glen and the narrow road from the Bridge of Muick will be unable to cope.

It was along this road that the drovers came in the old days, from the Bridge of Muick and south by Easter Balmoral to the river, which they forded before moving on to the Spittal. As the name indicates, there was once a hospice there and the key to it now hangs in the window of the Visitors' Centre at the Spittal. Not many people pay any attention to the scattering of stones on the right-hand side of the road as they approach the car park. These crumbling ruins are all that is left of the curiously-named Titaboutie, a house or inn where travellers stopped before making their way over the Capel Mount to Glen Clova.

For the most part, visitors picnic on the banks of the Allt Darrarie, walk the shores of the loch, or toil up Lochnagar. The distant hills swallow up the more adventurous walkers, who head for Broad Cairn and Bachnagairn, into the hollow of the Dubh Loch, or over the Stuic to Glen Callater. The increasing visitor pressure has not only disturbed wildlife in the reserve, but has seriously eroded paths around Loch Muick and on the route to the Lochnagar summit. At some points, the path up Lochnagar has been eroded to a width of thirty-five yards.

A few years ago I climbed Lochnagar to see the sun rise on the longest day. Celebrating summer solstice on the old mountain is a tradition that goes back to a time between the wars when Davie Glen, a Dundee cyclist and climber, set out to get a thousand people on top of Lochnagar. He almost succeeded. On the night I was there more than four hundred people had climbed to the top. Lochnagar must tremble under such assaults. Erosion creeps over the hill like a plague, but even worse are the bulldozed tracks that have scarred the hills on the Royal estate. We are trampling the land to death with boots and bulldozers.

The District Council believes that a management plan is needed for the whole of the Glen Muick and Lochnagar area, but it has also considered the possibility of spreading the load, taking the weight off Glen Muick and Glen Tanar and on the Muir of Dinnet. It takes the view that if a range of other facilities similar to those in the three main Deeside reserves were introduced throughout the area, the pressure could be spread over a number of locations. One of the tasks it set itself for the future was to find out if there were ways of exploiting the existing resources of Deeside for tourism and recreation.

Whether other areas on Deeside could be opened up to the same development as Glen Muick and Glen Tanar is debatable. Leaving aside landowner opposition, there are plenty of people ready to put up barriers, or even to man the barricades, at the first sound of tourist feet tramping into other wild places. Fear of over-development, of losing the qualities that make wilderness areas what they are, tends to lead to extreme thinking. The Scottish Wild Land Group, for instance, argue that on Speyside the Cairngorm chairlift should be closed to the public during the summer months. They also opposed the building of a footbridge at the Fords of Avon on the Lairig an Laoigh pass between Deeside and Speyside.

Certainly, Deeside has no shortage of 'undiscovered' glens.

Dark Lochnagar . . . and the loch which gave the mountain its name.
Hundreds of people climb it during the year, many of them unaware
that it can be a temperamental and dangerous hill. Byron
immortalised it with his lines about 'the tempests of dark Lochnagar'.

Some mark the old Mounth routes followed for centuries by
soldiers, packmen and drovers. Others are wilderness blind
alleys. For the most part, they are undisturbed by tourists and
uncorrupted by traffic, but time is not on their side. There are
glens like Callater, south of Braemar in Glen Clunie, which
seldom see tourists, yet motorists pack their cars and caravans
wantonly along the banks of the Clunie Water, turning the
road to the Cairnwell into a strung-out parking lot. Caravan
parking was eventually banned in Glen Clunie, but now a
caravan site has been opened in Braemar.

Take a three-mile walk to Loch Callater and you are in a part
of the glen which the Deeside Survey describes as 'idyllic'. It is
not an overstatement. I have always thought Loch Callater one
of the loveliest lochs on Deeside. It stretches away to the distant
Tolmount, following an old drovers' path that leads eventually
to Jock's Road and Glen Doll.

From the tableland above Loch Callater you can follow the
track that Queen Victoria took when she rode over the hills to

91

Caenlochan and Cairnwell, or cross the ancient Monega Pass to Glen Isla, or peer down into the black heart of Loch Kander – 'lonely, lonely dark Loch Candor', one Angus poet called it. When you walk across this plateau you get fleeting glimpses of the Cairnwell ski slopes, but it is only when you go downhill by the Glas Maol, following what Queen Victoria called the 'Month Eigie' road, that you begin to realise what sort of physical impact ski development has had on this mountain landscape. Victoria marvelled at 'the wonderful panorama'; she would not be amused by what she would see now.

But there are other less challenging areas to be discovered on Deeside. Just west of Ballater is Glen Gairn, which Amy Stewart Fraser wrote about so affectionately in *The Hills of Home*. It carries a heavy weight of traffic, cars rushing north over the old military road to Cock Bridge and the Lecht. Not many people stop for any length of time, except, perhaps, to look at the hugely humpbacked bridge at Gairnshiel Lodge, or the Teapot Cottage where the Queen and Princess Margaret played as children. Few venture away from the main road.

Here, there are paths over the hills from Tullochmacarrick and Easter Sleach to Corgarff, while a track follows the River Gairn west by Daldownie to Corndavon to Loch Builg and the cliffs of Ben Avon. The folk at Daldownie came to their door to wave to Queen Victoria when she passed that way on one of her Great Expeditions, but a few years ago the building was demolished. Nothing is left. Cattle raiders came through by Loch Builg from Tomintoul and Speyside, dodging Redcoats in outposts scattered about the hills, and in later years Glen Gairn itself became the haunt of freebooters and smugglers.

Deeside is riddled with old passes, forgotten tracks buried under the heather or trailing aimlessly into the hills. At present, hill-walking clubs and ramblers are rediscovering the old paths and 'ways', but in time even these will have commercial value, for there has been a sudden sprouting of 'activity' companies ready to cash in on the growing interest in the outdoors. The Scottish Wild Land Guides and Tramp the Gramps operate in the Deeside area and, with other organisations throughout Scotland, have formed themselves into a marketing congolomerate.

Feughside and Finzean, which have Clochnaben frowning

down on them near Banchory, are regarded by Kincardine and Deeside District Council as areas of considerable potential for the tourist trade, although there is some concern that development would destroy the special qualities of the valley. The Feugh rises on the slopes of Mudlee Bracks, where the ancient Firmouth and Fungle roads meet and push south to Tarfside in Glen Esk.

There are farms along the river whose names make me think of a verse written by a poet who obviously had no great opinion of Feughside folk:

> Easter Cleen and Waster Cleen,
> An' Percie and Dalsack,
> An' a' the boddies thereaboot,
> They are a middlin' pack.

Peterhill rises above Wester Clune. On today's OS maps its height is given as 617 metres, but older records show it as 2023 feet, while the Rev. Dr.George Skene Keith put it at 1930 feet. Keith, who was a minister at Keith-hall in the early nineteenth century, wrote an important book on the agriculture of Aberdeenshire, but he deserves a small niche in North-east history for other reasons. He was an ardent mountaineer who in July, 1810, took part in one of the earliest recorded rock-climbs. It happened while he was following the River Dee back to its source on Braeriach, when he had to climb a succession of huge rocks set at an angle of seventy to eighty degrees.

Before cartography became the skill it is, and long before people started bagging 'Munros', Dr. Keith decided to 'ascertain the Elevation of the principal Mountains of Marr'. He had an old-fashioned mountain barometer, a spirit level, a lot of enthusiasm, and little else. Peterhill was his first 'mountain', so it has some claim to fame. Two days later he checked the height of Clochnaben, which was said to be 2370ft. His finding was that it was 'not above 2000ft', and, in fact, he was on target, for it is 1900ft.

From there he went on to greater things. He climbed Lochnagar and got caught up in fog and drenched with rain; he visited the Linn of Dee, where he saw 'several foolhardy people' leap across the dangerous ravine; and he clambered up

Braeriach and diluted 'some good whisky' with water from the Wells of Dee. His notes describe an extraordinary scene on the summit of Cairn Toul, where he was soaked to the skin by rain and lashed by fierce winds. 'The wind battered us so much that two gentlemen holding umbrellas over my head could not protect me while I marked the height of the barometer in my journal.'

He and his party made their way down by the Poten Duon (the old name for the Devil's Point), lost their way and ended up exhausted in a shepherds' shieling in Glen Geusachan. They gave him oatmeal and bannocks, which he declared was 'the best meal I have ever tasted'. Some months later he was back in the hills again with his barometer and spirit level, puffing up 'Cairngorum' and 'Ben MacDouie'.

'The height of the principal mountains and the elevations of the Dee and the Don will render this country better known than it was formerly', he said. Well, that was true enough, but he could never have foreseen that the hills themselves might become too well-known, or that people would worry about erosion, rights-of-ways, conservation and the freedom to walk in these high places.

I sometimes think of him when I tramp over the Feughside hills. When he climbed Mount Battock and measured it he was 'quite disappointed' to find that it was only 2600ft. (he was 45ft. out) and he stood there for over an hour before going downhill. He probably had his umbrella over his arm and his notebook in his hand. At any rate, he left a message for future generations – 'to every man who undertakes a similar expedition'. He should, he said, always use a spirit level, along with his mountain barometer.

Chapter 6
The Balmoral Story

It was to the old Invercauld Bridge, on the fringe of Ballochbuie Forest, that Prince Charles brought his bride in August, 1981. The Royal newly-weds had just returned from a honeymoon cruise . . . and, as one newspaper put it, the world's Press was waiting for them 'like a shooting party waiting for the grouse to break'. As the Royal couple walked out of the Ballochbuie woods to talk to the seventy journalists, they said Deeside was the best place in the world. Princess Diana thought Balmoral was 'lovely'.

Ballochbuie casts its spell over every visitor. Like the Princess of Wales, Queen Victoria thought it 'most lovely'. It spreads its green cape across a great sweep of the Balmoral estate, reaching south from the River Dee to the high, rocky tableland around Lochnagar. It is one of the largest tracts of ancient pine forest in Scotland, although place-name purists argue that it should be called a wood, not a forest, because in this part of the country the word 'forest' means a deer forest.

Whatever the Ordnance Survey map says (and it plumps for 'forest'), Adam Watson and Betty Allan, co-authors of *The Place Names of Upper Deeside,* cast their vote in favour of the Wuid o' Ballochbuie. Queen Victoria had the same idea; she never called it a forest. After driving through it on her way to climb Lochnagar, she wrote about riding in 'the wood of Balloch Buie'.

When Victoria bought Ballochbuie from the Invercauld estate in 1878, she had a cairn built on Craig Doin with the inscription, 'The Bonniest Plaid in Scotland'. This is said to have come from a tradition that the last McGregor laird of Ballochbuie sold it to Farquharson of Invercauld for a tartan plaid. I have never been convinced that the story is true – no MacGregor worth his salt would give away land for a strip of cloth – and I would argue for an alternative theory that has its roots in Bovaglie Wood, a wind-shattered clump of trees in Upper Glen Girnock, east of Balmoral.

According to Watson and Allan, there is a local saying that the Glen Girnock wood 'haps (shelters) Bovaglie ferm like a plaid'. 'Bovaglie's Plaid' was the name of a Scott Skinner composition, and, since Bovaglie was Balmoral's neighbour, it is more than likely that Queen Victoria had heard it, and may even have listened to the Scots fiddler playing it when he performed at the castle. Later, when Victoria bought Ballochbuie, she probably remembered the tune – and the wood that 'happed' Bovaglie farm. She may have thought, with some justification, that Ballochbuie was a lot bonnier than any Bovaglie plaid. As far as she was concerned, it was the bonniest plaid in Scotland.

Ballochbuie has another place-name link with Balmoral. No one is very sure of the origin of the Royal estate's name. It has been called Bouchmorale, Ballmoral, Balmurral and Balmurrel. There have been endless arguments about its origin, but the most popular explanation is that it comes from Mor-choille, 'the big wood', which may have been the old name of Ballochbuie Forest. When a 'Both' or 'Bailie' was built on the outskirts of the forest it was called the 'bothy', afterwards the 'town of the big wood'.

From the main Deeside road, travelling west from Ballater to Braemar, you can look across the River Dee to Ballochbuie. This is as close as most people are likely to get to it, for it is closed to the public, although walkers sometimes stray into it from Glen Gelder and Lochnagar. Yet at one time you could have travelled the length of the Ballochbuie forest, starting at Easter Balmoral and coming out six miles later at the old military bridge at Invercauld. This was when the road through Ballochbuie was a continuation of the South Deeside Road, running through the Balmoral estate and going on to Braemar.

Albert and Victoria made sure that none of their subjects came too close to their 'dear Paradise'. Victoria put a stop to the proposed extension of the Deeside railway line because it would have invaded her privacy, and Albert took steps to have the road through Balmoral and Ballochbuie closed to the public. The official argument was that it was 'little used as a thoroughfare' and that it would lead to the evasion of tolls when the north Deeside turnpike road was completed. It is mind-boggling to think how much it would be used as a

Balmoral Castle in its mountain setting . . . a view seldom seen by the public. In the background is snow-covered Lochnagar, which Queen Victoria climbed, riding a pony, in 1848. The mountain was shrouded in mist. The Queen said it made her 'feel cheerless'.

thoroughfare today if it had remained a public road.

The Prince Consort had a new bridge built over the River Dee so that the turnpike road on the north side was carried across the river slightly west of the old military bridge and out of Balmoral territory. Now there are two bridges within a stone's throw of each other, one carrying traffic up and down Deeside, the other virtually unused, a picturesque tailpiece to the story of Victoria's determination to maintain her privacy at Balmoral. In the same year, 1859, the Balmoral Bridge was opened, as was the present East Lodge, replacing the suspension bridge half a mile to the east. The Prince Consort could never have foreseen that it would carry thousands of visitors across the Dee and into the castle grounds.

Not much has changed. Prince Charles and his young bride held their open-air Press conference so that photographers could get their pictures and leave them in peace during their Deeside holiday, although at Balmoral, probably more than anywhere else, the Royal Family can feel reasonably sure that their privacy will be respected. Nevertheless, on the south side of the Invercauld Bridge there is a sign pointing out that this is a private estate – strictly no admittance. Not even Queen Victoria was quite so rigid. One of the tracks on the south side of the bridge leads to the Falls of Garbh Allt, a well-known Ballochbuie beauty spot, and Victoria allowed the public to visit it on certain days of the week. It was said to be 'much frequented by tourists'.

There was a lodge at the Garbh Allt before Queen Victoria's time, according to the Aberdeen historian Joseph Robertson. It had its visitors' book, like many of today's shiels and bothies, and it also had its graffiti merchants. Robertson complained that some of these 'pitiful nincompoops' carved their names 'with a fifteen penny pen-knife on the door-post, table or window-sill'. He reserved most of his venom for 'would-be poets' who tried to out-Byron Byron with passages about lofty hills, tumbling torrents, and foaming falls rushing on 'the stun'd ear'. In particular, he picked out an Andrew Johnston, from Aberdeen, who visited the lodge on August 3rd, 1831. Johnston wrote:

> Garrowal thy romantic Sylvan scenes
> With admiration and great delight we view
> But from thee with reluctance do depart
> With tearful eyes do bid thy bowers adieu.

Well, it may not be great poetry, but it is better than the

obscenities I have seen scribbled in the visitors' book at Gelder Shiel. At any rate, the book, the poets, the tourists – and the lodge – have all vanished. Victoria spoke about admiring the view from 'the little bridge'. In 1867, it was replaced by the present bridge, built in 1878. It is a first-class piece of engineering, although it has virtually become redundant. They should let the public have access to the 'romantic sylvan views' at Garbh Allt when the Royal Family is not in residence.

In the maze of tracks that run through Ballochbuie, one leads to a lovely shieling in the heart of the forest south-west of the Falls, while another follows the Feindallacher Burn on an old right-of-way known as the Smugglers' Shank. It was used by smugglers carrying illicit whisky on the backs of garrons (hill ponies) to Glen Doll and Glen Clova in Forfarshire. Hill-walkers still occasionally take this route on their way to Lochnagar.

Balmoral had its share of illegal stills. Glen Girnock, east of Abergeldie Castle, had as many as a dozen 'black bothies' in the upper part of the glen, and it is said that the remains of old stills can still be found in remote corners of the estate. There is, in fact, an 'illicit still' almost on Balmoral Castle's doorstep, in the grounds of Lochnagar Distillery, but it is there only for display purposes. In the early nineteenth century, when at least half of Scotland's whisky production came from illicit stills, a whisky smuggler called James Robertson, from Crathie, turned from illicit whisky-making to legal distilling. His first distillery was in Glen Fearder, on the north side of the Dee, but it was burned to the ground by unlicensed distillers who disliked his new-found respectability. He then built the Lochnagar Distillery, becoming a licence-holder in 1826-27, but in May, 1841, the premises were reduced to ashes by another mysterious fire. It looked as if old resentments died hard.

In 1845, John Begg bought the distillery. Three days after its opening, Queen Victoria and Prince Albert visited the premises and tasted Mr Begg's whisky. They obviously liked it, for he was granted a Royal Warrant and his *Royal Lochnagar* became firmly established. For the next half-century or so, the story of Balmoral is punctuated by polite hiccups. Queen Victoria had a remarkably tolerant attitude to the drinking that went on in her Deeside home, perhaps because she liked a dram herself.

The last official portrait of Queen Victoria at Balmoral, taken by the Deeside photographer Robert Milne. Milne never reached the heights attained by George Washington Wilson, but he took many pictures of the Queen and members of the Royal Family.

Gladstone caught her lacing a glass of claret with a stiff shot of *Royal Lochnagar,* which by any standards must have been a potent mixture.

Tyler Whittle, in his book *Victoria and Albert at Home,* paints an appalling picture of drunkenness at Balmoral, where 'tippling was almost an occupational hazard in the royal service'. Prince Albert's garderobier, a man called King, was 'in the grip of drink', and his successor, Bray, 'showed signs of tippling', while the famous John Brown knocked them back with gusto.

The Queen's private secretary, Sir Henry Ponsonby, said that no festivity at Balmoral was complete without 'a case or two of Begg's best'. Certainly, whisky was served up on every possible occasion. When a cairn was raised on Craig Gowan to mark the purchase of the castle, the Queen noted that 'whisky was given to all', and when a bonfire was lit to celebrate victory at Sebastopol, Prince Albert described the celebrations on Craig Gowan as 'a veritable Witches dance, supported by whisky'. Willie Blair, the Queen's fiddler, was living proof of Victoria's belief that a drop of the hard stuff was good for your health. Willie, who frequently over-indulged, lived to be over ninety.

Whatever discreet drinking goes on inside Balmoral Castle nowadays, it can never match the binges that took place when Mr Begg delivered whisky to the castle 'in bottles with an attractive blue and black label, or, more generally, by the gallon in casks'. Interestingly, the Lochnagar Distillery no longer holds a Royal Warrant, and for a time the 'Royal' tag had to be dropped because of the Duke of Edinburgh's objection to it. It was later restored.

Today, Lochnagar Distillery is looking forward as well as back, and in 1988 it opened a museum and a restaurant to cater for the visitors who want to see where Deeside's illicit hooch was once made. There is still one vital link with the past – the distillery's water comes from springs in the foothills of Lochnagar, the mountain that gave the whisky its name.

The distillery stands in Easter Balmoral, which was a village in its own right when Queen Victoria came to Deeside. From the distillery a track – a disputed right of way – runs south to Inchnabobart on the River Muick, which the Queen often forded on her way to Loch Muick. Easter Balmoral still gives the appearance of a community on its own, its cottages clustered around the entrance to Balmoral. It has its own shop, post office and village hall. The shop was there in Victoria's time and was often used by members of the Royal Family, as it is today.

Easter Balmoral can claim to have two Royal residents living in the village, or almost, for Prince Charles and Princess Diana have their Deeside home at Craig Gowan, which stands just off

the track running from Strachan's 'shoppie' towards Glen
Gelder. It is a useful 'back door' for the Prince when he escapes
into the wilds. You could always tell when the Royal couple
were in residence, for a London policeman, resplendent in old-
style 'bobby's' helmet, stood at the end of the drive leading to
the house. The London 'bobbies' have gone, and now a neat
little wooden office has been erected outside the house.

The Royal golf course and a curling pond lie between Easter
Balmoral and the Gate Lodge at the main entrance to
Balmoral, while in the opposite direction is Clachnanturn, a
hamlet which once had a large market. Less than a mile to the
east is Abergeldie Castle, a Gordon property, which Prince
Albert tried unsuccessfully to add to his Deeside estate. He was,
however, given a long lease of it and Abergeldie housed many
Royal visitors over the years, including the present Queen's
father, George VI.

George's brother 'Bertie' (Edward VIII) thought its bat-
infested tower was haunted by 'the ghost of Kitty Rankie', who
was burned as a witch on nearby Craig nam Ban. The name of
the hill means 'the woman's crag'. Kitty Rankine – French Kate
– was a maid at Abergeldie who is said to have dabbled in black
magic. Patricia Lindsay, daughter of a local doctor, used to tell
how in Queen Victoria's time Old Effie, the housekeeper, told
bloodcurdling tales of mysterious noises and bell-ringing.

Balmoral is the melting pot of a curious mixture of romance,
superstition, ghosts and gory legends. Queen Victoria knew
about the witches of Deeside. Up to the middle of last century a
'witch-burning' ceremony was held at Balmoral on Hallowe'en.
This was called the 'Shandy Dann' ceremony, the name coming
from the word 'shane', meaning to break the spell of witchcraft.
On Hallowe'en, the effigy of a witch – 'Shandy Dann' – was
burned in front of the castle. Scores of marchers gathered to
hear an indictment read out accusing 'Shandy Dann' of
witchcraft. Then, as the bagpipes skirled and the crowd
cheered the witch's effigy was thrown on to a blazing fire.
Victoria wrote in her *Journal* about Hallowe'en celebrations at
Balmoral in 1867 – 'Louise looking like one of the witches in
Macbeth . . . the keepers and their wives and children, the gillies
and other people . . . all with torches'.

If any ghost haunts this lovely corner of Deeside, it is the ghost of Queen Victoria. Her presence is everywhere . . . in the statues and memorials scattered about the estate, in the castle, in the woods and gardens where she walked with Albert, and along the dusty tracks that took her into the hills on her Great Expeditions. Balmoral is steeped in Victoriana. Inside the Ballroom, which is the only part of the castle open to the public, the exhibition is completely Victorian. John Brown looks down on it with a disapproving eye. The simple fact is that the Royal Family regard Balmoral as a home, not a museum, and they have not flung open the doors to the outside world.

Across the River Dee, over the bridge which Prince Albert built when he closed the road through Balmoral, tourists poke about in the old kirkyard of Crathie, resurrecting history from the tombstones. There is a tablet erected by Victoria to the memory of James Bowman, who was her gamekeeper for seventeen years. Aged seventy-one, he was killed in 'a sad accident' in the Ballochbuie. There is also a stone erected by the Queen in memory of Peter Farquharson, her gamekeeper for twenty-seven years, and one (not erected by the Queen) to Hugh Brown, 'Highland attendant of Queen Victoria, brother of John Brown'. He died in 1886 at the age of fifty-seven. Then there is John Brown's own stone, marking the last resting place of the 'devoted and faithful attendant and beloved friend of Queen Victoria'. It is kept in good order. The most unusual one is to John Spong, who was the Queen's 'travelling tapissier' for nineteen years. He died at Balmoral in 1870.

The words 'Crathie Post Office' are inscribed below the name Thomson on one of the stones. You might think it an odd thing to find on a gravestone, but the Thomson family were postmasters of Crathie for 130 years. The post office, now a private house, sat on a hillock above the main road, near the drive up to Crathie Church. It did a roaring trade in ice-cream and picture postcards, and when it closed down a number of years ago Crathie lost its only tourist attraction, apart from the kirk.

There are few bed-and-breakfast signs at Crathie. There is virtually no accommodation for visitors in the area, although some houses take in people without advertising the fact. It wouldn't do to be seen cashing in on their Royal neighbours.

Crathie Church, where the Queen worships when she stays at Balmoral. There have been five Crathie Churches. The present church was built between 1893 and 1895. Thousands of people turn up at Crathie on Sunday to catch a glimpse of the Royal Family on their way to kirk.

Perhaps this will change, for even Balmoral is discreetly commercialising its attractions. Kincardine and Deeside District Council, in its Deeside Survey, commented on the lack of accommodation. 'Considering its significance', it said, 'it is remarkable that for most of the year there is little for the visitor to see or do at Crathie, except visit the church'.

For about two months of the year, Crathie Church has a congregation that any kirk would envy – and an overspill of hundreds. Sadly, it is Royalty, not religion, that draws them to its door. It is a remarkable fact that each year thousands of people flock to Crathie on Sunday just to catch a fleeting glimpse of the Queen and members of the Royal Family as they drive past them on their way to church. It is not a new phenomenon, for Queen Victoria became so disenchanted with Sunday sightseers that she often attended service in a specially-prepared room in Balmoral Castle.

Nor is there anything new in devout worshippers trying to catch a glimpse of the Queen inside the kirk. In an earlier

Crathie Church, Queen Victoria sat in an open gallery with every eye fixed on her. There have been five churches at Crathie. The first was established three miles east of Crathie by a ninth-century saint called Manire (there is a standing stone on the spot), the next was in the old kirkyard of Crathie, and the third was on the site of the existing church. The fourth was a temporary building used when the present church was being built.

The modern church sits in a strip of woodland high above the North Deeside Road, looking across the Deeside hills and the thirty-five-foot high memorial pyramid which Queen Victoria built on Craig Lowrigan to the Prince Consort. From it you can see the field on the south side of the Dee where the Grand Bazaar was held in 1894 to raise money for the new church. It was called 'the event of the season on Deeside', and special trains were run from Aberdeen to Ballater for it.

Robert Milne, the Aboyne man who became one of Queen Victoria's favourite photographers, caught two historic moments with his camera. One was the laying of the foundation stone by Victoria on September 11, 1893, the other was the two-day Bazaar. His pictures vividly mirror the excitement of the event. One shows the Balmoral Stall, manned by Princess Louise and Princess Beatrice. Royal contributions included a book-rack made by the Princess of Wales, embroidered cushions by Princess Christian, and a table cover by the Duchess of York. There were silver-mounted inkwells, stags' heads, Bohemian jam-pots, anti-macassars, pin-cushions, and a paper-knife made from the wood of Nelson's ship *Victory*.

Milne had competition from another photographer – Prince Henry of Battenberg. The Prince had turned photographer for a day, snapping visitors and charging them five shillings for a 'Cabinet' photograph. The Queen was the star of the show. She arrived in the Royal carriage and walked slowly to the entrance porch, helped by Scottish and Indian attendants. There she climbed into a bathchair and was wheeled inside the marquee to tour the stalls. That night, 6000 lamps and 1000 Japanese lanterns lit up the field. Over the gateways were white and red lights forming the letters 'V.R.'

All that was long ago, but for the crowds who stream through the wrought-iron entrance gates and walk up the long drive to the castle there are reminders everywhere of Victoria's years on Deeside. Tucked off the road which leads from the entrance to the stables is Karim Cottage, built for the Queen's Indian servant, the Munshi Abdul Karim, who was even more disliked than John Brown. Along a path on the west front of the castle is a sculptured memorial to her pet dog, Noble, 'for more than 15 years the favourite Collie and dear and faithful companion of Queen Victoria'.

The Queen had a passion for cairns and statues. Balmoral is peppered with them. It was a habit that began when Victoria built a cairn on Craig Gowan in 1852 to mark 'our taking possession of this dear place'. Probably the most impressive statue is the one of Prince Albert, unveiled on October 15, 1867. A contemporary picture shows it standing boldly against the skyline east of the castle, but today it is half-buried in trees on the edge of the golf course.

Nowadays, visitors can wander round the grounds and the tracks above the castle 'collecting' cairns and statues like souvenirs. The one they probably want to see most is the hardest to find. The path to it passes the Old Dairy and cuts back through thick woodland. There he stands, Victoria's faithful John Brown – 'Friend more than Servant, Loyal, Truthful, Brave, Self less than Duty, even to the Grave', says the inscription on the plinth.

He is magnificent in his kilt, two small medals at his breast, one a Devoted Service Medal, the other the Faithful Servant Medal. Faithful, Loyal, Brave, Truthful . . . Victoria must have run short of adjectives. This near-adulation of the rough-spoken Brown fuelled the fires of a controversy that has rumbled on for more than a century. If their friendship was platonic, why did the Prince of Wales attempt to wipe out every trace of him when the Queen died? I remember hearing about a group of men from Ballater who, early this century, went hunting in the woods of Crathie for a bust of Brown which was said to have been dumped there.

There is a portrait of Brown in the Ballroom exhibition, drawing admiring glances from the ladies. He was a good-looking man. The Prince Consort is also there, his portrait almost insipid against that of the servant who claimed so much of Victoria's affection. Landseer, another of Victoria's

John Brown – 'Loyal, Truthful, Brave'. But some people say that this statue of Queen Victoria's famous servant has been tucked away in a corner of Balmoral estate where few visitors can see it.

admirers, features prominently in the exhibition, as does Carl Haag, who painted many pictures of the Royal outings at Balmoral. There is one showing the Queen and her party crossing the Ford of Tarff on their way home from Blair Atholl. The Queen is seen sitting calmly on her pony, while two Royal pipers blow away bravely on their bagpipes, up to their kilts in water. The Queen's pony was called Inchrory and there is a silver inkstand in the Ballroom incorporating two of its hooves.

The Ballroom at Balmoral is impressive. You enter by the west door and go down the stairway to the hall, making the grand entrance. This was where the annual Gillies' Ball was held. A painting of the 1859 ball gives the impression that it was a sedate affair, but gillies' balls were never that. They were originally held in a specially-erected marquee and organised by John Brown, and the mildest description of them was 'Bacchanalian'. Gladstone, who enjoyed Balmoral more than most of the jaded London guests, said it was 'nearly the best fun I ever witnessed'. It lasted until three o'clock in the morning, and next day Gladstone was up and off on a nineteen-mile tramp up Lochnagar.

The Deeside Survey indicates that the opening of the ballroom and the castle grounds to visitors has brought 'an expansion of tourism'. It describes Balmoral as a major attraction, vital to hotels on Deeside and drawing large numbers of visitors from overseas as well as from other parts of Britain. The estate is said to get 'a very substantial income' from its tourist takings, although the season runs through May, June and July only.

There is an interesting melding of past and present at the Balmoral stables. Here they have introduced pony-trekking for visitors, who can now explore the tracks and trails around Balmoral in the same way that Victoria did a century ago. Her ponies had names like Lochnagar and Fyvie – 'Dear Fyvie is perfection', she wrote – and one carried her own name, Victoria. The modern generation of ponies are called Dawn, Bramble, Martin, Ebony and Roy.

Ebony and Roy are used to pull the Balmoral 'bus'. That is what the staff call the canopied carriage which runs up and down the drive to the castle gates. Its passengers feel a bit like the old Queen herself, waving regally to bemused passers-by. The illusion might be shattered if they knew they were riding on an old Edinburgh milk float, converted to its present 'Victorian' grandeur by the St Cuthbert's Co-operative Association in Edinburgh. St Cuthbert's made the four-wheeled Balmoral dog-cart which is on display in the castle's entrance hall. At one time, it was driven four-in-hand by the Duke of Edinburgh, who uses the estate's stalking ponies to practise carriage-driving in the grounds.

The Duke laid out a practice driving course at Balmoral, as he did at Windsor and Sandringham. The little village of

Tarland, near Ballater, runs an annual carriage-driving event. It was started on the suggestion of the Duke, who himself took part in it a few years ago. He has also acted as host to members of the British Driving Society when they have been invited to Balmoral for a day's 'friendly'.

There are ten traps, dog-carts and carriages at Balmoral, including a governess carriage which the Queen uses while staying in the castle. But, when there is no Royal Standard fluttering from the mast, it has a commercial use; it is included in the 'Rides around Balmoral' plan, carrying four passengers at a time. Another carriage, which carries two people, is used to take deer down from the hills during the shooting season. There is also a carriage which Queen Victoria used – with a heated floor.

It is estimated that over 80,000 visitors pass through the gates of Balmoral in its short season. Coaches full of camera-carrying foreigners (German and Dutch tourists lead the way, with the Americans in hot pursuit) pour into the grounds every day. The car parks across the bridge at Crathie are choc-a-bloc. It is only in recent years that the estate has taken advantage of this tourist potential by opening up shops in the grounds. Queen Victoria would not have been amused by such vulgar commercialism, but there are no complaints from the customers. The only murmurs of protest come from shopkeepers in Ballater, who feel their trade is being taken away.

There are three shops inside Balmoral, one near the main gate, another at the stable, and a third inside the new cafeteria which opened in 1988, while a stall is set up outside the castle when things get busy. The souvenirs are tasteful, usually with the Royal insignia. There are books on the Royal Family, teaspoons, tablecloths, pencils and pot plants. The new cafeteria, completed in August 1987, is in what has been called the Queen's Buildings. It replaces a corrugated iron building – the 'Tin Building' – built in Queen Victoria's time.

Lucky white heather is also on sale, which makes me wonder when they will cash in on the story of Princess Victoria and her bashful beau, Prince Frederick William of Prussia, later Emperor Frederick of Germany. She was only fifteen, the Prince twenty-six, when romance blossomed. He was ready to wait, but the Queen had no objection to his approaching 'our dear Victoria'. When they were on a ride up Craig-na-Ban the Prince spotted a sprig of white heather, plucked it, gave it to the Princess, and popped the question. They were married in 1858 while she was still under eighteen.

I never found any lucky white heather on Craig-na-Ban, but I got it later in a neat little packet marked *Calluna vulgaris*. They were selling it in one of the Balmoral shops, with instructions on how the seeds should be sown in the autumn. The real thing can also be bought in Balmoral, but, while some has been grown in the Royal gardens, most of it has been imported from Scottish nurseries. I wonder how many visitors go off clutching sprigs of white heather in the belief that they were plucked from the hills around Balmoral, just like the one that sealed the romance of Prince Frederick and Vicky.

Away from the Victoriana and the tourist broo-ha-ha, the everyday work of the estate goes on. Some forty-eight people are employed on Balmoral, including nine game staff and eight foresters. Seventeen more are taken on during the season. Dominated by 3789ft-Lochnagar, the estate covers just over 50,000 acres, with sporting leases on a further 11,750 acres. There is little arable land, mostly in pockets on the edge of the estate. Over 2000 acres are afforested.

Ballochbuie is one of the main wintering grounds for red deer. While going through the woods there in winter, I came upon a herd of deer near the Garbh Allt Shiel, or Danzig Shiel as it used to be called. I was taking some photographs when a keeper in a Land Rover appeared and shouted me over. I expected some brusque words about my presence in this part of Balmoral; instead, he asked if I wanted pictures of the deer. When I said 'Yes,' he blew on his horn and they came running out of the woods in their hundreds, ready for their food. Winter feeding is carried out from December onwards.

What the future holds for Balmoral, only time will tell. There is little doubt that when he becomes king Prince Charles will hold to the tradition established all those years ago when Queen Victoria arrived on Deeside. Whether it will be as much a home to Charles and Diana as it has been to their predecessors remains to be seen. Despite what she said that day at the old Invercauld Bridge, there are rumours that the

Princess of Wales is not totally captivated by this corner of Scotland – or its weather. The average annual rainfall on Deeside is 33½ inches. Perhaps Diana feels as Queen Mary did back in 1909, when she wrote, 'It really is not so bad when the weather is fine, but in bad weather, oh!!!'

If, like Victoria, she walks around Balmoral talking to the staff, the language must baffle her. There is a story that a sketch performed by the comedy team 'Scotland the What?' was really a re-enactment of what happened when Princess Diana went shopping in Ballater for gifts for Prince William and Prince Harry. The shopkeeper tried to sell her some 'beets', but eventually had to spell it out – 'B-O-O-T-S, beets, fitba' beets he'll grow into'. Also on offer were a 'futrut' – a ferret – and a rubber 'duke' – a duck. When the same sketch was performed at a Royal Command Performance in the King's Theatre, Glasgow, Prince Charles told the 'Scotland the What?' trio that when he was taken to a toy shop in Ballater as a boy the shopkeeper spoke exactly like that.

Like his mother and grandmother, the Prince has always had a soft spot for Deeside. The Queen is relaxed and happy at Balmoral. Former Prime Minister Harold Wilson tells the story of how, during a visit to Balmoral, he went with the Royal Family on a picnic to one of the shiels. When it was over, the Queen and Mary Wilson washed up the dishes. As a schoolboy at Gordonstoun, Prince Charles spent many weekends at Birkhall with his grandmother, the Queen Mother, who encouraged his interest in fishing. He knows the Balmoral hills well, particularly the area around Lochnagar, which Queen Victoria often gazed at from the windows on the west front of the castle. He also knows the Old Man of Lochnagar, who lives in a cave on the mountain and feeds on loch haggis.

Prince Charles wrote the story of the Old Man of Lochnagar for his younger brothers, Prince Andrew and Prince Edward, who were nine and five years old at the time. Produced as a book and later turned into a play, it told of how the Old Man tried to get to London but was held up at Aberdeen when snow blocked the track. 'Secretly he was rather pleased', wrote Prince Charles, 'for he hated leaving his cave and his friends who lived in the hills around him.'

Was the Royal author really writing about the Old Man of

Lochnagar – or was he putting into words how he himself felt about that wild and lovely land stretching out from the doorstep of Balmoral Castle?

DONSIDE

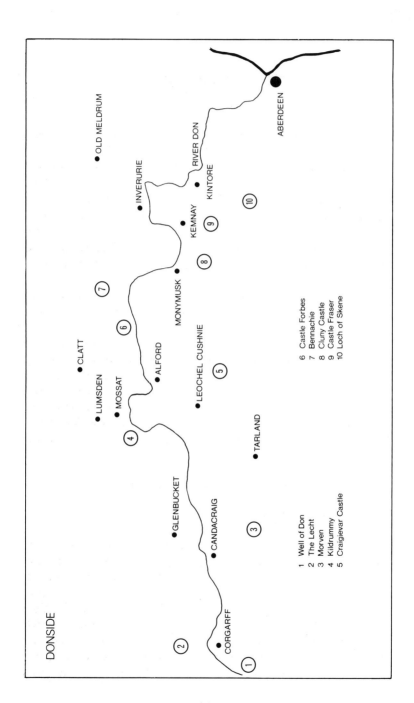

DONSIDE

- CORGARFF
- GLENBUCKET
- CANDACRAIG
- TARLAND
- LUMSDEN
- MOSSAT
- CLATT
- ALFORD
- LEOCHEL CUSHNIE
- MONYMUSK
- OLD MELDRUM
- INVERURIE
- KEMNAY
- KINTORE
- ABERDEEN

RIVER DON

1 Well of Don
2 The Lecht
3 Morven
4 Kildrummy
5 Craigievar Castle

6 Castle Forbes
7 Bennachie
8 Cluny Castle
9 Castle Fraser
10 Loch of Skene

114

Chapter 7

One Rood of Don

While the River Dee rises majestically in the heart of the Cairngorms, gushing powerfully from the Wells of Dee at a height of 4000ft., the River Don splutters into life on a bleak hill-slope near the old drove road from Inchrory to Cock Bridge. Here, on the Aberdeenshire-Banffshire boundary, a stream known as the Allt an Mhicheil, Michael's Burn, spills from the Well of Don, crosses the road to Cock Bridge, and runs eastward to join a jumble of other headstreams at Inchmore, where the map makers finally give it the name of the River Don.

The two rivers race each other over eighty miles to the sea, but the Dee is always one jump ahead. Despite the fact that Aberdeen lies between both rivers – 'twixt Dee and Don' – the tendency is to think of the city as belonging to the Dee. The majority of tourists pass through Donside, rather than staying to enjoy what it has to offer. Donside folk say that this is because the Scottish Tourist Board, seduced by the Dee's Royal tag, has shown a long standing disregard for the attractions of the Don. It may never have heard the old couplet which claims that a rood of Don (a hundred and sixtieth of a Scots acre) is worth two of the Dee:

> Ae rood o' Don's worth twa o' Dee,
> Unless it be for fish or tree.

Even this judgement no longer holds good. The Don is one of the premier salmon rivers in Scotland, and when it comes to trees the balance has been put right by the rash of afforestation on Donside in recent years. Even without this development, which gives environmentalists some cause for concern, the Don valley has always been well endowed with woodlands. One version of the couplet suggests that Deeside is also best for 'stone,' but Donside has nothing to be ashamed of. It is steeped in history, bristling with ancient kirks and castles (so much for the *stone* theory), claims its share of the North-east's industrial

Corgarff Castle on its site near Cock Bridge, above the River Don at Corgarff. It was built in 1537, burned down in 1571, burned again in 1607, and put to flames a third time in 1689. It was restored by the Ministry of Works.

wealth, and can boast some of the loveliest country in Aberdeenshire.

On the road from Inchrory to Cock Bridge there is a Royal lodge which threatens to join Donside's historic ruins. This is Delnadamph, which is said to have been bought by the Queen for Prince Charles. Local folk say that the 'Royals' wanted the land for shooting, but not the Lodge. It has seldom been used, and now it is falling into disrepair. It stands empty and neglected, the harling peeling from its walls and the slates tumbling from its roofs. The old bell over its door is tolling a death sentence for this decaying building, for it is likely to be demolished.

Delnadamph is less than two miles from Corgarff Castle, which stands guard over the Lecht, with its back to the old trails over the hills to the Gairn. In its latter years as a garrison it was used as a watch-post against whisky-smugglers, while in the eighteenth century Government troops were quartered there to combat cattle-lifting. It was held by both the Jacobites and the Hanoverians, but it is best known as the setting for 'Edom o' Gordon', the tragic ballad about a Forbes laird's wife, family and servants who perished in a fire there in 1571.

The land around Corgarff can be cold and uncompromising in winter. In March, 1746, Captain Alexander Stuart led an expedition north 'to destroy a Magazine of Rebels at Corgorff, which lies near the head of the Don'. He wrote a letter to his brother in which he said it was 'such a country that a hundred men might beat a thousand from the hills above them'. They had to spent two nights in the open fields – and sit on horseback all night. If it had snowed another night, he said, they would never have been able to return.

Nowadays, they spend the night in cars, not on horseback, when snow closes the notorious Lecht Road. The castle at 'Corgorff' is still there, dominating the approaches to the Lecht, where the A939 climbs unwillingly up the Hill of Allargue on its way to Tomintoul and Speyside.

The Lecht has become a busy ski centre, smaller and less testing than Glenshee and the Cairngorms, but nudging its way into greater prominence. In 1987 the Lecht Ski Company embarked on a three-year plan to spend around £700,000 on improving facilities and providing new tows. This means that the uplift capacity will be extended from 5500 to 7500 skiers an hour.

The community generally has benefited from the ski development, partly from an improvement in the roads and an increasing awareness on the part of the authorities that they must be kept open. The Allargue Arms Hotel at the foot of the Lecht is a popular 'watering hole' for skiers before they struggle uphill into the wilderness. When I was there in late September, Charlie Dent, the host, was sniffing the air for snow. For him, snow means business, and that year he was forecasting an early winter. The deer were down among the 'neeps,' the swallows had gone, and there were robin redbreasts in the field.

West of the hotel, up the Burn of Loinherry, is Tobar Fuar, the Cold Well, the second largest spring in Scotland. Its waters are supposed to have cured the blind, the lame and the deaf, but some say this was Tobar Ruadh, the Red Well, up the Cock burn, while others plump for the Fae Well at Inchmore. Today, travellers look for something stronger when they go to the Allargue, sipping their drams and listening to the poems of Wullie Gray, a local farmer known as the Bard of Corgarff.

The last of the winter snow lingers on the slopes at the Lecht ski centre. Ski-ing developments at the Lecht have brought new life to the people in this remote and storm-struck corner of Aberdeenshire. The Lecht road is inevitably one of the first roads to be blocked in winter.

Wullie scribbles dialect poetry on old envelopes and cornflake packets, and he talks tongue in cheek about 'taking the literature' to the *literati* at the Allargue Arms. He will give you a long, contemplative look if you ask him to recite 'The Motor Bike', a work that has won him a measure of fame far from the hills of Strathdon. It is the story of what happened when 'a lad ca'ed Wullie Gray' took a girl for a spin on a motor bike:

> Wull thocht that he wis jist g_y smart
> Tae hurl about at this young tart.

It is not the sort of poem you would read to the Corgarff ladies' guild. Wullie, while agreeing that it is too indelicate for most tastes, nevertheless claims that it has given him an international reputation. Visitors from abroad take it down on their cassette recorders and go off with a permanent reminder of the tousle-haired shepherd whose poetry is reminiscent of Burns's bawdy verse. 'The Motor Bike' is probably being recited with lipsmacking relish all over the world.

But Wullie gets his inspiration from the hills and moors as well as from the smoke-filled bar of the Allargue Arms. He finds that ideas and phrases come easily to him when he is lying in the heather during the grouse season. Everybody goes beating when the guns are out. They showed me a photograph of old Jimmy Troup, who was a cobbler in Corgarff, standing on the moors with his pipe in his mouth and a white flag in his hand when he went beating at the age of seventy-six.

Sitting in Wullie Gray's farm kitchen at the Luib, I listened to him recite 'The Glorious Twelfth', a poem about a shoot on the Canadcraig estate, with beaters toiling and sweating up the hills, 'girning' about their pay and the 'poorin' rain', while the shooters – the 'toffs' – wandered about watching their dogs pick up the grouse. The Twelfth wasn't always glorious for the beaters:

> They'll travel on oor aifter oor,
> God help a lad that's feeling dour.

Wullie is self-effacing about his work, dismissing much of it as 'stite', but he has a sharp and observant eye and his poetry opens up small windows on life in Strathdon. Through it you can follow the changing seasons – 'winter's early, spring is late' – and taste the long summer days. You can meet the 'toun folk' on holiday, and learn how shepherds dig for blackfaced ewes 'buried deep in drifts o' snaw'. There is nothing romantic about the daily routine in Upper Strathdon, where they

> Dig fur neeps, muck the byre,
> Tak' in peat tae stoke the fire,
> Feed the hens, milk the coos,
> Sort the feet o' cripplin' ewes.

I first saw an example of Wullie's work in a leaflet publicising an exhibition in the village hall at Corgarff. It carried this invitation:

> So if ye are aboot the Lecht,
> An' o' the past ye'd like a sicht
> O' glen life as it used tae be,
> Or maybe hae a cup o' tea,
> It's worth yer while,
> Just mak a call,
> Ye'll find us in the Corgarff Hall.

The Allargue Arms Hotel, which often plays host to motorists stranded by storms on the notorious Lecht Road. The old Lecht road is seen on the left, while the modern road climbs up the steep hill to the Lecht ski centre and goes on to Tomintoul.

In winter, the village hall at Corgarff is used for dances, concerts and Burns Nichts, but in summer it becomes the setting for a remarkable experiment in community self-help. The Corgarff Rural Exhibition is intended to reflect rural life, past and present, but it is also the linch-pin of a project aimed at holding the community together. The exhibition provides employment for a number of people and serves as an outlet for local crafts and produce, but its main achievement has been to bring hope to an area in which life was in danger of withering away.

The prime mover behind the scheme is an Edinburgh woman, Mrs Isobel Conboy, who lives at Ordachoy and came to Corgarff eight years ago. She found the winters frightening. She learned that if you were careless you could die within a few yards of your front door, and she discovered what it meant to have your brain made numb by the cold. There are days, she says, when the track to her house fills in with snow so quickly that it is almost a waste of time clearing it.

Old people were moving out to sheltered housing further down the glen, but no one was moving in to replace them.

Empty houses remained empty. 'Everybody was moving out,' said Isobel. 'All the facilities were going. We were down to the pub and the school – and the school was constantly under threat.' Now, with the community project firmly established, she feels that there is a new spirit in Corgarff.

The exhibition, which has been running since 1986, is a plunge into nostalgia. The exhibits include an old magic lantern, a branding iron, a room with a box bed, a display of Percy Topliss (the gunman who shot his way out of a cottage in the Lecht), skis used in Strathdon in 1890, and a poker-like instrument call the Puir Man, which was used to fix wire fencing. There is also a barn door from Shinnach, covered in graffiti. They didn't smear obscenities on doors in the old days. The graffiti on the Shinnach door tells of 'a terrible blizzard' sweeping over Scotland in 1906 and of how the Shinnach farmer started ploughing on 7th February, 1908, and finished on the 21st.

It isn't only at Corgarff that things are happening. All down the glen you have the feeling that the folk of Strathdon are pulling themselves up by their own bootstraps, proving that one rood on Don *is* worth two of Dee. Perhaps it has something to do with new blood coming into the glen, or with the fact that the winter gap, that long isolation when the snows come, is being shortened and made tolerable by the developments at the Lecht. There was a time when the Lecht was closed and the people of Upper Strathdon sank into a kind of resigned lethargy; now, with hundreds of people making for the ski slopes, things are different.

Down the road from the village hall at Corgarff a knitwear enterprise flourishes; at Inverernan House, once the home of 'Black Jock' Forbes, a familiar figure in the 1715 Rebellion, Andrew Lawson Johnston is producing a distinctive range of engraved glass; Candacraig House, whose south wing was designed by John Smith ('Tudor Johnie') and reconstructed after a fire in 1955, became a guest house and has now returned to its original role as a private house, but the old walled garden at Candacraig, established as a formal garden in 1820, has been taken over by Liz Young and opened to the public for the first time in its history. These are only a few of the developments.

E

The knitwear project is opposite Corgarff cemetery, where soldiers from Corgarff Castle were buried. Back in 1938, a member of one of the oldest families in Strathdon was laid to rest there, brought to his grave while they played a lament he had written for his own burial, 'Hame to the Glen'. He was Pipe-Major James McHardy, piper to Queen Victoria, whose story is told in a booklet entitled *My Father, the Bagpiper* which was on sale at the Crogarff exhibition. It was written by 'McHardy', the name given to Mrs Edith Paterson, the Pipe-Major's daughter, who lives in Fife.

Jamie McHardy often travelled with Queen Victoria when she went abroad, sometimes under an assumed name and without John Brown. There was no love lost between the two men, possibly because the Queen had a soft spot for the Strathdon piper, and when Jamie left Royal service Brown gave him a testimonial which carried the cryptic report, 'James McHardy left. Gave no offence. Signed: John Brown'. 'My Father, with youthful impatience, tore it up,' said Mrs Paterson. 'A wonderful relic lost!'

Jamie also attended Victoria when she went driving or tramping through the hills of Deeside and Donside. He was piper/valet to the Queen, carrying her cloaks, umbrella and picnic-hampers. Long before he joined the Royal Household, Victoria travelled along the old track from Inchrory on one of her expeditions. She came by Inchmore and 'Dal-na-Damph Shiel', which was then a shooting lodge belonging to Sir Charles Forbes, and she took the old military road to Gairnsheil by 'Dal Choupar' and 'Dal Vown'.

The road can still be followed, cutting off a corner of the A939 and passing Delachuper and Delavine. The route takes in three old 'Wade' bridges, one of which is still intact. They were actually built by Wade's successor, General Caulfield. From Delavine, a faded track with the curious name of the Ca climbs over the hills to Glengairn. It was the old route to Gairnside from Corgarff and it takes its name from the Gaelic word 'Cadha', meaning a way over the hill range.

From the former military road you look down on the small chapel of Tornahaish. A century ago, mass was held in various houses in the district and the local priest, Lachlan MacIntosh, complained, 'I am suffering a most wretched condition through want of a place for divine worship. Tis' in a dark kiln I officiate at present'. They built the chapel in 1880 and mass is still held there by visiting priests during the summer. To the east of Tornahaish is Tom a' Bhuraich, where a treasure was found in 1822. Several hundred silver coins and two rings were dug up when the foundation of a dyke was being laid.

Life is returning to the valley, but the old tracks through the hills remain unchanged. I went up Glen Nochty in search of Belnabodach. The word 'bodach' means either a spectre or an old man and Belnabodach, or *Baile nam bodach,* is known as 'the town of the ghost' and 'the town of the old men', depending on your place-name source. I wasn't sure which I'd meet, old men or ghosts, but in the event I ran into Charlie Gordon, who looked remarkably spry for his 85 years.

Belnabodach lies beyond his farm, which has an even more peculiar name – Lost. There used to be two 'Lost' signs at the road-end, but one disappeared after a Lonach Gathering. It turned up in a car, but was never replaced. Lost has been in Charlie's family for 200 years and now his son is carrying on the tradition. He thought that the name was from a Gaelic word meaning 'a small meeting place'. The original name was said to be Losset.

Charlie told me that Belnabodach has been a ruin for twenty or thirty years, then, pointing his stick up the glen, he said he could remember when there were 'forty reekin' lums' there. Forty reekin' lums ... the phrase said more about the depopulation of the glens than any official report. Go north through Glen Nochty and Glenbucket, cross the Aberdeenshire boundary at the Roch Ford, and eventually, west of the Cabrach, you will come to a place called Reekimlane. The story is that when hard times struck the area every family moved out except one, so that a single reekin' lum was left in the district. There is also a Reekitlane near Coull on Deeside.

Alexander Laing, who wrote *The Donean Tourist* in 1828, said that Belnabodach was the ancient seat of the Forbeses of Auchernach. It was later held by a family called Nairn, who killed a marauding cateran and secretly buried him there. Many people are supposed to have seen his ghost, which is how the place got its name.

Wullie Gray, the Bard of Corgarff, outside his home in Strathdon. A local sheep farmer, he scribbles dialect poetry on the backs of old envelopes and corn flake packets and recites his verse to audiences in the Allargue Arms Hotel.

Laing, however, could never be relied on for historical accuracy. He was a packman, nicknamed 'Stachie' and sometimes called 'Gley'd Sandy' because of his squint, and he sold books at cottar houses and castles. He also wrote some of the works he sold, including *The Donean Tourist,* which he said gave 'an account of the Battles, Castles, Gentlemen's Seats, Families with their origin, Armorial Ensigns, Badges of Distinction, carefully selected from the best Authorities'.

'Stachie' was a familiar figure in the glens of Strathdon. Nochty's names must have stirred his imagination . . . Downie's Loup, beside the Auchernach bridge; Glackanlochan; Paul's Cairn on the top of Breckach; the Hill of Three Stones, and Duff Defiance, a ruin of the old track to the Ladder Hills.

There are differing stories about how Duff Defiance got its name. One says that a squatter called Duff defied the laird, the Earl of Fife, when he tried to evict him, and another says that Duff defied the gaugers by operating an illicit still.

It is tempting to plump for the latter, for Glen Nochty was the old smuggling route from Glenlivet to Strathdon. Sir Charles Forbes of Newe and Edinglassie, who was a Member of Parliament, told a meeting in 1825 that he regretted that illicit malting and distillation had become so prevalent in the area. He laid it down that a tenant's lease would be cancelled if he was found guilty of smuggling.

It was a Deeside shoemaker who brought fame to Nochty's whisky-makers. John Milne married a Glenlivet woman and moved to the area, where, encouraged by his wife, he dabbled in illicit whisky-making. He was a nineteenth-century Wullie Gray and he wrote a poem about a clash between an Exciseman called M'Bain and the Glen Nochty smugglers. 'I composed thirty-seven verses between breakfast and dinner-time,' he said, 'sitting making shoes, and minded the whole without writing a line of it.' The poem, 'Nochty Glens', sold at threepence a copy and was an instant success. The gaugers came off worst in the Battle of Glen Nochty. They were sent packing with the warning ringing in their ears:

> Burn no more bothies in Mount Sack,
> Case the mist come on and you win not back,
> But be forced to lodge in some peat stack,
> Among Noughty glens in the morning.

Poaching was as common as smuggling in Strathdon and it was in Glen Nochty that one of the North-east's most notorious poachers, Alexander Davidson, was found dead. Sandy Davidson, who was born at the Mill of Inver on Deeside, was himself a whisky smuggler before turning to poaching. He was a crack shot and respected by many of the lairds. He loved freedom and he once said that when he died he hoped it would be among the heather. That was what happened. He was found lying on his back in the hills of Glenbuchat with his dog, a little brown pointer, keeping watch over him.

Sandy Davidson's father was a noted Deeside athlete and a friend of Robert Dinnie, whose son, the famous Donald Dinnie, often competed at Lonach. They were 'buirdly chiels' (stalwart men) in those days and there were plenty of sturdy Donsiders to compete with the mighty Dinnie. Mrs Paterson tells in *My Father, the Bagpiper* that Pipe-Major McHardy's grandfather and his five brothers were all over 6ft. tall except one. He was 6ft. exactly and nicknamed 'The Infant'. There is a story told in Strathdon that on one occasion Lonach sent '38 feet of McHardys' to a Games in the south.

Even 'Stachie' Laing was impressed by the muscular McHardys. In *The Donean Tourist* he wrote of 'a peasant named M'Hardy' who was noted for his 'feats and corporeal strength'. It was said that the Earl of Mar arranged a meeting between McHardy and a 'celebrated pugilist' from England. When the Englishmen saw his rival turn up at Kildrummy wearing a flannel jerkin, kilt and bonnet, he 'laughed immoderately'. McHardy was brought down in the first and second rounds, but in the third round he buried his head in the Englishman's belly and 'grasped his side with such firmness that he broke several of the ribs'.

Things are less violent now, but the 'heavies' look no less heavy. The Lonach games started in 1836, a number of years after the founding of the Lonach Highland and Friendly Society 'for the preservation of the Highland garb and language'. It wasn't until the 1860s that they were thrown open to all comers.

One of the unique features of the Lonach Gathering is the March of the Lonach Highlanders, who, armed with pikes, start the day by tramping six miles round the area to pay their respects to the 'big houses'. There are generous drams for the marchers at each stop – and a horse and cart taking up the rear in case anyone falls by the wayside.

Before Highland games became popular, the Lonach lads tested their strength at the Lifting Stones. These stones, often found in rivers, were well-known locally. In Strathdon, they were in Glenbucket, near the Roch Ford on the way to the Cabrach. The stones were of different sizes and had to be lifted and piled on top of a pointed rock. The Glenbucket and Cabrach men held contests at the Roch Ford. Today, the modern equivalent is putting the stone at Ballabeg during the gathering. On Deeside, there is a Clach Thogolach, a lifting

Jimmy Troup, a Corgarff cobbler who went beating on the grouse moors at the age of seventy-six. This photograph, showing Jimmy with his pipe and bonnet and carrying a beater's flag, was put on display at the Corgarff Rural Exhibition.

stone, near the junction of the Luibeg and the Derry, west of Braemar. There was also said to be one near the head of the Boonie in Glentanar.

From Lonach to Deskry, where the Don writhes and wriggles

on its way east before turning north to the Bridge of Buchat, the land south of the river stretches away to Mullachdubh and Morven – Byron's 'Morven of Snow', which forms a natural barrier between Deeside and Donside. It is an area whose forgotten glens and tumbling streams once had the pulse of life in them. Now, snow-poles stick up like giant toothpicks on roads that lead to nowhere, larachs pockmark the landscape and roofs go red with rust over empty cottar houses. There are few reekin' lums in this vast wilderness between the Dee and the Don.

Drovers, horse-dealers, squatters, tinkers, cattle raiders . . . these were the kind of men who made their mark in this inhospitable terrain. There were squatters in Glencarvie and Glenconrie and along the banks of the Deskry. In the seventeeth century there was a hamlet on Deskryside with the name of Tollaskink, but there is no longer any trace of it. These old names draw intriguing pictures of the past, but many leave questions unanswered. Belnagauld is a farm at the end of a road which peters out on the approaches to the Craig of Bunzeach. The name means 'the town of the strangers of lowlanders', which suggests a link with the squatters who made their homes in ramshackle sheilings in this part of the country.

The Craig of Bunzeach was better known as The Bunnyach, pronounced The Boonyach. It was the name given to grazings on the north side of the Deskry, and a charter going back to 1600 shows it as 'the sheiling and pasture in the hill of Morving (Morven), called Bunzeoch'. The route by Glen Deskry and Morven was one of the busiest drove roads between the Don and the Dee, and people living in Donside no more than forty years ago can remember seeing cattle resting in Badnagoach, near the top of the Deskry Water. Boultenstone Inn, at the mouth of the Deskry glen, was a drovers' inn. Before it was built there was a hostelry nearby at a spot called Pantieland. This is thought to have been a form of Punder-land or Pund-land, a place for impounding stray cattle.

Where there were cattle there were cattle raiders. The hills between the Don and Dee were the haunt of cateran. It was said that dying cateran chiefs told their children to go to the 'yellow glen of Morven' if they were ever in want, for there they would find plenty of fat cattle.

Near the source of the Water of Carvie there is an outcrop of rock called Castle Wilson, which takes its name from a freebooter who hid there, while up in the Bunnyach is Gilderoy's Cairn. Patrick Gilroy MacGregor was the leader of a band which plundered and looted all over Deeside and Donside. He was 'the red lad' or 'bonny boy' of ballad fame:

> It was, I ween, a comelie sight
> To see sae trim a boy,
> He was my joy, and heart's delight,
> My handsome Gilderoy.

Another of Gilderoy's hiding places was the Burn o' Vat, a spectacular cave on Easter Morven, not far from the main Deeside road. It draws hundreds of visitors each year, many of whom are under the impression that another MacGregor, Rob Roy, hid there. Despite the ballad, Gilderoy lacked the charisma of his famous kinsman. The 'bonny boy' was betrayed by one of his girlfriends, Margaret Cunningham, and hanged at the Market Cross in Edinburgh in 1658. A tributary of the Cock Burn, the Burn of MacGregor's Thicket, is called after him.

Back on the right bank of the Don, there is a startling contrast to Morven's empty lands in a church that would look more at home in a busy city centre than in this rural backwater. The Church of Strathdon, built in 1851, is so large and imposing that it had been called the Cathedral of the Strath. According to the Statistical Account of Scotland, there was a time when local ministers in Strathdon were given rough treatment by 'haughty and cruel' lairds. One clergyman had his head cut off at his manse door by a laird wielding a Lochaber axe, while another, the Rev. Donald MacSween, was attacked and almost smothered with a wet canvas when at family prayers.

The lairds behave themselves today, although a Lochaber axe or two might be seen at the Lonach Gathering. On the north bank of the Don, nothing disturbs the tranquillity of the tiny roadside communities. They have a charm of their own . . . Roughpark, where farm buildings rub shoulders with the local shop and Post Office; Lonach, taking its name from the hill crowned by a huge cairn erected in honour of Sir Charles

Forbes's elevation to the Baronetcy; Bellabeg, home of the Gathering; and, away from the main road, the Kirkton of Glenbucket.

RUFIS, the Rural Facilities Information System, set up by Grampian Regional Council to establish the existing level and distribution of rural facilities (shops, libraries, schools, halls, old people's homes, surgeries and so on), pinpointed Upper Donside as one of the places where basic services are least well represented. In Strathdon's defence, it should be said that it has a particularly attractive scheme of sheltered housing. But Glenbucket is picked out as a parish with few settlements and limited facilities. It is, in fact, a badly depopulated area, and that, sadly, is one of its main attractions for city-weary visitors.

It is a remote, forgotten place, its narrow winding road pushing north to Badenyon, which gave its name to another Donside ballad, 'John o' Badenyon', by the Rev. John Skinner, which Rabbie Burns called 'this excellent song':

> I still was pleas'd where'er I went,
> And when I was alone,
> I tun'd my pipe and pleas'd myself
> Wi' John o' Badenyon.

This is a land of ballads, among them 'Edom o' Gordon'; 'The Earl of Mar's Daughter'; 'Glenkindie'; and 'Glenlogie', which is supposed to have associations with the Gordons of Glenbucket. The ruins of Glenbucket Castle are a reminder of the last Gordon laird of Glenbucket. He was known as 'Old Glenbucket of the '45', and it is said that George II – German Geordie – had nightmares about him, waking up in the middle of the night screaming, 'De great Glenbogget is coming!'

Before reaching the Bridge of Glenbucket from the west, two roads branch off to Deeside. One is the main A97 to Boultenstone and Logie-Coldstone, with other routes turning east to Migvie and Tarland. In the days when creels were used to carry both dung and peat, and cattle were sold to south-country drovers, Strathdon sent its butter and cheese to market at Tarland.

The second road is a minor route, a short cut from the main Strathdon road to Boultenstone, passing through what is left of

The bag after a day on the Donside moors . . . a picture that captures the atmosphere of the old-time grouse shoots. The picture was shown at the Corgarff Rural Exhibition.

the old hamlet of Heughhead. Heughhead Inn is now a private house, but still retains much of its character. A short distance away is the Old Semeil Herb Garden. It is a curiously delicate and old-world name, sounding as if it had been thought up to match the fragrance of the garden's products. Semeil, however, was there long before the herbs arrived. There is a farm of the same name near the garden and the word comes from the Gaelic 'suidhe maol', which means 'bare seat'.

East of the Bridge of Buchat, the main road runs to Glenkindie. It is an attractive hamlet, small in size but big in ambition. Corgarff has its Rural Exhbition, Glenbucket can tell of 'de great Glenbogget', but neighbouring Glenkindie has the great Memorabilia Loft Museum. The store run by Barrie and Eileen Davies at Glenkindie is in the tradition of the old country shoppie. There isn't much room to move, but everything you want is there, even a 'tearoom' – two tables – with home baking.

When they have done their shopping, had their cup of tea and tasted the home baking, visitors make for the stairs at the back of the shop, where there is a sign saying 'Museum'. Up there is the loft – and an Aladdin's Cave of homely treasures.

Barrie points out that he is not displaying antiques, just things that will bring back memories for the old folk and create interest for youngsters.

The first thing I came across on the stairs was a curiously shaped stone – a bannock stone, used in the making of bannocks. If was said to date back to 1000 or 2000 BC. Then, inside the loft, I was confronted by a dazzling array of bottles, lamps (front and rear from the postie's bike), old clocks, pewter, a doll's pram and a mangle. There was an advertising sign urging me to 'Insist on Mitchell's XXX Bogie – original and best', and if I had taken out my clay pipe and dropped ash on the floor I could have cleaned it up with Beesway Wax Polish.

The loft was originally earmarked for a local agricultural museum, but this fell through and Mr Davies decided to open his Memorabilia Loft Museum. He himself does glasswork, so glass candlestick holders and an old steam engine made from glass are on show – Glenkindie bottlecraft, he calls it. There is an old fireplace with a girdle or griddle for making oatcakes, and there is also a Blickograph duplicator, forerunner of the photocopying machine, a tattie chapper (potato masher, a note explains), an ancient wireless set and a pair of spats.

What sights these spats must have seen. Perhaps they adorned a pair of shoes that swung and tapped to the music of reels and jigs at the Lonach Ball, or whirled around the Lonach Hall beneath walls decorated with tartan, targes and claymores. There was always plenty of music in Strathdon, and not all from the pipes. A reconstruction of a cottar's kitchen at the Corgarff Rural Exhibition showed a fiddle resting on the mantlepiece, and nothing could have been more appropriate.

The fiddle came close second to the chanter in Strathdon. Pipe-Major Jamie McHardy was a fiddler as well as a piper, and he not only played them but made them. The famous Scott Skinner was a frequent visitor to the area, and one of his works was composed while he was a guest at Auchernach House.

The musical instrument that caught my attention at the Glenkindie exhibition was an old gramophone on a stand. My music teacher used to wind up one of these things with the quip, 'Music by Handle'. Here, again, I could imagine the pleasure it must have given some family in the long winter evenings on Donside. There was a note beside it which read, 'If there is a record you would like to hear please ask downstairs and we will do our best'.

I wondered what request I would make ... a schottische, perhaps, or an old-fashioned waltz like the ones that made the lairds and their ladies take to the floor at the Lonach Ball. I was never able to play a record. Barrie and Eileen Davies were away for the weekend and the assistant at the counter didn't know where the records were kept. Some day, however, I will go back to the Memorabilia Loft Museum and claim my tune.

Chapter 8

Kirks and Castles

The Hill of Coilliebhar, halfway between Kildrummy and the Bridge of Alford, was where Donside folk built a monster bonfire in 1887 to celebrate the Jubilee of Queen Victoria. From its summit they could see between sixty and seventy other fires stabbing the darkness on hilltops all over Aberdeenshire, but Coillebhar was the biggest and the best. It is a modest hill, not much more than 1000ft. high, but from it you can pick out all the great peaks of the Cairngorms, nod your head towards the Mither Tap of Bennachie, and stretch your gaze northwards as far as the Bin of Cullen.

From where I stood I could see the route the drovers took when they went over the Socach to Pressendye, above Tarland, or south from Towie to 'Bouties', the old drovers' inn at Boultenstone. 'Stachie' Laing, the chapman whose *Donean Tourist* had taken me down the Don, ended his days at 'Bouties'. He died in 1838 and was buried in an unmarked grave. For a man who spent much of his time collecting epitaphs, many of them scurrilous, it was a sad kind of irony. One of his favourites went:

> Here lies the D----'d godson,
> Who never loved the poor,
> He lived like a hog and
>   died like a dog,
> And left what he had to a Whore.

'Stachie' claimed to have found this epitaph in Coull churchyard, but there is no trace of it today. I often wondered if he made them up, for he produced a whole volume of them. One of his haunts was an old kirkyard at Leochel, which was one half of what is now the combined Leochel Cushnie charge. It lies in a tiny woodland south-west of the present Leochel Cushnie Church, just off the Corse road, up a rutted farm track to the Kirkton of Leochel. Nearby, the Rumblie Burn gurgles past the farmyard.

All that remains of the kirk is a broken gable and an empty bell tower. Weeds twist forlorn fingers round broken tombstones, and nettles and willowherb rise shoulder-high as you push your way through the kirkyard. Among the ancient tombstones that lurch grotesquely from the undergrowth is one with the inscription, 'Here lies the dust of the late James Leslie . . .'

There are plenty of graveyards like Leochel in Aberdeenshire, offering rich pickings for tombstone hunters. Not that there is anything wrong with this macabre pastime. Books of epitaphs have become a literary fad, and it is true that old stones mirror much of the history of an area. In some ways it is a pity that nothing is done to decipher the epitaphs or restore them. The Church of Kildrummy also came under Laing's gley-eyed scrutiny. Here, the kirkyard is in the five-star tombstone category, with so many ancient stones lying around that I thought that the ground had been laid out in flagstones. The church, which stands on a mound not far from the main road, was known as the Chapel of the Lochs before the land around it was drained.

Leochel Cushnie lies south-east of Kildrummy. It can be reached by a maze of back roads skirting Coilliebhar Hill, taking you through countryside where life seems to trail languidly behind the twentieth century. There are crofts and cottar houses which have lain unchanged for decades, unlike Leochel Cushnie itself, where modern bungalows have replaced many of the old buildings. The Rumblie Burn and the Cushnie Burn rise in the Cushnie hills, linking up with the Leochel Burn, and somewhere in the centre of this gurgling triumvirate, about halfway between the Dee and the Don, is Craigievar Castle.

The National Trust looks upon Craigievar as its fairytale castle. The late Cuthbert Graham, who was an authority on the castles of the North-east, once described Craigievar's appearance as 'slender, like a flower of chivalry', while Stewart Cruden, one of HM Inspectors of Ancient Monuments, said it was a work of art, claiming a Scottish place in the front rank of European architecture. Above the stairway is a crest with the motto, 'Do not Vaiken Sleiping Dogs'. It is a Forbes crest, but William Forbes, the colourful Forbes laird who completed

Craigievar Castle against the distant backdrop of the Bennachie hill range, with the Mither Tap on the right. This lovely 'fairy castle' is under the care of the National Trust. It was completed in 1626 for a Forbes laird known as Willie the Merchant, who made his fortune in the Danzig trade.

Craigievar in 1626, was no sleeping dog. It was his acumen as a merchant – 'Willie the Merchant', he was called – that brought him the money which enabled him to build Craigievar. He made shrewd speculations in the Danzig trade, which also won him the nickname of 'Danzig Willie'.

Craigievar is not a defensive casle, but Danzig Willie must have had defence in mind when he built it, for there is only one entrance. The heavily studded outer door and the turnpike stairs provided a problem for Craigievar lairds, for if someone died they were unable to get the corpse down the stairs and out at the door. Now it keeps tourists in their place. The setting of Craigievar is superb, which may have something to do with the fact that the Barony Court once fined an offender one merk 'for despoiling the trees of Leochel'.

Back at Kildrummy there is a different kind of castle. This impressive ruin could never be described as a fairytale castle, yet it has a compelling fascination for visitors. They get a lesson in one of the seven deadly sins when they hear the story of Osbarn, the Smith, who betrayed the Scots defenders when King Robert the Bruce's brother, Sir Nigel, defended the castle against Prince Edward of Caernarvon, the future Edward II. Osbarn, who was bribed with as much gold as he could carry, set fire to the castle with the red-hot blade of a plough-coulter. When the castle surrendered and Sir Nigel was beheaded, the blacksmith got his gold – heated until it was molten and poured down his throat.

The Toll of Mossat, two miles from Kildrummy, is an important junction for traffic coming through the Howe of Alford, bound for Corgarff or going north to Strathbogie and Huntly. Here, a few years ago, stood the famous Mossat shoppie, which drew hordes of motorists to its doors at the weekend. It had a country flavour that attracted the town dweller, for it sold everything from wooden egg cups to tackety boots. Success eventually ruined it, for it began to sell more sophisticated fare and lost many of its customers. There is still a small shop there, but the old charm has gone.

At Mossat the A97 goes north into the heart of Gordon country, where the tidy town of Huntly sits in the shadow of Huntly Castle, whose impressive ruins whisper of a dark and stormy past. From Lumsden and Rhynie you can strike west through the Cabrach to Dufftown and Speyside. At the entrance to Lumsden you are liable to meet a man in a top-hat

Modern sculpture and ancient walls. The sculpture is from the Lumsden Sculpture Workshop, which holds exhibitions in the grounds of Kildrummy Castle. Some people have complained about using the site for a sculpture exhibition.

playing a flute, or see a keep-fit fanatic doing press-ups, or spot a brightly-beaked puffin peering at you from the undergrowth. These fantasy figures are found in a Sculpture Walk which has been set up in Lumsden, for this small village, rather to its own surprise, has become the home of the Scottish Sculpture Workshop.

Near Rhynie, the Tap o' Noth, with its vitrified fort, glowers down on the passing world, its volcano-like summit a landmark for miles around. Up there, cupped in the hollow of the hill, you feel a chill that goes beyond anything caused by the winds off Clashindarroch. Betty Allan, who was co-author of *The Place Names of Upper Deeside*, once told me of an inexplicable fear that gripped her when she was on Tap o' Noth with her small son. She wrote about it in a poem called 'Ghaists o Noth':

> Some ither mither's terror, strang an stairk,
> Cauldrife* and seenister, smored* me aa aboot;
> An eldritch* dreid, a fleg* the likes o me
> Could niver ken in my douce, ordered life.

* *Cauldrife* – cold; *smored* – smothered; *eldritch* – ghostly; *fleg* – fright.

To the north-east on the road to Insch is Leith Hall, one of the showplaces of the National Trust for Scotland, and further east by the Shevock is Dunnideer, whose name dances out of the old Harlaw ballad – 'As I cam in by Dunidier, and doun by Netherha . . .'

Druminnor Castle, which dates from the fifteenth century, is about a mile from Rhynie. It was the original Castle Forbes, seat of the Lords Forbes, and the gloom of its turbulent history is lightened by the fact that it has a Happy Room. In a vaulted chamber next to the kitchen there is a fireplace with the inscripton A HAPPY ROOM 144– I.R., which links it to King James II. How it came to be called that seems to be a mystery; perhaps they had a Happy Hour there, just like they do in modern times.

Less than two miles from Druminnor is Clatt, hiding away at the foot of the Correen Hills. The word Clatt comes from *cleith*, meaning concealed, and it is not a bad description of this sleepy little hamlet. An information board on top of Suie Hill reminds you that Clatt was made a burgh of Barony by James IV in 1501 and had its own provost and baillies. It has also had some eminent sons, not least among them the Bard of Corgarff. Wullie Gray came from Clatt and his literary efforts have won him more recognition than Sandy Low of Clatt. There is a four-line verse which runs:

> Beneath this stane upon this knowe
> Lies single-handed Sandy Low,
> He wrote a book nae man could read,
> Noo book an' author baith are deid.

Clatt has another link with Corgarff. It set up a Forum to sell its local crafts and home-made baking to visitors, and it was from this enterprise that the folk of Corgarff got the idea of starting up their Rural Exhibition.

Climbing the Suie Hill, you look down on Knockespoch House, home of the Fellowes-Gordon family, where the Inverurie weaver-poet William Thom found patronage. I left Suie behind and went down into the Howe of Alford – and into the 'Arms' of another poet. The Forbes Arms Hotel at the Bridge of Alford is where Charles Murray often stayed when home on leave from South Africa. It was there that a lassie,

The massive walls of Huntly Castle in the heart of Gordon country. Its ruined walls speak of a stormy history. Its main feature is a great oblong keep of six storeys.

'reid-cheekit, snod an' fair', made such an impression on him that he cried, 'O lassie fae the Forbes Airms, come owre the Brig to mine'.

Murray's poetry floats over the Howe of Alford like thistledown. You think of it in the Spring, when there are 'burstin' buds on the larick'; at harvest-time, when the crops are 'weel in an' stackit'; and when 'cauldrife winter' comes, riding through the Howe 'wi' angry skirl'. You see it in a youngster 'roadit at last' and creeping to school, and you feel it in the undulating hills of Donside – 'Fae the Buck o' the Cabrach thro' Midmar, Whaurever your tryst may lie'.

Murray has been called the inheritor of the Scottish Makars' mantle, the forerunner and inaugurator of the Scottish Literary Renaissance, and there is little doubt that it is true, but it is unlikely that Alford thinks of him in terms so grand. They have a way of keeping things in perspective. If you were going a bit over the top they would offer you the advice given in one of Murray's poems, 'Be wise an sit siccar (tight) – ye're safe on your doup (bottom)'. They have a careful, down-to-earth approach to things that Murray's father, Peter Murray, a local vricht (wright), showed when someone asked him if he was addressing the father of Charles Murray. 'Weel, sir', said Peter cannily, 'his mither aye said I was'.

Murray himself had the same kind of humour and the same kind of philosophy. 'Very little matters and nothing matters much', he used to say. For all that, he encapsuled in his poetry a way of life that has all but vanished from the North-east. He marked out the route for the Doric poets who followed him, and in many ways he was the inspiration for the movement which today, more than eighty years after his death, is fighting to preserve the North-east tongue.

The Howe of Alford must be rich soil for nurturing poets. At the turn of the century, when Charles Murray became a Lieutenant of the Railway Pioneer Regiment in South Africa, a rank he held during the early stages of the Boer War, Alexander Robertson Birnie, from Clochforbie in King Edward, was following a different kind of railway career. He worked with the old Great North of Scotland Railway at Aberdeen and in 1909 he was transferred to Alford, where he wrote one of his first poems.

A bowl on display at the Alford railway station museum reminds visitors of his best-known work. It is an example of the 'Nae crackit stuff' from Staffordshire which a local 'Pig and Ragger' merchant sold in the Alford area. His name was Charles Wright, but he was always called Pig Charlie, and the phrase 'Nae crackit stuff' came from a poem, 'A Tale o' Pig Charlie', written by Alexander Birnie, who was a station signalman at Alford.

It paints a marvellous picture of the old rag and bone merchant, who has long since disappeared from our streets. The 'Pig and Ragger' he was sometimes called. Everyone knew Pig Charlie – 'The Alford folks a' ken me brawlie'. His aul' bald pow was brown with exposure to the sun, he had whiskers 'like a scaffie's broom', and he had a timmer leg. He sold crockery 'richt up Donside and roon the Vale', paying for rags with cash or dishes:

> Nae crackit stuff, but a' things richt,
> They get the best frae Charlie Wicht.

The Tap o' Noth rises behind the little village of Rhynie. There is a vitrified fort on top of the Tap and also a stone known as Clochmaloo, the Stone of St Moluag, the famous Celtic missionary.

These itinerant pedlars were always given nicknames by their customers. Because they often belonged to the army of the Great Unwashed, the word 'Fool', meaning dirty, was frequently used. Charlie, whose face and hands had never been washed 'for mony a year', was no exception. 'Fule Charlie, Pigger, Wicht or Swine, Auld Screw' – these were some of the names they threw at him, but he didn't mind. He quoted a piece of homespun Aberdeenshire philosophy; they could call him anything, he said, as long as they didn't 'ca' (knock) me ower'.

The Alford Valley Railway Museum, where 'Pig Charlie's' bowl is on show, is part of the Grampian Transport Museum, which opened in 1983 and in 1987 attracted 40,000 visitors. Here, surrounded by a gleaming array of vintage cars, carts and cabs, not to mention penny-farthing bikes, you are transported back to a more dignified age in which the speed limit was 4 mph and a man with a red flag walked in front of your vehicle. There is a photograph of a driver who dared to exceed the speed limit. He was Dr P.E. Howie, of Strathdon, who is said to have had the first horseless carriage in

Aberdeenshire. His car was unpacked and running on the morning of July 17, 1896, at Alford railway station. He was in trouble with the police for going faster than 4 mph, but no charges were brought. This may have been because he was something of a local hero. When he was invited to exhibit his machine at Huntly Show, half the population of Strathbogie stayed up all night in case they missed the car's arrival.

Whether Dr Howie was the first car owner in Aberdeenshire may be open to argument. Deeside also laid claims to the honour. John Milne, who was road surveyor at Aboyne, was the owner of the first car on Deeside. He got it from Lord Granville Gordon, brother of the Marquess of Huntly, who found he was unable to start the 'horseless carriage' and gave it to Milne. John Milne often drove it over the hills to Strathdon to have a chat with Dr Howie about their roadsters. It is more than likely that the two pioneers met up with J.C. Barclay-Harvey, laird of the Deeside estate of Dinnet, who owned the *third* car in Aberdeenshire. This was a 1902 Arroll Johnston double dog cart, which the Transport Museum has on loan.

The vehicles on show range from a Rolls Royce Silver Ghost to a Victoria carriage (given the name because Queen Victoria liked it) and an 1896 Aberdeen horse tram. There is also a Marshall portable steam engine from Balmoral. Called the Birkhall, it was donated to the museum by the Duke of Edinburgh. The old vehicles carry the day, catering for a nostalgia which yearns for the days when there were no such things as angry motorists, honking horns, meters and traffic wardens. The vintage car rally is one of the most popular of the many outdoor events organised by the museum.

The pride of the museum is the famous Craigievar Express, which its creator claimed was the first steam car in the North of Scotland. This remarkable machine was built at Craigievar by a local postman called Postie Lawson. He once told Sir Ewan Forbes, the 11th Baronet of Craigievar, that its fire box and boiler came off a little boatie that plied on the River Thames. He used his inventive genius to improve his work, building a small horse-drawn wagon with windows all round a shelf in front of the driving seat. That was where he kept the mail – in a kind of portable sorting office.

Thus the motor age dawned in Strathdon and the Howe of

Leith Hall, near the village of Kennethmont, is under the care of the National Trust for Scotland. The earliest part dates from 1650 and it was the home of the Leith and Leith-Hay families for over three centuries.

Alford. The age of the train had already arrived. Forty years before, when Dr Howie and John Milne were struggling over the Donside hills in their horseless carriages, the first train had come snorting into Alford railway station on the new line from Kintore. Work on an extension of the Great North of Scotland Railway's line from Kintore to Alford, via Kemnay, Monymusk and Tillyfourie, had been held up for a number of years by shortage of cash. Other proposals popped up, among them a plan to continue the Deeside line from its terminus at Banchory to Lumphanan and via Cushnie to Alford. In 1856, work began on laying a line from Kintore to the Bridge of Alford, but shortage of cash again threatened it. For a time it looked as if it would end at Whitehouse, but the people of the Vale of Alford raised a guarantee of £5000 and the line eventually reached a point about a mile and a half short of the Bridge of Alford.

Just as bypass roads affect local communities today, the decision to shorten the railway line changed the face of Alford. The old centre of the village was cut off from the rail terminus and a new market town quickly developed around the railway station. For a time there was a happy marriage between road and rail, with steam traction engines hauling heavy loads to and from the rail terminus. That was when Alexander Birnie wrote an ode to Bella Craigmyle, a traction engine carrying goods from Alford into the foothills of the Cairngorms:

> Wi' a stop noo and then for a drink on the road,
> Through the wilds o' Strathdon Bella trips wi' her load,
> She's a muckle stoot jaud and her wark is nae toil,
> She's my ain charmin' lassie is Bella Craigmyle.

Clunking and groaning, Bella has long since gone to her last resting place, but engine buffs can now pay court to a sweeter jade – Saccharine. That is the name of an 0-4-2 steam locomotive built in Leeds in 1914 and currently operating over the Alford Valley Railway, Scotland's only 2ft. gauge passenger railway. It rumbles out of the reconstructed station (which is also the local tourist office), away from the original station platform, and takes its passengers on a journey through Haughton Country Park and the Murray Park. The Murray Park was donated to the community by Charles Murray and is a permanent memorial to its famous son.

Haughton Country Park is another example of how this small Aberdeenshire village has put itself on the tourist map. Haughton House, originally the home of the Farquharson family, has been a hotel, a residential boys' school, and a convent, and today it is the focal point of the caravan site run by Grampian Regional Council. It houses a shop, holiday flats, and amenities for the caravan dwellers. The mini-rail track passes the 'MacDonald Walk', a nature trail leading to outdoor curling and skating ponds.

For those who like a full-scale track, and yearn for the old GNSR days, there are still stretches of the Alford Valley line that can be walked, even if uncomfortably. There has never been any suggestion that this should be turned into a walkway, as there has on Deeside. Too much of it, at any rate, has

One of the miniature trains operating on the Alford Valley Railway, Scotland's only 2ft. gauge passenger railway. The trains take people on a trip round the Haughton Country Park and the Murray Park.

disappeared. For most of the way the railway hugs the main road, firstly the A944, then the B993. Curving down through Whitehouse, once a staging post for the stagecoach on its way from Aberdeen to Strathdon, it turns away from the main Aberdeen road at Tillyfourie and heads for Monymusk, Kemnay and Kintore.

You can pass through Tillyfourie and not even know that it is there, yet it is more important than you would think. The old trains that came clanking up from Alford were puffing their way through the history of the granite industry in the North-east, and publicists who invent tourist trails – castle trails, heritage trails, whisky trails – should give a thought to starting a granite trail at the Hill of Tillyfourie.

They have kept Rubislaw Quarry locked away from the public eye for long enough, and they are doing the same at Tillyfourie; or, rather, at Corrennie, which is across the road from Tillyfourie. The notice at the start of the steep track up to Corrennie Quarry discourages prying eyes, but this may be because they still take some stone out of it. Pink Corrennie granite was used in the building of Aberdeen Art Gallery and Gray's School of Art, and was also used for the pillars of the Tay Bridge, while Tillyfourie was the main centre in Aberdeenshire of the kerb trade. They ranked high in the 127 working quarries which Aberdeenshire had at the turn of the century.

Pink stone, pink soil. The quarry itself is tucked away in thick woodland, as is Tillyfourie. There is no outward despoliation of landscape here. If they ever turn Corrennie into a tourist attraction they can shout aloud about the magnificent view. The Mither Tap pokes its head inquisitively out of the hills to the north and, nearer at hand, there is a different kind of stone. This is a 12ft. monolith called Luath's Stone, which rises on the Green Hill and is said to mark the grave of Lulach or Luath, Lady Macbeth's son.

Down below, I could see traffic crawling toy-like towards Alford, and at the base of Tillyfourie Hill a line of dilapidated wooden cottages. These were the bothies of the quarrymen who worked at Tillyfourie. Wood panelling and old-fashioned grates suggest a reasonable degree of comfort, but vandals and graffiti-writers have had a field day inside the buildings.

Outside, I was told by a local man that I was standing on the Alford railway line. He spoke about the huge blocks of Corrennie stone that lay at the side of the track waiting to be carried off to Kintore. For stonemasons looking for a richer vein to mine, Paradise lay ten miles to the east – at Kemnay. It is odd to think that this small village on the banks of the Don, described at the beginning of the nineteenth century as 'a paltry hamlet', became world-famous through stone hacked from a hill called the Hill of Paradise.

Kemnay takes its name from 'kame' or 'kem', the gravelly ridge on which it stands. This part of Aberdeenshire has always been noted for its stones ... the Lang Stane o' Craigearn, a 12ft. monolith south-west of the village, the Clovenstone, the Camiestone, and a croft with the name of Great Stone, which the locals call Gryties. Here, the actual stone is as big as a haystack. Great Stone has the same meaning as Grey Stone, and accounts of witchcraft trials on Deeside mention a grey stone or gyrt stone at Lumphanan. The Great Stone is one of a number of huge stones, glacier-borne from the Cairngorms,

The famous Craigievar Express in the Grampian Transport Museum. It was built by a local postman called Postie Lawson, and its creator claimed it was the first steam car in the North of Scotland.

which can be seen in the area. Tradition has it that the Devil hurled one from the top of Bennachie at the parish priest of Kemnay.

Despite the Devil, Paradise triumphed. The first quarry on Paradise Hill was opened by the owner of Kemnay estate, John Burnett, for alterations at Kemnay House, and a quarry at Whitestones, on the east side of Leschangie Hill, supplied massive granite blocks for Waterloo Bridge in London. But the man who made Kemnay granite famous was John Fyfe. The firm he founded in 1846 is still in existence; when the high costs forced other companies out of business, Kemnay turned to the making of a new type of building block called Fyfestone.

In October, 1987, I was at the opening of the firm's new Westhill Granite Works in Aberdeen. There was word that new 'good' granite had been found at Kemnay and a few months later Fyfe's were awarded an £800,000 contract for the supply of 4000 tonnes of granite for external cladding of the Bon-Accord Centre. Today, the firm imports granite from

Scandinavia, which means that they can compete strongly with their European competitors. I watched huge automatic polishers at work and a giant saw cutting through 30-ton blocks of granite, but here and there a handful of masons chipped away at stones with hammer and chisel. The old skills haven't completely disappeared.

The great gash on the face of the Hill of Paradise is an ugly monument to John Fyfe's enterprise. Between the mid-nineteeth century and 1900 the population of the parish of Kemnay rose from 600 to nearly 3000. Kemnay granite has gone all over the world. London took its share . . . for the Thames Embankment, the Tower, Blackfriars, Southwark, Kew and Putney Bridges. The Queen Victoria Memorial, opposite Buckingham Palace, has Kemnay granite in its steps and landings.

There are stones from Kemnay at Sunderland and Newcastle and in the foundations, piers and approaches of the Forth Road Bridge. They are the real memorials to Fyfe's work. He was an inventive, progressive businessman who was always on the look-out for new ideas to improve his quarrying operation. He introduced a steam derrick, the first of its kind, but discovered that there were limitations to what it could do. He found what he was looking for during a visit to Braemar to check on a bridge-building contract, when he saw a 'postie' delivering mail to Abergeldie Castle.

There was no bridge over the River Dee at Abergeldie at that time and the postman had to send his letters across the river on an endless rope. Until a footbridge was built there in 1885, people used a 'cradle' to get over the Dee. It gave Fyfe the idea of building a cableway for quarry work instead of cranes. When he began to think of a name for it he remembered the little Frenchman, Jean Francois Gravelet, who came to Aberdeen in 1861 with a tightrope act, stringing a rope across an open space in Golden Square and thrilling hundreds of spectators by crossing and re-crossing it. Gravelet was better known as Charles Blondin and John Fyfe's new cableway was named the Blondin. The first Blondin was erected at Kemnay in 1873 by the engineering staff at the quarry, and other cableway 'Blondins' sprang up in quarries all over Scotland.

The road to Paradise led to more than the granite stones of

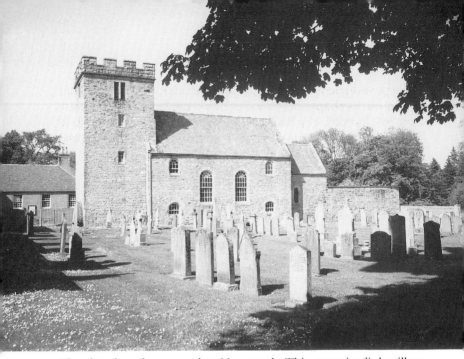

The church and graveyard at Monymusk. This attractive little village was once the home of the famous Monymusk Reliquary, which contained a bone of St Columba. It is now in the National Museum in Edinburgh.

Kemnay. Paradise was a term used in the seventeenth and eighteenth centuries for an area that had been enclosed and planted. Queen Victoria twice travelled from her own 'dear Paradise' at Balmoral to visit Paradise at Monymusk. Here, the names dated back to 1716, when Lord Cullen, previously Sir Francis Grant of Cullen, laid out a landscape garden about two miles from the village. Sir Archibald Grant spectacularly topped his father's efforts by planting nearly 50,000,000 trees in Paradise Woods. It is a staggering total, a figure to toy with today when widespread afforestation has become a controversial subject.

Sir Archibald was one of the great eighteenth-century improvers, far-sighted North-east lairds who brought new thinking and new techniques to agriculture. They supported the ideals of the Society of Improvers in the Knowledge of Agriculture in Scotland, set up in 1723 with a membership of forty-two peers and 260 commoners. Twenty-nine men from Aberdeenshire were among its members. Sir Archibald, whose farms were reported about 1720 to be 'ill-disposed and mixed',

150

also spearheaded the move to improve Aberdeenshire's roads, urged on, perhaps, by his wife. He complained that he 'could not, in chariote, get his wife from Aberdeen to Monymusk'. But it was in agriculture that he made his mark, introducing new methods of husbandry and persuading farm workers that if they changed their ways they could have 'all the comforts and credits of life'.

He criticised the time they 'spent in idleness, or sauntering about, or upon trifles'. He was sorry for their poor living, he said, but it was their own fault. Monymusk is one of the loveliest villages on Donside and it is hard to believe that it was once a squalid collection of dirty huts. The description came from Sir Archibald himself – 'the farme houses, and even corne millns and mans (manse) and scool, all poor dirty huts'. Sir Archibald lived in Monymusk House, but he didn't think that *it* was much to write home about. It had 'granaries, stables and houses for all the cattle and of the vermin attending them'. He was advised to pull it down, but happily that demolition never took place.

The Monymusk that visitors see today, with its ancient church and Tudor-style cottages grouped around a small village green, was the creation of Sir Arthur Grant, the 9th baronet, who rebuilt it at the turn of the century. There are inscriptions above a number of the buildings showing when they were built. Few villages in Aberdeenshire can boast so much history. Here, the Culdee missionaries had one of their earliest seats in the North of Scotland; here, too, Malcolm Canmore stopped on an expedition against rebels in Moray in 1078. The church, built of Kildrummy sandstone, has its own fascination, and it is here that the parish records, dating back to 1678, are preserved, as well as silver cups dated 1671 and a 1772 silver bowl for baptisms. Monymusk has always been known as the home of the Monymusk Reliquary, a seventh-century casket containing a bone of St Columba. It was known as the Brecbennoch of St Columba and was carried before Bruce's forces at the Battle of Bannockburn. The reliquary is now in the Royal Museum of Scotland in Edinburgh.

While Sir Archibald Grant was busy trying to teach new farming methods to the folk of Monymusk, the 'scool' that he mentioned had a teacher who was to become famous both as a churchman and poet. He was the Rev. John Skinner, author of *Tullochgorum*, which Robert Burns said was 'the best Scotch song that Scotland ever saw'. Skinner, who was only eighteen when he became assistant schoolmaster at Monymusk, wrote his first poems there. While he liked the laird's 'Paradise' (he wrote a poem about it), he had little time for Sir Archibald's agricultural improvements. He thought they would put some nasty temptations in the way of simple farmers.

He probably thought a good hard game of football would be better for their souls. Football in those days was what present-day sports writers would call 'physical', but modern soccer is puerile stuff compared with the mayhem that went on when John Skinner was a dominie at Monymusk. During the three days' holiday at Christmas, the men and boys of the village took part in a game of football known as the Christmas Ba'ing. The kirkyard was the pitch and there were no referees to blow the whistle on any fouls. Skinner wrote about the game in a poem called 'The Monymusk Christmas Ba'ing', and some idea of the sort of 'sport' it was can be got from these lines:

> In Monimuss was never seen
> Sae mony well beft* skins;
> Of a' the Ba' neb* there was nane
> But had twa bleedy shins.

> * *beft* – struck; *neb* – point.

Skinner put himself into the game as the 'insett Dominie' (acting schoolmaster), who joined the throng 'riftin (belching) frae his dinner' and was coupit (overturned) 'heels-o'er-goudie (topsy turvy)'. The poem is crowded with marvellous characters like Francis Winsy, 'a sauchin slivery slype (sour, slobbering, worthless fellow)', Petrie Gib, who got a crack on his crown that made him 'yow'll and claw'; and a competitor who was as cross-eyed as 'Stachie' Laing. He was called Gley'd Gibby Gun, and his fate in the game was to be thrown 'o'er the grave divine, on's bum that day'.

Chapter 9

Down the Lord's Throat

The wind snaps and snarls through the Glens of Foudland, throwing great wreaths of snow across the fields, piling them in drifts against the frozen paling posts. There is a never-ending battle to keep the Glens open in winter, for Foudland is the gateway to Strathbogie and the north. It was once regarded as the most difficult and dangerous stretch of the road between Aberdeen and Inverness, and it is still treated with caution. There are names on it which today's drivers pass without a glance, yet they were once important milestones on the long trek through the Foudland hills. Pitmachie, Bainshole, Newtongarry, Sheelagreen, Clinkstone ... oyster-like, they hold the secrets of this bleak tract of uplands west of the River Urie.

Despite oil developments and heavier traffic flow, there has been no dualling of the roads north of Aberdeen, but today's drivers have an easy run compared with that of the men who first blazed a trail through the Foudland glens. They must have had something of the pioneering spirit of the old American West. At any rate, they had covered wagons, although they called them Caravans. It is a pity that no one thought of raising a monument to diminutive Alexander Scorgie, whose vision went beyond the post horses and post chaises that clattered out from Aberdeen to penetrate the wilderness of Foudland nearly two centuries ago. He was the first to start a passenger 'caravan', a vehicle with two wheels, drawn by one horse, and covered over with painted canvas.

There were four passengers inside and one outside, seated beside the driver and the flat board. The Scorgie Caravan ran from George Street, Aberdeen, to the West Wynd, Huntly, and the little man's business quickly expanded. In September, 1807, he extended his run to Keith, where horses and gigs took passengers on to Fochabers, Elgin and Forres. He also built a bigger and better Caravan, painted black and yellow, with glass windows, a padded interior, and space for eight passengers – six inside and two outside, although eight could be squeezed in if necessary. The speed of the new Caravan averaged five miles an hour – one mile an hour faster than the permitted speed of the first car on Donside.

But there was competition. A Huntly man, Alexander George, also started a caravan between Aberdeen and Huntly, charging 'seven shillings the whole way'. Both had their followers. Scorgie, reaching Pitmachie, a well-known staging post, on a particularly stormy day, was asked, 'Foo'll ye win through the Glens the nicht?' The Caravan proprietor replied calmly, 'I'll gae throu in coorse'. When the Marquis of Huntly wanted to get to Pitmachie during a severe snowstorm, he put his trust in Mr George. On the return run through the Glens they stopped at Bainshole, where a pair of fresh horses was waiting to complete the journey. The Marquis was impressed by such foresight.

Bainshole was one of the main hostelries in the Glens, but it had an unsavoury reputation. Norman Thomson, who farms Newtongarry, remembers how in recent years, when Bainshole was no longer an inn, you could still get a drink there. When it ceased to be a public house it was turned into a general merchant's store, but regular customers knew they could always get a dram in the back shop. The shop, however, also went out of existence and today it is a private house.

There was another hostelry at the Thomsons' farm at Newtongarry. The farm, which is still called Newtongarry Inn, is said to be haunted. There have been stories about strange noises and crockery mysteriously shaking and rattling on the shelves, but Norman Thomson and his wife Anne told me they have never heard anything that made their hair stand on end. Maybe the people who saw the ghosts had drunk too much Foudland whisky, for there was never any shortage of it. If you couldn't get it at one of the inns, you could always get it at Jericho.

Jericho was a distillery which operated near Colpy at the beginning of the last century, using the waters of Jordan for its whisky-making. The Jordan is a small burn that runs down the River Urie. The malt whisky produced at the Benachie Distillery (its official name) must have been marvellous stuff, for the distillers didn't tell you how good it was; instead, they boasted that it didn't give you a hangover. 'There's nae sair heids in Benachie' claimed one of their advertisements.

There was no Bennachie Distillery when Alex Scorgie's Caravan first ran through the Glens of Foudland, but it is more than likely that his passengers got their drams from illicit Foudland stills when they stopped at Bainshole. In the early days of the distillery another kind of 'caravan' was often seen in the Glens – a long line of carts, nose to tail, taking barrels of whisky from Jericho to the railway station at Insch. It was said that there was seldom a sober carter among them. There are still people in Foudland whose fathers or grandfathers worked at the distillery, which closed just before the start of the First World War. But the walls of Jericho have long since come tumbling down and there are few signs of the old distillery at the farm of Nether Jericho, where it was originally situated.

The old road through the Glens, skirting the Hill of Foudland and running parallel with the present road, passes a farm called Clinkstone. Old spellings show the name as Clinks-town, not stone, and one theory is that it was a personal name, like Clinkie's Well in Huntly. A much more interesting, if less likely explanation, is that the name came from the clinking sound of slate slabs being struck together. The two principal slate quarries in Aberdeenshire were on the Hills of Foudland and Tillymorgan, and there was also a quarry on the Hill of Skairs. The Foudland workings can still be seen from the main north road.

Foudland slate, which was light blue and classed as 'semi-hard', was used to roof Balmoral Castle. Farmers and crofters earned some extra cash in the slack season by carting the slate from Foudland to Deeside. There were about sixty-five men employed at the Foudland quarries in the first half of last century, four in each quarry, the remainder working on the breaking up of new veins and in splitting and dressing the slates. Their wages ranged from twelve shillings to sixteen shillings a week, with the quarriers and splitters getting the highest wages. The rock was generally split with wedges, but gunpowder was used if it was very hard. The number of Foudland slates sold in a year varied between 800,000 and 900,000.

East of the Skirts of Foudland is a farm called St Sairs. It is a reminder of two great fairs that were once held there. One was

St Serf's or St Sair's Fair, which was said to be one of the oldest in Aberdeenshire. It was held at Monkeigie, now Keith-hall, and later transfered to Culsalmond. The other fair was St Laurence Fair, better known as the Lourin Fair, which ranked alongside the most important horse and cattle markets in Scotland. It was held at Old Rayne and has its place in North-east ballad lore in a song about a woman who lost two of her lovers there:

> The tane was killed at Lourin Fair,
> An' the ither was drooned in Dee.

The old Cadgers' Road is still marked on OS maps, cutting across the Hill of Tillymorgan. This was the way they came to the Lourin Fair, drovers and pedlars, chapmen ballad singers and recruiting sergeants. Tents were strung out along the banks of the Urie, the pungent smell of cooking rose from huge, boiling pots of broth, and smoke from open fires spiralled and drifted away to the Mither Tap of Bennachie. It was a boisterous, bawdy affair and 'many a bloody racket' was seen there. Charges laid down by the Privy Council in 1621 show that two pennies were charged for every foot length of a merchant's stand, four pennies for every 'kow, ox and horse', and a similar sum for every 'cordonner's stand for shoone'. There was also a charge for 'everie tent or pavillion for selling meate or drinke'.

In recent years the Lourin Fair has been revived. It is one of the few events in the North-east to bring back the authentic atmosphere of the old horse and cattle trysts. It is still very much a horse fair. The great, clomping Clydesdales have made their comeback, primped and pampered, manes combed and tails plated. The organisers dress for the part; bunnets, sarks and galluses are required dress for the bothy concert.

You can taste hot bannocks straight off the girdle, smothered in lip-smacking syrup, and you can throw sponges at the stocks, just as they used to do to the tinkers, although they probably threw something more damaging than sponges.

Old Rayne was the home of Charlie Leslie – Mussel-mou'd Charlie, a chapman poet and ballad singer, who learned his trade at the Lourin Fair. Charlie became a familiar figure throughout Scotland and was lauded as 'the street laureate of

Three things for which Aberdeenshire is famous . . . castles, farms – and Bennachie. The castle, which rubs shoulders with farm buildings a mile north of Monymusk, is sixteenth-century Pitfichie Castle. In the background is the familiar outline of the Mither Tap of Bennachie.

Aberdeen'. He lived to the ripe old age of 105, dying in 1782, when the 'Bells o' Raine' rang out in tribute to the fact that he had 'danced and sang five score years and five'. His portrait hangs alongside those of lords and ladies in a room at Fyvie Castle, one of the great houses he visited during his travels throughout the North-east.

The Urie carries its memories south to join up with the Gadie at the Back o' Bennachie – 'Up at the back o' Bennachie, far Gaudie rins sae sweet'. There are a number of ways you can approach the Mither Tap. One is from the Back o' Bennachie, near Oyne, another from Essons car park by the Maiden Causeway, and a third by Millstone Hill, across the River Don from Paradise Woods. The Donview Centre at Millstone Hill is popular with visitors, not only walkers bound for the Mither Tap, but picknickers lolling at the riverside and enjoying a glimpse of Paradise. Inside the centre there are some excellent drawings by Mary Wilson, Nairn, with verses specially written by Flora Gray, the Buchan poet, who now lives in Comrie. One is called 'The Hill Fort':

> The Romans marched by Don,
> Herriet the laich* countrie,
> But heich in their fort in the Mither Tap.
> The Picts fan sanctuary.

laich – low

Folk in this part of the country used to tease visitors with the riddle, 'How do you get to Paradise?' The answer was, 'Down the Lord's Throat'. The Lord's Throat is south of Bennachie. Charles Murray wrote about spending 'Fine cheery days' in this area – 'Up Nochtyside or throu' the Cabrach braes, Doon the Lord's Throat an' ootower Bennachie'. There is a Satan's Well north of the hill at Chapel of Garioch, so the Mither Tap lies between the De'il and the Deity. I once heard two people having a solemn discussion about the Lord's Throat. They could understand the Devil's Elbow at Glenshee, but the Lord's Throat baffled them. If they had looked at the map more carefully they would have seen that it is *My* Lord's Throat.

The 'Lord' is the Laird and the word 'throat' means a ravine, which in this case is on the Keig-Monymusk road. The pass is said to have been named My Lord's Throat in honour of Lord Forbes, the Premier Baron of Scotland, whose ancestral home, Castle Forbes, stands at the south-west corner of Bennachie. Castle Forbes, which was originally called Putachie, was designed by Archibald Simpson and built in the early nineteenth century. It isn't open to the public and is well screened from sightseers, but you can catch a glimpse of it among the trees from the Keig road.

One of the treasures at Castle Forbes is a black sculptured bear's head in stone. The stone is supposed to represent the bear traditionally slain by the founder of the family (three bears' heads are shown in the Forbes arms) and there is an interesting tale about the origin of the name Forbes. The name can be pronounced as it is read, or as Forbess. I always thought that the For-bess pronunciation was a piece of upper-class affectation. Now I am not so sure. The story, at any rate, says that nine young women were slain by a boar at the Nine Maidens Well on the Craigs of Logie, near Mossat. The boar was killed by the lover of one of the women, whose name was Elizabeth, and when her sweetheart slew the animal he cried,

'It's a' for-Bess!' That, according to tradition, is how the family got its name, although in the story the bear becomes a boar.

Whether you believe the legend or not depends on how much romanticism there is in your soul, but anyone living within sight of Bennachie knows that it is a place for romantics. No other height has aroused such an explosion of emotion as this lumpy Aberdeenshire hill. There has been a vast amount of literature written about it ... poems, prose, dreadful doggerel, books, calendars, exruciating songs; it pours out in a never-ending torrent.

Just over a century ago, Deacon Alexander Robb, an Aberdeen merchant, who was something of a versifier, wrote a poem in which he complained that Lochnagar was getting too much attention. He mentioned 'the Lordly Poet's praise', which was presumably a side-swipe at Byron, and asked why there was no Scottish minstrel 'to sing of lofty Bennachie'. Leaving aside the fact that lofty Bennachie is only 1733ft. high, there is not, on the face of it, a lot to sing about. It has, for instance, neither the grandeur of Macdhui nor the symmetry of Mount Keen. No one seems to know what its name means, and some fanciful theories include the Hill of Sight, the Hill of the Rain (there might be a good case for this one), and the Hill of the Dog. John R. Allan said that one clergyman described it as Bend-up-High because its shape made it look like someone touching his toes. I have a suspicion that this may have sprung from a book, *Travels through Scotland,* written in 1834 by a P. Finlayson, who was known as 'the observing farmer'. 'There is a hill in the Gerioch called Benahee', he wrote, 'but the proper name is Ben-up-High', and then he went on to mis-spell the name, declaring that 'Many of Bend-up-High stones are sent to London'.

So what is it that makes canny Aberdeenshire folk go daft over the Mither Tap? 'To hell with your Alps, Rockies and Himalaya,' declared the late Lord Aberdeen. 'Bennachie is the hill for me'. Charles Murray, sitting at starlight banquets in South Africa, thousands of miles from home, could think only of wading through the bracken at Bennachie. Alexander Rodger, the Rayne-born dominie and poet, living in the 'steerin', reekie toun' of Glasgow, longed for 'the hamely crack o' Bennachie' and the Garioch poet, J. Pittendrigh McGillivray, wanted to be off 'the hard steen streets' and up the back o' Bennachie.

I have never been able to put my finger on the fascination of the hill, but I have a feeling that the answer lies in the foreword which Sir Maitland Mackie wrote for *Bennachie Again*. He mentioned Flora Garry's poem, 'Foo Aul's Bennachie?' and said it didn't seem to him to matter. 'What is important is that it is there,' he declared, 'it's aye been there and it will aye be there. In a changing world that is comforting'. W. Douglas Simpson's description of Bennachie as the sphinx of the Garioch suggests an incomprehensible timelessness. It is a staggering thought that the granite forming the Bennachie ridge is something like 400 million years old. It puts most things into perspective; perhaps that is Bennachie's secret.

It is a miracle that the Mither Tap hasn't been trampled flat by the boots of invading walkers. It certainly gives them problems, but a voluntary conservation group called the Bailies of Bennachie was formed in 1973 to fight litter and vandalism, preserve rights of way, and look after footpaths. The idea was to have a membership of fifty, but within three years there were about a thousand bailies on the roll. So it looks as if Bennachie will be in good shape for another 400 million years.

I left Bennachie and Paradise and went east, through the Chapel of Garioch, down past the ruins of Balquhain Castle, where Mary Queen of Scots spent a night in 1562, and on by Red Harlaw towards Oldmeldrum. I was looking for another hill, a mere knoll compared to Bennachie, but I thought that if I stood on its summit I might feel a sense of history.

Barra Castle is a small but attractive castle standing on the edge of the B9170 road from Inverurie to Oldmeldrum. It was built in the early seventeenth century by a family called King, whose connection with Barra went back to the mid-thirteenth century. It raises the interesting question of what was there when Robert the Bruce passed that way in 1307, for the castle is at the foot of the Hill of Barra, which is linked with Bruce's victory over Sir John Comyn, the Earl of Buchan. The Comyn's first clash with Bruce was at Slioch, south-east of Huntly. Repulsed, Comyn had another go after Bruce returned to his camp at Inverurie. He gathered about him, as John Barbour put it, 'a full gret company of men arayit jolily' and headed for 'ald Meldron'.

Busy with the sheep at Tarland Show. Tarland is one of the few places where the atmosphere of the old-style agricultural show is still retained.

There is a track opposite Barra Castle leading to the top of the Hill of Barra. Comyn spent the night there before the Battle of Barra and the spot is known as Comyn's Camp. Bruce came forth from his camp at Crichie, near Inverurie, and the two armies met at what is now the North Mains of Barra. There are the usual tiny crossed swords on maps to show that a battle took place at Barra, but there is nothing on the site to indicate that this was where Bruce won a significant victory. The North-east doesn't seem to regard King Robert as a tourist attraction.

'Ald Meldron' is an interesting little town. Nobody calls it Oldmeldrum, simply Meldrum. A gazetteer published a century and half ago said that the town was 'a respectable edifice' and that the streets of Oldmeldrum were 'very irregularly built'. Both observations are still true. The town hall, with attractively ornamented chimneys and an Urquhart heraldic decoration on its wall, is now the headquarters of the North East Library Service. The narrow, dipping streets and lanes *are* irregular, but they give the burgh a certain charm.

Heavy traffic used to push awkwardly through these streets, but a by-pass has taken care of that.

Outside the Meldrum Arms Hotel there is a statue of a Jack Tar clutching an anchor, which is not the sort of thing you expect to see in an inland agricultural community. It was suffering from an acute case of verdigris when I was there. Nobody seemed to know much about it, but it was apparently put there by an old sea captain who owned the hotel in the 1930s. The other oddity for which Oldmeldrum is known is a pyramidal boulder on the golf course known as the Groaning Stone.

Perhaps the groans come from drinking too much Rob Roy, which is a blended whisky produced at the old-established Glengarioch Distillery. Whether Glengarioch, like Jericho, can boast 'nae sair heids' I do not know, but its malt stands high in the taste-buds of whisky-drinkers. Moreover, there is an interesting example of rural enterprise at the distillery. In 1977 it became the first distillery to grow tomatoes to use up its waste hot water, starting with half an acre under polythene. Now it has one and three-quarter acres, mostly under glass – one and a half acres for tomatoes and a quarter-acre for pot plants. In 1987 its yield for tomatoes was 130 tons.

Inverurie, the so-called 'capital' of the Gairloch, is about fives miles to the south. It was at one time the home of the Inverurie Locomotive Works and when they were shut down it was regarded as the biggest catastrophe in the royal burgh's long history. Dole and disaster stared the town in the face. Today you would never know there had been a Loco Works. They are still there, but the premises have been taken over by industrial and other firms like Seaforth Maritime, and Inverurie is as busy and bustling as it ever was. The only reminders of its time as a railway town are inside the local museum. Here, too, is a link with another transport era in the Garioch, a wooded sign announcing that 'The Passage Boat sails from Inverury for Aberdeen every afternoon at half-past 2 o'clock, Sunday excepted'.

It is a long time since the Passage Boat pulled out of Port Elphinstone en route for Aberdeen. Flags flew, a band played, and a gun on board the *Countess of Kintore* boomed out in celebration as the first barge set off on its historic journey along the Aberdeenshire Canal in 1806, but less than half a century later the dream dried up with the canal. It was drained to make way for the Great North of Scotland Railway.

At one time, twelve boats plied between the Port and Aberdeen Harbour. Their cargoes included slates from the Foudland quarries. On Fridays, carts piled high with sacks of grain gathered at the Canal Head to load their goods on to the barges. The landlady at the change-house toiled through the night baking oatcakes to feed the farm servants driving the carts. Prosperity at the Port was measured by the number of eggs consumed at breakfast – the average was two apiece. The barges took from ten to fourteen hours to make the journey from the Port to Aberdeen.

Passengers as well as goods were carried on the canal. Two fly-boats, each pulled by two or three horses, driven in tandem fashion, with a boy riding on the first one, made the return journey twice daily at a speed of about 8 m.p.h. On one stretch of the canal at Stoneywood you can still see a milestone indicating a distance of 5½ miles from Aberdeen. The explanation is that journeys on the barges were charged by the half mile. In Aberdeen, names like Canal Street and Canal Terrace are reminders of the days when barges and fly-boats passed through Woodside on their way to Waterloo Quay.

Although stretches of the canal can still be traced, most of it will ultimately vanish. History is slipping through our fingers and nothing is being done to preserve it. Port Elphinstone, where it all started, has never been very good at saluting the past, as experience has shown. Apart from its role in the rise and fall of the Aberdeenshire Canal, the Port's only other claim to fame is that it is the birthplace of J. Pittendrigh Macgillivray, the man who wanted to be off 'the hard steen street' and up Bennachie. Macgillivray became the King's Limner for Scotland, but it wasn't only as a poet that he won recognition; he was also a sculptor, painter, architect and scholar, which was no mean achievement for a lad born in a humble cottage in the Port and taught at the 'Port school'.

One of Macgillivray's principal works was a statue of Byron, which now stands in the grounds of Aberdeen Grammar School. Aberdeen Art Gallery owns eleven of Macgillivray's works, including bronze busts of Sir George Reid, the

Aberdonian who was president of the Royal Scottish Academy, and William Alexander, author of *Johnny Gibb of Gushetneuk*.

Words like 'genius' and 'one of Aberdeenshire's few great men of art and imagination' were used when a granite plaque was unveiled on the wall of 3 Victoria Terrace, Port Elphinstone, in 1951. The plaque, chosen by the sculptor himself, read 'Pittendrigh Macgillivray was born here MDCCCLVI'.

That was thirteen years after his death. Five years later, on the centenary of his birth, the North-east's morning paper, *The Press and Journal*, carried the headline, 'Town Forgets Famous Sculptor'. There were no centenary celebrations, no exhibitions, only mumbled apologies. The then director of Aberdeen Art Gallery, asked about a centenary exhibition, said it would 'be very expensive to move heavy statues about the country'. One could almost hear the ghost of Pittendrigh Macgillivray shouting the lines from one of his poems:

> I'll gang nae mair to yon toun,
> Whate'er may be the plea.

The Gallery made amends with a superb exhibition in 1988, the fiftieth anniversary of his death, although it hinted that previous neglect was due to Macgillivray's own character. He wasn't called 'Macdevilry' for nothing; he had a tendency, on his own admission, 'to tell the mob to go to hell'.

Macgillivray had a passion for the Mither Tongue. 'The Norlan' Fiddle' was about the preservation 'o' Lallan Scots or Aiberdeen'. 'They say our fiddle's auld and deen,' he declared, but he himself didn't believe it. The Norlan' fiddle, the Mither Tongue, would never 'gae deen', for 'the bairn-time words', the old familiar speech of Buchan and the Garioch, would always stay green in people's hearts.

Not far from Pittendrigh Macgillivray's birthplace in Victoria Terrace, a section of the old canal carries water from the River Don to Inverurie Paper Mills. This, at least, is an unbroken link with the past. The building of a canal was talked about as far back as 1795. When it finally got underway the motivation came from the Taits of Inverurie, a family who had been in the Garioch since about 1650.

A village shoemaker – the souter – sits in the sun mending a pair of ploughman's tackety boots, his tools beside him. This striking picture was taken by Aberdeen's pioneer photographer, George Washington Wilson, back in the 1880s. Picture by courtesy of Aberdeen City Libraries.

As well as being leading farmers in the area, they owned a meal mill. They wanted the canal so that grain and ground oats from their mill could be transported to the docks at Aberdeen. Even in those days they were leaders in new ideas and new technology. They were the first to use an iron boat to carry their grain to the Aberdeen docks, but it was so badly designed that it had to be scrapped. It can still be seen rusting on the banks of the Don. They also owned a small snuff mill near the intakes of the Lade at the Don Bridge. When the canal was shut down to make way for the railway, the Taits were paid compensation, and they used the money to start a paper mill. Today, the name of Thomas Tait and Sons ranks high in the papermaking industry.

Inverurie is the start of the Donside paper trail. Downstream are giant papermaking conglomerates like Wiggins Teape and the Bowater Group, but the Inverurie Mills are showing that local enterprise and local pride can match anything the 'big guns' put up. The man at the head of the company is Thomas John Tait, still in his thirties, who, when his father was killed in an accident, took over the running of the mill at the age of twenty-one.

He shies away from the well-dressed businessman image, preferring to turn up at work wearing a pullover and open-neck shirt. He calls his employees by their first name, speaks with a broad Aberdeenshire accent, and talks jokingly about his 'foreign' wife. Sheila, who is his personal assistant, is English. Behind Tom Tait's homely exterior and North-east tongue is a shrewd and calculating business brain. With £23.5 million worth of investment at his back, giving his mills the largest and most advanced papermaking machine in the country, he has been taking his company through a period of decline in the papermaking industry towards the new opportunities of the 1990s. Tom Tait likes to show visitors round his factory in Inverurie. One day, perhaps, like Grandholm Mills further down the Don, he will have a museum there, showing how it all began when the flags went up, the guns boomed, and the first barge sailed proudly out of 'The Port'.

The other major mills on the Don – Stoneywood, Mugiemoss and Donside – have also been planning for the future, with millions of pounds' worth of investment paving the way to the twenty-first century. The manufacture of paper in Aberdeenshire goes back to 1696. The Stoneywood Paper Mills were established in 1770 and became almost a self-contained community, with houses for its workers, playing fields, and a school built by the company for the children of its workpeople. It was, according to a report at the turn of the century, healthy work, for 'the girls and women have a fresh, healthy apperance which is striking, and they are all smartly dressed'.

Just as Mugiemoss and Stoneywood are names that have become synonymous with paper, Crombie and Grandholm mean only one thing – cloth. Like the Inverurie Paper Mills, the Grandholm enterprise started with a canal, but it was only a mile long, carrying water from the Don to drive the machinery at Gordon's Mills, on the haugh of Grandholm. J. & E. Crombie, who had a mill at Cothal, took over Grandholm in 1859 when it was vacated by the linen firm of Leys, Masson and Co. Today, the name Crombie is known throughout the world.

In August, 1987, a new Visitors' Centre was opened at Grandholm, with a museum, a shop and a coffee shop. The museum and an audio-visual show turn the pages back on Grandholm's past ... on the mill girls of the Twenties and Thirties, on a visit by the Queen (now the Queen Mother) and Princess Elizabeth in 1944, and on the Grandholm Big Wheel, the biggest water wheel in the world, which was demolished in 1905. It was 26ft. in diameter, 20ft. 6in. wide, and used 115,000 cubic feet of water per minute.

Grandholm has always had its finger on history. During the American Civil War it sent rebel grey cloth across the Atlantic to make uniforms for the armies of the South. Crombie cloth has draped many famous shoulders. The firm has a large export trade to Russia, and when Mr Gorbachev is seen striding across our television screens the workers at Grandholm smile and nod their heads knowingly. He is wearing a Crombie coat.

The mills that live off the Don have often repaid it by polluting its waters, but in recent years large amounts of money have been spent to put it right. Now, cleaned up, it sweeps past Grandholm below the high-rise flats at Gordon's Mill Road on the last stages of its journey. They have always aimed high at Grandholm – the first spinning mill there was seven storeys high and had 386 windows. Two miles on, the old river loops round Seaton Park and under the Brig o' Balgownie, then out under the Bridge of Don to swirl and dance and disappear into the grey North Sea.

BUCHAN

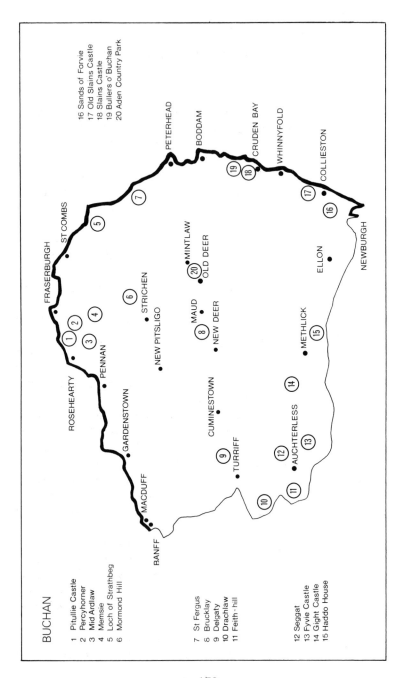

BUCHAN

1 Pitullie Castle
2 Percyhorner
3 Mid Ardlaw
4 Memsie
5 Loch of Strathbeg
6 Mormond Hill

7 St Fergus
8 Brucklay
9 Delgaty
10 Drachlaw
11 Feith-hill

12 Seggat
13 Fyvie Castle
14 Gight Castle
15 Haddo House

16 Sands of Forvie
17 Old Slains Castle
18 Slains Castle
19 Bullers o'Buchan
20 Aden Country Park

FRASERBURGH
ST COMBS
ROSEHEARTY
PENNAN
GARDENSTOWN
MACDUFF
BANFF
NEW PITSLIGO
STRICHEN
TURRIFF
CUMINESTOWN
AUCHTERLESS
METHLICK
MAUD
NEW DEER
MINTLAW
OLD DEER
PETERHEAD
BODDAM
CRUDEN BAY
WHINNYFOLD
COLLIESTON
ELLON
NEWBURGH

Chapter 10
Cyaaks and Carlins

The folk in the little shop at Balgaveny, on the road from Rothienorman to Aberchirder, had heard of Dr John Burnett Pratt, but they had never heard of the Oof Stone. It was Dr Pratt, author of the classic North-east work *Buchan,* who declared that the Oof Stone could be found south-west of Auchterless. It was also known as the Woof Stone, indicating a fairy or wicked sprite, and it marked the old county boundary of Buchan. The Balgaveny folk knew all about boundaries. They knew about a farmer at Lenshie who could stand in a field with one foot in Aberdeenshire and the other in Banffshire, and about a steading at Lenshaw that was cut in half by the boundary, but the Oof or Woof Stone defeated them.

Then someone remembered the *Wolf* stone. That's what it had always been called, and an Ordnance Survey mapmaker who visited Balgaveny said that the word 'Wolf' meant a boundary stone. It lay less than a mile away, up a road marked Haremoss, but it was buried in the tangled undergrowth of a ditch and nobody could recall seeing it for many years.

I never found the Wolf Stone, although I came upon a stone that might have passed for it, but I tracked down another boundary marker mentioned in Pratt's *Buchan.* This was the Hare Stone on the farm of Feith-hill. There are a number of Harestones or Hare Cairns in Aberdeenshire and all refer to land boundaries. Haremire means the boundary mire, and the famous Harlaw in the Garioch should be Hairlaw, the boundary hill.

Go two miles north of Feith-hill to the Hill of Drachlaw and there is a boundary stone which has sinister links with witches and warlocks. This is the Carlin Stone ('cyarlin' is the local pronunciation) and a carlin was an old woman, a witch or a hag. Its Gaelic equivalent is *cailleach,* a name more familiar in the hill country of Deeside than in the flat lands of Buchan.

When you try to follow the boundaries in this part of the North-east you feel like the Lenshie farmer doing the splits in his field, for you are never very sure if you are on one side of the boundary or the other, or simply straddling it. The boundaries of Buchan have always been confusing to the modern traveller. Thousands of commuters making their daily run from Aberdeen to Ellon think they are in Buchan when they cross the Bridge of Don, but they are, in fact, travelling through the ancient Thanedome of Formartine. 'All that country which lyeth betwixt the rivers Don and Diveran (Deveron)' was once thought to be Buchan, but now it is recognised that its boundaries enclose all the country lying between the Rivers Ythan and Deveron.

When I set out to explore Buchan, I started on a hill at Ythsie, north of Pitmedden, which was somewhere near the boundary. One of the reasons I was there was that it offered a grandstand view of Buchan. Here I could look down on the world and think of the lines from one of J.C. Milne's poems – 'O Lord look doon on Buchan and a' its fairmer chiels'. Behind the farm of North Ythsie, at a point where visitors leave their cars, a notice reminded me that this was not a right of way, but, nevertheless, welcomed me to 'the best view in Buchan'.

It *is* the best view in Buchan, but I was there for something more than that. In a field at the end of a farm track was a tall stone monument – the Prop of Ythsie. Not many people, I imagine, see it at close quarters, although it is a well-known landmark. The word 'Prop' means landmark, and this one was built as a memorial to George Gordon, 4th Earl of Aberdeen, the Laird of Haddo, who was Prime Minister of Britain from 1852 to 1855.

He is a shadowy figure in the country's history. Despite the fact that he was Foreign Secretary for seven years and Prime Minister for two, he was regarded as a grey character, humourless and austere, an incompetent leader and a bad Prime Minster – the man who made a mess of the Crimean War.

I once saw a sculpted head of George Gordon in the Statesmen's Aisle at Westminster Abbey. He was set apart from other leaders, dwarfed by towering statues of men like Disraeli, Pitt and Gladstone. Glowering across the aisle was Palmerston, who once cruelly described him as a piece of antiquated imbecility. It is a far cry from the cloistered quiet of

The Prop of Ythsie, erected by the tenants of Haddo estate to the memory of their laird, George Gordon, 4th Earl of Aberdeen, who was Prime Minister from 1852 to 1855. From the Prop, they say, you can get the finest view of Buchan.

Westminster Abbey to the dubby fields of Buchan, but I couldn't help thinking that here in the North-east he had been better thought of. There is nothing on the Ythsie monument to indicate that the man it honours was once Prime Minister. It was erected by his 'grateful servants', who were less concerned with what he had done for the country than what he had done for them.

Looking down on Haddo from the top of the monument, I thought of how Gordon, taken away from the estate at the age of eight, had returned to it on his coming-of-age. He found the land neglected and Haddo House virtually in ruins. He wanted to turn on his heels and leave the place; instead, he decided to bring it back to life. He spent nearly £3000 on improvements in the first ten years, and when he died in 1860 he had planted fourteen million trees and spent £60,000. Farms were improved, new schools were built, and peaty moorland was turned into fields of corn.

Haddo House and its estate are today in the care of the National Trust for Scotland. Hundreds of people come to walk in the grounds and stroll around the stately house where George Gordon played host to Queen Victoria in 1857. The garden at Haddo is open all the year round, as is the adjacent country park run by the local authority. Haddo has also become a cultural centre, a development that would have met with the 4th Earl's approval. He was a lover of the arts, a competent poet, if not a particularly original one, and a keen amateur actor. As he put it in one of his own verses, he loved to 'tread with Shakespeare's music the buskin's stage'.

They are still treading the buskin's stage at Haddo more than a century after his death. The tradition set by the 4th Earl of Aberdeen is being maintained by June Gordon, the Marchioness of Aberdeen, a softly-spoken women of great charm, who is herself an accomplished musician. With her husband, the late David Gordon, 4th Marquis of Aberdeen, she decided after the Second World War to make Haddo a rural centre for music and drama. The Haddo House Choral and Operatic Society became known, not only throughout Britain, but internationally.

Vaughan Williams, Benjamin Britten and Sir Michael Tippett are among those who have conducted at Haddo, while the Prince of Wales and Prince Edward have performed on the stage of the modest wooden hall at Haddo House. In 1987 the Haddo House Trust was set up so that the tradition of music and drama at Haddo could be continued into the future. The Trust, working with the National Trust for Scotland, has ambitious plans to modernise the hall, introduce educational programmes for the young, courses for senior citizens, art exhibitions and performances of traditional Scottish music. Prince Edward is a patron of the Trust.

Standing on the hill of Ythsie (the name is pronounced Icy, which seemed to be particularly appropriate), I took one last look at the best view in Buchan. I could see the Mither Tap in the distance. Pratt's *Buchan* makes much of the fact that Bennachie, although not belonging to Buchan, can be seen from almost every part of it, which seems a poor attempt to gain some reflected glory for this endlessly flat and treeless country.

From the Prop I could pick out a Buchan hill of some height and importance, although its familiar summit was despoiled by a radar defence system. Every time I see the fretwork of masts on Mormond Hill I think of another of J.C. Milne's poems, 'Atomic War', in which two boodies (scarecrows) are talking in the aftermath of an atomic war, one saying to the other, 'Faur's Mormond that wis stanin here?' The White Horse of Mormond must sleep uneasily in its heather bed these days. Across the woods of Haddo lay the village of Methlick, where the Gordon Earls of Aberdeen are buried. It sits on the edge of the River Ythan, which comes looping down from Fyvie, some eight miles away. There are Haddo farms in the Fyvie area. The name is derived from half-dauch, a measure of land, and the Gordons adopted it in the early seventeenth century when they became baronets of Haddo. The old name of Haddo and its park was Kelly.

From Methlick you can follow the Ythan to the gloomy ruins of Gight Castle. Byron was a Gordon of Gight and the castle became a ruin in the lifetime of his mother, Catherine, the last of her line of Gordons. Byron's father, 'Mad Jack' Byron, gambled her fortune away and Gight passed to the Haddo family. Curiously, the 4th Earl's father, Lord Haddo, was killed by a fall from his horse at Gight only two months after the death of Byron's father.

To the south of the Prop of Ythsie is Pitmedden, whose magnificent gardens prove to the world that Buchan is not flowerless as well as treeless. The Great Garden of Pitmedden was founded by Sir Alexander Seton, second son of John Seton of Pitmedden – 'Fundat 2 May 1675' says the inscription above the entrance. The estate was bought in 1894 by a well-known farmer, Alexander Keith, whose son, Major James Keith, gifted it to the National Trust for Scotland in 1952.

When the Trust took over Pitmedden, three acres of the Great Garden had been turned into a kitchen garden. The original plans had been destroyed in a fire in 1818, but both lower and upper gardens have been lovingly recreated. It is a marvellous garland of colour on grey old Buchan's shoulders. The colours in four parterres are provided by 40,000 plants, and three miles of boxwood hedges have to be kept in trim.

Pitmedden has always meant farming as well as flowers. The estate stands in the centre of rich Aberdeenshire farming country and James Keith, who died only a year after giving Pitmedden to the Trust, was a forward-thinking agriculturist. This has been recognised by the setting up of a Museum of Farming Life, where you can open the door on a fascinating slice of the North-east's farming past . . . the farmhouse, the bothy, the byre and turnip shed, the stable and hay-loft. There is also a small collection of rare and interesting breeds of Scottish livestock.

Udny Green lies to the south of Pitmedden Gardens, with Udny Castle on its doorstep. It is an attractive little village, but the castle is closed to the public. The only other thing it can offer the tourist is a huge round mort-house, built to keep out body-snatchers. Inside the mort-house is a circular turntable for the coffins. The whole structure looks disconcertingly like a baker's oven. When I peered through the doorway I had a mental picture of corpses lying around the turntable like the spokes of a wheel. I hastily withdrew.

Udny Green has never really cashed in on the fact that it is the home of Jamie Fleeman, the Laird of Udny's Fool. Wandering around the village, I wondered if I should stop someone and ask, 'Fa's feel are you?' That was Jamie's reply when a pompous visitor asked him whose fool he was. 'I'm the Laird o' Udny's feel,' he said, with a glint in his eye. 'Fa's feel are you?'

Lots of lairds had their 'fools' in those days. They were status symbols, rather like the butler or chauffeur in modern times. Jamie was the last of the jesters. He won his place in history by saving the family when fire broke out in their castle at Knockhall, near Newburgh, in 1734. The other Fleeman

Pitmedden Gardens, a seventeenth-century garden originally laid out by Sir Alexander Seton, the first baronet of Pitmedden. The garden was recreated by the National Trust for Scotland.

remark that has drifted down the years is the one he made when he was dying. 'Dinna bury me like a beast', he said. The phrase is inscribed on his tombstone in Longside cemetery.

Jamie, whose real name was James Fleming, was born in Longside in 1713 and died in 1778. He would have done well on today's stage. He looked like an eighteenth-century Spike Milligan. His hair stood on end, he dressed eccentrically, and he had piercing eyes and a loud voice. But he was no fool; he had a quick, deflating wit that made his detractors think twice about crossing swords with him. His humour was often dipped in vitriol. When he was seen leading a donkey, a passer-by cried, 'Is that your brither, Jamie?' 'Na, na!' replied Jamie, 'jist a casual acquaintance like yersel'.'

During a long sermon in church, half the congregation were falling asleep, but Jamie stayed wide awake. 'My brethren', said the minister, pointing to Jamie, 'you should take an example from that poor fool'. 'If I hidna been a feel', said Jamie, 'I would hae been sleepin' tae.'

There is a Fleeman's Country Shop in the village. Inside it is

Jamie Fleeman's Kitchen, which boasts mouth-watering fare the Laird o' Udny's fool would never have tasted ... salmon quiche, navarin of lamb, chocolate mousse, fruit dumpling and blackcurrant tart. There is also a whisky boutique in the shop, but Jamie would never have approved. He had a horror of strong drink, declaring 'Auld Nick hides in the bottle. Every time you taste it, he gie's you a kiss'.

I got a kiss from Auld Nick in the local hostelry and went north to the land of bonnie lasses. According to an old ballad, there are plenty of them in the Howe of Auchterless, but you have to go to Fyvie to find the best. The Trumpeter of Fyvie obviously thought that 'the flo'er o' them a'' was in Fyvie, O. The story of the ill-fated love affair between Mill o' Tifty's Annie – the miller's daughter, Annie Smith – and Andrew Lammie, the Trumpeter of Fyvie, is enshrined in North-east balladry. When the miller, opposed to his daughter marrying a lowly trumpeter, locked her in her room, Lammie climbed on the top of Fyvie Castle and blew a despairing love call towards the Mill o' Tifty. The trumpeter was sent away and Annie died of a broken heart. A stone figure of the trumpeter can be seen on top of one of the castle towers, still blowing his horn.

Fyvie Castle is the jewel in the National Trust's crown. It has everything that a castle needs to attract tourists ... a rich history, a priceless art collection, a ghost and a secret chamber. The ghost that haunts the castle is the Green Lady. There is a reddish-purple stain across the floorboards of the room where Alexander Seton is said to have killed his first wife, Lillias Drummond, who stalks the castle corridors in a dress of shimmering green satin. The Secret Chamber is a windowless inaccessible chamber at the bottom of the Meldrum Tower, an evil place they say, and it has never been opened. There is also a Weeping Stone, which mysteriously exudes water. It is said to be one of three stones mentioned in an old curse.

Not surprisingly, Fyvie Castle has become one of the National Trust's most popular properties, and art has as much to do with it as things that go bump in the night. The Treasures of Fyvie, as the art collection is known, went on show at the Scottish National Portrait Gallery in Edinburgh and at Aberdeen before the opening of the castle in 1986. There are paintings by artists of the calibre of Romney, Reynolds and Raeburn. Pompeo Batoni's full-length portrait of Colonel

Fyvie Castle, one of the most important – and popular – castles in the care of the National Trust for Scotland in Aberdeenshire. It has five great towers, a ghost, a secret chamber, memories of a tragic love affair, and a unique art collection.

William Gordon, one of the lairds of Fyvie, is the most famous of the paintings in the castle.

Alexander Leith, or Alexander Forbes-Leith as he later became known, bought Fyvie in 1889 after making a fortune in the American steel industry. He was the man who created the Fyvie collection. There is an odd man out in the collection, a painting of Charles Leslie, Mussel-mou'd Charlie, the Old Rayne hawker, by a relatively unknown Peterhead artist, James Wales. It was found stuck away in an old chest of drawers when the National Trust took over the castle. Mussel-mou'd Charlie is supposed to have called at Fyvie when he wandered the country selling his wares and singing his songs.

Mussel-mou'd Charlie lived to be 105, but this was not particularly uncommon in the eighteenth century. 'Aberdeenshire', said a report in 1785, 'hath the reputation of being remarkably healthy, and the inhabitants are distinguished by their longevity.' In the second half of the century a list taken from the *Aberdeen Journal* showed that there were seventy-two centenarians in the North-east counties.

They not only lived long, they usually kept active. William

Barns, who was a mere youngster of 100, was enjoying a game of fencing only a month before he died in 1759, while Agnes Christie, of Midmar, who was 'hale and vigorous to the last', walked sixteen miles in one day two months before she died at the age of 104 in 1762. Robert Williamson, from Countesswells, didn't quite make the century. He died at the age of ninety-eight, after being married for seventy-four years. His wife, Isobel, was 100 and still walking to the market in Aberdeen to sell her poultry and eggs.

Alexander Christie, of Auchleuchries in Cruden, had two wives before he died in 1791, aged 101. His first wife, Christian, was in her 105th year when she died and Alexander was eighty-four when he married again. A Peterhead beggar-woman, Jean Petrie, lived to be 113 and was still wandering through the country till within a few days of her death. Her father died at the age of 114.

Fyvie air seemed to be a recipe for long life. Grizel Strath was 102 when she died there in 1777, which may have been due to the fact that 'she was most regular in her habits'. But the centenarian's crown went to Peter Garden, from the Chapel of Seggat at Auchterless. The *Aberdeen Journal* reported on January 30, 1775, that 'On the 12th curt. died near Chapel of Seggat in the parish of Auchterless, Peter Garden, at the extraordinary age of One Hundred and Thirty-One'. He had lived under ten rulers and sovereigns, starting with Oliver Cromwell and running through to George III.

A painting of him, sitting on a huge stone in full Highland dress, with a snuff box in his hand, carried the caption: 'The Celebrated Peter Garden of Aberdeenshire, famous for uninterrupted Health, Gigantic Stature, and Longevity, having lived to the uncommon age of 131 years with his faculties entirely to the last'. Peter, who was a farmer, was able to work on his farm until a few years before his death, when his sight failed him. He married his last wife at the age of 120. She had been his servant and married him 'for a bit of bread'.

Peter may even have been older than was thought. He often boasted that he had served under Montrose and had been at the Battle of Fyvie in 1644. He was between ten and twelve years old then, which would have made him at least 141 years old when he died. He used to say that in his young days he was a 'gey loon' (great rascal).

There is, sadly, nothing at Seggat, or anywhere else in Auchterless, to indicate that Peter Garden ever lived there. Nor is there anything to mark the birth of another 'gey loon' at Seggat – Lewis Grassic Gibbon, or James Leslie Mitchell. The Mecca for lovers of Gibbon's classic *Scots Quair* is in the Mearns, and few people know that he was born at a farm called 'The Hillies', Hillhead of Seggat, tucked away in a hollow at the end of a dusty farm track near the Chapel of Seggat.

Coming over the Darley hill from Fyvie to Auchterless, I thought of the new minister who is supposed to have arrived by the same road and, looking down on the village and its church, said: 'Plenty of siller and plenty of sin – I'll stay'. The first thing you notice about the kirk is that the clock has only three faces. There is a blocked-up hole where the fourth one should have been. The story is that a local farmer gave a clock to the church, but laid down that there would be no face on the north side. He didn't like the folk at Seggat and wasn't going to give them a clock face to see the time.

The church was built in the late 1870s, but the spire was added in 1896. Until the steeple was built, the congregation used the bell in the gable of the old church, whose ruins, with the bell, still stand in the grounds. Some budding poet wrote a jingle about it:

> The folk of Auchterless are a curious people,
> They built a kirk without a steeple,
> They weren't able to raise a bell,
> So they rang the aul' een that hangs on the ga'le.

The lines reminded me of a familiar verse from Lewis Grassic Gibbon's *Cloud Howe:*

> Oh, Seggat it's a dirty hole,
> A kirk without a steeple,
> A midden heap at ilka door,
> And damned uncivil people.

The Segget of Gibbons' Mearns and the Seggat of Auchterless may have been separated by miles, but they were probably one and the same place in Mitchell's consciousness. He lived at Hillhead of Seggat until he was seven, and it is more than likely that the childhood impressions he gained there lingered in his mind when he wrote *Cloud Howe.* Was it the Auchterless jingle that planted the seeds of the Seggat verse? And did the Chapel of Seggat, half a mile from Hillhead, become the Chapel of Seddel in *The Thirteenth Disciple?* The book was a thinly-disguised autobiographical novel and it is not too difficult to see young Leslie Mitchell in Malcolm Maudsley, the black-haired boy with the brose-bowl haircut, woollen stockings and heavy-soled boots.

'The Hillies' is derelict now, the life sucked out of it by an eternity of toil. It is like all the other old farm touns that were once scattered across the face of Buchan. 'A grey, grey life', wrote Mitchell. Here at the 'Hillies', as at the fictitious Chapel of Seddel, the boy Mitchell awoke to the clanking of milk-pails and the sound of 'brown beasts oozing through the midden glaur'. Mitchell described in *The Thirteenth Disciple* how the young Malcolm Maudsley was taken to a window to watch a great bonfire that was lit at midnight on New Year's Eve, 1900. 'He was elevated in friendly arms and bounced and danced ecstatically at the sight which greeted his eyes. They were burning out the nineteenth century.'

Soon they will be burning out the twentieth century, and there is no knowing what the next century will bring, but, looking back on the old one, it is clear that life has changed almost beyond belief since Lewis Grassic Gibbon wrote about ploughmen in sodden bothies, old, bent and wrinkled people, and the 'grey servitude' of the farm worker. Still, as you travel through Buchan there are reminders enough of what it was like in those hard, scarring days.

To the north of Auchterless lies Turriff, a prosperous little town which always reminds men of three things. One is the Turra Coo, the white dairy cow that caused a riot when it was confiscated and auctioned off during an insurance stamp row in 1913; the second is the Turra Show, which is still a major event in the agricultural calendar; and the third is the famous bothy ballad, 'The Barnyards of Delgaty', where the farmer was wealthy and the men hard done by:

> Sae fare ye well, ye Barnyards,
> Ye'll never catch me here again.

I passed the Barnyards on my way to the lovely Idoch valley, into the heartland of Buchan. James Cowie, of Cuminestown, who was said to be one of the most talented painters to have worked in Scotland this century, was born there, at Netherton of Delgaty. Cowie's uncle lived across the Idoch valley at the Mill of Haremoss and it was this countryside that became the background to many of his paintings.

The names at the road-ends are as Buchan as Buchan Humlies . . . Sprottyneuk, Bodiechell, Fadliedyke, Tillypestle, Clackriach, Glasslaw, Pundlecroft. A pundler was an impounder of stray animals in the days before land was enclosed. Glasslaw figured in an old rhyme which went:

> Cyaard, Cyaak and Cairnywhing,
> An' scum the lums o' Glassla.

Glasslaw, where the lums needed cleaning, is about two miles south-west of New Aberdour, and Cairnywhing is in Tyrie. Cyaak is how you pronounce Cavoch, the original name of New Pitsligo, where they still make Pitsligo lace. The wool carders from the Highlands who plied their trade in that part of the country were known as 'The Cyaarders o' Cyaak'.

The name Clackriach comes from glack, a ravine or a hollow. There used to be a castle of Clackriach beside the Mains of Clackriach, near Maud. When I was looking at the origin of field names a few years ago I discovered that the Pantons of Clackriach had fields called Frostyhill, Frostybrae, Lady's Well (the site of the well is still marked on the map), Lang Rigs and Scrapehard. Scrapehard, I was told, was very aptly named. At one time many farm names reflected the poor condition of the land. There were names like Bakebare, Thirstyhillock, Hadagain and Piketillum. Pike meant 'pick', a small helping, and when a farm was poor, with only a bare living for a tenant, it was said that it was 'a pike till him'.

New Pitsligo, New Byth, New Deer, New Aberdour . . . they were all new at one time, some built for the linen industry during the second half of the eighteenth century. There is a row of ruined cottages, buried under ivy and weeds, at Invereddie, a few miles from Longside. It was known as the Creeshie Raw.

The cottages were occupied by women working in the carding and spinning departments of a wool mill at nearby Kinmundy. 'Creeshie' meant greasy – the Greasy Row – and youngsters taunted the 'creeshie' folk with a piece of doggerel that went:

Creeshie beagle*, tatie thief,
Four and twenty airn* teeth.
Yin to ca'* and yin to girn*,
An' yin to ca' the creeshie pirn*.

* *beagle* – oddly dressed figure; *airn* – iron; *ca'* – drive;
girn – catch; *prin* – reel.

The 'new' villages now seem as old as Buchan itself, forgotten communities whose streets are strung out in long, straight lines, keeping a lazy eye on the world as it whirls past their doorsteps. In New Deer kirkyard, where the Dingwalls of Brucklay have a burial enclosure, there is a monument to rival the Prop of Ythsie. It stands on top of the Hill of Culsh and, like the Haddo tower, was erected in 1875 by the tenants in memory of their laird, William Dingwall Fordyce of Brucklay, MP.

I remember riding up to Brucklay Castle before the war in a truck carrying a huge block of ice for the pantry. My uncle, Alex Murdoch, was grieve on the home farm of Shevado, and Brucklay seemed a fairy-tale world, a magic place where pretty streams gurgled under quaint old-fashioned bridges. It was always sun-dappled and peaceful; memory, at any rate, paints it that way. Now the castle is gone and the childhood images have gone with it.

Changes are putting a testing finger on Buchan, the 'land o' plenty'. The legacy of success is there, but the future is uncertain. It is a cliché to say that farmers complain about bad times as they drive about in luxury cars, but in recent years there has been good reason for their concern. Changes in consumer tastes and the influence of CAP, the Common Agricultural Policy, have brought new patterns of agricultural output, not least being the growing concentration on cereal production. The problem of surpluses is increasing and the forecast is that it will get worse. The result will be that there will be a reduced requirement for agricultural land, and already the question of alternative uses for agricultural land has been under discussion.

Farm incomes and profitability have been on a downturn since the early 1970s. More than half the farmland in the North-east is under grain. Bad weather and poor harvests have taken their toll; in 1987 cereal yields were drastically reduced and the experts said there would have to be a re-examination

The restored farm buildings in the Round Square at Aden, centre of a 230-acre country park between Mintlaw and Old Deer. The North-east of Scotland Agricultural Heritage Centre is also sited at Aden.

of farming enterprise. Well, there may be lessons to be learned from the past. The North-east of Scotland Agricultural Heritage Centre at Aden Country Park, Old Deer, provides a telling illustration of how innovations in farming methods and implements radically altered farm life and landscape in the North-east.

Aden is a crossroads where past and present come together. The Heritage Centre, which spans the period from the eighteenth century to the present day, attracts nearly 30,000 visitors each year. Its focal point is an agricultural collection known as the Adamstown collection, which mirrors the farm life of the North-east over the past two centuries. Andrew Hill, the curator, has used North-east poetry and music as a background to the picture it unfolds. The Heritage Centre turns its eyes to the future as well as to the past. Developments in new crops, mechanisation and chemicalisation are examined, and their impact on farm production and the landscape is considered. Aden is a living museum, not a dusty exercise in nostalgia. It has its own farming demonstration plot, where youngsters from local schools come to actively practise farming.

The agricultural centre is only one part of the Aden scene.

There were two large estates in this part of Buchan at one time, Aden and Pitfour, and a none too friendly rivalry existed between the Ferguson and Russell lairds. The boundary line was the bridge crossing the Ugie near the Abbey of Deer. One half of it is narrower than the other, and this is because the Laird of Pitfour had a larger carriage than the Laird of Aden and widened his half of the bridge to accommodate it. The Laird of Aden refused to widen the other half.

The Aden estate, once the home of generations of the Russell family, covered over 10,000 acres at the turn of the century. Today, 230 acres of it have been turned into a recreational playground, a place where people can stroll in the grounds, gaze at the shell of the once-great mansion house, and find out how their forbears lived. One of the main developments at Aden has been the restoration of the farm buildings in the Round Square, including the Horseman's House, where Mary Jane Thomson, a latter-day 'horseman's wife', bakes bannocks and oakcakes for the visitors. The room she sits in was her mother's kitchen, for her father, Jimmy Thomson, lived there when he worked for the Lairds of Aden back in 1919.

It was through the Heritage Society that Aden was able to put on permanent display a rare and important collection of photographs recording the folk and times of the North-east up to and after the Great War. The photographs, which were discovered in a trunk in a farmhouse loft, were taken by James Morrison, who ran a cycle agent's business in the Balmedie area. Morrison carried his cumbersome camera equipment with him when he travelled around the countryside on his motor-bike, so that day by day, year by year, he built up a fascinating record of life in the North-east . . . farm lads at Savoch sitting on corn kists in front of their bothy, barefooted salmon fishermen on the Ythan estuary, a pair of horse in dress harness, the first Aberdeen-Newburgh bus, with luggage above and passengers below, and an orraman at Easterton farm smoking a clay pipe. More than 500 plates were found in the old trunk at Balmedie.

As Sir Maitland Mackie said in an introduction to a booklet about the James Morrison Collection – 'A clearer understanding of the past must certainly help us to face a future full of challenges'.

Chapter 11

Smugglers' Coast

The coastal villages of Buchan have always had a fragile hold on the land. Some, like Pennan and Crovie, stand uneasily on the edge of the sea, the waves raging up to their doorsteps, yet they survive. If it isn't the sea, it's the sand, blown over exposed stretches of coastline by onshore winds to form great billowing dunes rising to a height of 60ft. or more. From the wastes of Forvie to Gamrie Bay, where the boundary of Buchan creeps into Banffshire, there are sharp and dramatic contrasts . . . shelving coastal reaches smoothed into long stretches of golden sand, towering headlands, rock gnawed into grotesquely sculpted shapes and pitted with hidden caves.

Back in the nineteen-thirties, an English visitor to Collieston, a fishing village three miles north of the Ythan estuary, wrote a letter to a friend in which he described this 'fighting of the sea against the land'. 'Imagine', he told him, 'whole systems of slate-like slabby rocks, flung flatwise and acres square, thrusting out into the maddened North Sea which heaves and foams over them in deafening surges.' He painted a picture of a Nor'-easter, full of rain and 'so misted that our smarting eyes can peer only two or three hundred yards into it', lifting the waves bodily into the air and smashing them on to the rocks.

The visitor was Lawrence of Arabia, T.E. Lawrence, on leave from the R.A.F. and hiding away from the world in a rented cottage – 'the nearest hovel to the high-tide mark' – in Collieston. He walked across the 'sand-tussocked desolation' of the links, ate pounds of peppermints ('pandrops they call them: Aberdeen and excellent'), read books, and threw scraps of food to the gulls that wheeled and squawked above his cottage roof. 'They have the saddest, most cold, disembodied voices in the world', he wrote. He also ate speldings, fish that were split, salted and dried in the sun, but he thought the local people tasted more in them than he did. Speldings are no longer made in Collieston, which is a pity, for they would make tasty seafood for the holidaymakers who have taken the place of the fishermen.

Looking down on Collieston, once a busy little fishing port. Today, many of its cottages have been taken over as weekend hideaways by people from Aberdeen. It was at one time well-known as a centre for smuggling.

It is more likely that Lawrence wandered about the Sands of Forvie looking for its lost village, remembering the sands of Akaba. Today he would find the Forvie Centre catering for visitors and standing guard on the nature reserve, while across the Ythan in Newburgh is the Culterty Field Centre, run by Aberdeen University's zoology department, where the birdlife of Buchan comes under the scientist's microscope. The area is a birdwatcher's paradise. Forvie is a well-known breeding ground for eider duck and terns, while along the Ythan estuary there are shelduck, redshanks, dunlin, sandpipers and sanderlings . . . an almost endless variety of birdlife.

In late September and October, thousands of pinkfoot and greylag geese come winging in to the fields of Buchan at the end of their long migration from Iceland and the Arctic. At the Loch of Strathbeg, further north, as many as 20,000 pinkfeet have been sighted on one October day, and at the other end of the season a day's count marked up over 4000 greylags. I have been out on more than one occasion with Bill Murray, a field technician at Culterty, who knows more about birds and animals than most people. He took me to the Meikle Loch, a few miles from Newburgh, where he has seen 10,000 geese flighting in at sunset. Two-thirds are pinkfeet.

The caves and inlets along this rugged coast have names like the Smiddy Cave, the Twa E'en (a double arch), the Bleedy Hole, the Auld Water Moo (Old Water Mouth), the Pricker and the Seggie Pot. Dick Ingram, an old Collieston worthy, once told me of a cave called the Gin Hole. 'I'll get gin oot o' it afore I dee', he said. It was inside these caves that casks of gin from Holland were hidden by smugglers, the so-called free-traders who operated at the end of the eighteenth and beginning of the nineteenth centuries.

Two luggers, the *Crookit Mary* and the *Crookit Meg*, were heavily involved in the smuggling trade. *The Crookit Meg* was the title of a book by Sir John Skelton, a nineteenth-century essayist and historian, who graphically described a cargo of contraband being landed on the Buchan coast: 'silks from Lyons, gin from Holland, lace from Brussels (and one golden cross set in pearls from Antwerp)'. Just how much the local population was involved is shown in Skelton's account of the contraband being carried in panniers on the backs of thirty or forty hill ponies, guarded, not only by the crew, but by fishermen and farm labourers. Although Skelton's book was remarkably true-to-life, it could never match the grim reality of a stone in St Ternan's churchyard, on the outskirts of Collieston. It marks the grave of Philip Kennedy, a local smuggler who died on a bleak December night in 1798 at the age of thirty-eight, his skull riven by a gauger's sword.

From the kirkyard a road winds its way along the coast to Whinnyford, passing a dusty track to the ruins of Old Slains Castle, which sticks up like a jagged tooth on a windy headland site. Behind it, a little incongruously, stands a modern house built by the Countess of Erroll on what was her ancestors' courtyard. There was actually a village of Oldcastle at one time, a thriving little fishing community which fell into disuse at the turn of the century.

Whinnyfold, less than three miles along the coast, was also a fishing village. T.E. Lawrence would have found his speldings there, for old pictures show them strung out to dry on fences all round the village. North-east fishing villages seem to teeter on the top of cliffs or cower at the foot of them, but the original Whinnyfold (or Finnyfaul', as the locals call it) was half

The Ythan estuary, where terns breed among the sand dunes. The area is a well-known haunt of naturalists. Newburgh, on the shore of the River Ythan, houses Culterty Field Station, where Aberdeen University researchers carry out studies in ornithology, zoology and biology.

a mile inland, almost as if Finnyfaul' folk had recoiled from the storms that lash this naked Buchan coast. Fishermen going out on what they called sma' line fishing had to clamber up and down a steep cliff path to the shore, and fishwives had to do the same to reach the 'scaups', the beds of shellfish which they used as bait.

The modern Finnyfaul' is a huddle of houses with little charm, and not much character. Interestingly, though, it has a house called the Crookit Lum, which provides a link with the old smuggling days. It has a crooked lum, or at any rate, a tilted gable. Whinnyfold still draws its quota of visitors, but gone are the days when wealthy guests from the palatial Cruden Bay Hotel walked across the nearby bay to take afternoon tea in the village. Standing on the cliffs, looking out to the notorious reefs called the Scaurs of Cruden, I thought of one visitor who discovered Whinnyfold long before the Great North of Scotland Railway built its palatial hotel at Cruden Bay. He was Bram Stoker, the creator of Dracula, who often stayed at Whinnyfold, and eventually retired to the village. His *Mystery of the Sea* was based on a legend which says that when there is a full moon at the Lammas tide, those with the 'sight' can see the bodies of victims claimed by the Scaurs rising out of the sea. Dracula, however, was Bram Stoker's most famous creation, and inspiration for this is said to have come from New Slains Castle.

It is surprising that he never used the Bullers o' Buchan as a setting for one of his books, for this 'monstrous cauldron', as Boswell called it, is the kind of place you would expect unthinkable things to happen. In the days of the Buchan railway, wide-eyed tourists travelled by train from Cruden Bay to peer nervously down into the great sea hole known as 'The Pot'. Now they come by car and coach, treading carefully along a narrow path 200ft. above the Bullers. Most people make the mistake of thinking that the name comes from the French 'bouillir', meaning to boil, but in fact it is an old Scots word meaning 'rushing of water'. Either way, it is no place to be on a stormy night. There is a tidy little hamlet at the entrance to the Bullers, its inhabitants cheerfully resigned to sightseers peering in at their windows and wondering why anyone should live on the edge of a watery abyss. The answer lies in the name of one of the houses, 'Breathing Space', which is what you get in plenty in this gusty corner of Buchan.

Beside the Bullers is the Bow of Pitwartlachie, which the Old Statistical Account described as 'a grand arch to which the kitty-weaks resort'. The kittywakes are still there, crowding the broken granite cliffs during the breeding season, along with razorbills and tubular-nosed fulmars. The Bullers of Buchan and Troup Head are two important seabird colonies on the Buchan coast. So the ragged shoreline creeps north, up past the Rocky of Dunbuy and the Manaarna Howp (howp, they say, is the Buchan sound of hope, a sea inlet), and on by Yoags' Haven and the Cave o' Meackie to where the remains of Boddam Castle sit between two deep gullies south of the village.

The Buchan coast is studded with ruined castles and mansion houses. No laird worth his salt was without his great house. On a headland near Boddam Castle is another ruin, a burned-out building that was an elegant retreat for Lord Aberdeen, the laird of Haddo, who built it in 1840, twelve years before he became Prime Minister. Facing across the water to Buchan Ness Lighthouse, it was known as the Marine Villa. It

The ruins of Slains Castle stand in sinister silhouette on a grassy headland called the Bow north of Cruden Bay. For three and a quarter centuries the Earls of Erroll, chiefs of the Clan Hay, had their home here. The castle was rebuilt three times before it was finally abandoned. Perhaps it was a scene like this that gave Bram Stoker inspiration for his macabre works. The author spent many of his holidays at Cruden Bay and is said to have got his inspiration for *Dracula* while staying there.

later became the Earl's Lodge Hotel, but a number of years ago it was destroyed by fire, and the only link with its Victorian past is the inscription on the lintel, *Procul Negotiis Beatus*. Sir John Skelton, author of *The Crooked Meg*, who for some reason or other was known as 'Shirley', lived in a Georgian mansion on the other side of Boddam at Sandford Bay.

Long before you reach Boddam, the giant stack of Peterhead Power Station beckons you towards the Blue Toon, which stands above Sandford Bay. The North of Scotland Hydro-Electric Board laid out a viewpoint on a hill overlooking the station and awarded a £10,000 commission to an artist to build a sculpture on it. It is shaped like a pyramid, but its symbolism escapes me, and I can't help thinking that canny Buchan folk would have been better pleased if they had taken a leaf from Lord Aberdeen's book. He built granite seats for the villagers to sit on and, while they may have given them cold bottoms (I'm told there are wooden slats on them now), they were at least functional.

The view itself is not much to write home about. Apart from the seascapes, the eye grates over a panorama of RAF huts, the power station, which could never be described as a thing of beauty, and the scars of the Stirling Hill quarries. Peterhead grew out of Stirling Hill in the way that Aberdeen grew out of Rubislaw Hill. It was up there that the North-east's most exclusive railway ran – a train carrying convicts from Peterhead Prison to work on the Harbour of Refuge. They travelled in specially constructed coaches with no windows.

If there had been a seat on the viewpoint, it would have been a good place to contemplate what has been happening in this grey Buchan town in the past decade – and to ponder what the Brochers, fifteen miles to the north, have been thinking about. It must irritate the folk of Fraserburgh to know that Peterhead has always been called the 'capital' of Buchan, and that it has now become Europe's biggest white fish port. There has always been fierce rivalry between the two towns. The Buchan poet J.C. Milne, in his advice to a young dominie, warned:

> Hae a' the toons and coonties in ye heid,
> For, loshtie man, I doot there's naething waur
> Then mixin up the Broch and Peterheid!

It isn't that Fraserburgh hasn't been doing well; it's just that Peterhead has been doing better. Not only has it taken a slice of the oil cake, it has also cashed in on the problems created in Aberdeen by the National Dock Labour Scheme, with the result that Peterhead now handles more than twice the amount of fish going through the Aberdeen market.

Peterhead is the main landing port for a fleet of about 300 vessels. It tops the landings league with a figure of about £40m a year compared to Aberdeen's £23m. The scene in the Buchan port is reminiscent of the great days of the herring fishing. The place sings with life. The fishing is concentrated on the inner harbour; outside, in Peterhead Bay, the Harbour of Refuge accommodates drilling rigs, pipelaying barges and oil supply boats. The number of supply boat movements is about 60% of the Aberdeen figure. There are two major oil bases within the harbour, the biggest on reclaimed land on the south side of the bay.

History takes a back seat to oil in ancient Keith Inch, or

Caikinche, as it was once called. I went there in search of Petrie's Loup, but found my way blocked by a barrier at the entrance to the Aberdeen Service Company's premises. The company has oil service bases at both the North and South Bays. Petrie's Loup is said to be the most easterly point in Scotland, but Ron Morrison, who was acting as security guard at the North Base, argued that the furthest east point was Buchan Ness Lighthouse, because Keith Inch had been an island. He was correct in that, for in 1739 the narrow channel between Keith and the mainland was closed up with stones and rubbish, and a causeway made. It was called the Queenzie, pronounced Queenie, and people said they were going 'ower the Queenie'.

On the other hand, Buchan Ness is also separated from the mainland. Some people argue that the rock island on which the lighthouse stands was called Boddam, and people spoke about going 'ower the Botham'. Ron has a vested interest in claiming the honour for Boddam. He comes from there, working with his brother at the gill-net fishing, and had 'migrated' to Keith Inch to take a job as a security guard while a new boat was being made ready. The Castle Street on Keith Inch led to a castle built by George, fourth Earl Marischal, in the late sixteenth century, modelled on the Palace of the King of Denmark. There is also a Pleasure Walk at the entrance to the Service Company's base, but oil developments have made the name a mockery. Still, a trace of romance lingers on, for Ron Morrison thought that courting couples had strolled in the Pleasure Walk in the days when a castle stood there.

The Earl Marischal's castle went into sad decline. It eventually became a fish-house and a gunpowder magazine, and in 1813 it was pulled down. The stones, slates and wood were sold for £57 17s 1d. Its demolition was speeded up by the need for space for the whaling industry, which is still recalled in Peterhead's Heritage Trail by names like Blubber Jetty and Jaw-bone of a Whale. Peterhead, despite its oil and its fish, is conscious of its attractions as a holiday centre, and the Heritage Trail takes its visitors through centuries of history. In 1987, its

---

A cluster of cottages sits above the famous Bullers of Buchan on the Buchan coast. The Bullers were visited by Boswell and Johnson and Dr Johnson, who was awed by their 'dreadful elevation', explored them by boat.

quatercentenary year, it opened the new Dales Country Park. There is also a Dales industrial estate, given over almost exclusively to oil-related businesses, so in a sense oil and leisure live in harmony at Peterhead.

When Nigel Tranter mapped out the North-east in his series of *Queen's Scotland* books in 1972, he said of a village five miles north of Peterhead: 'Probably comparatively few know of the existence of St Fergus, or could place it on the map. It is one of those rural Buchan parishes, medium-sized, of 9000 acres, but with no very important or outstanding features'. In the sixteen years that have passed since that was written, Tranter's statement has become woefully out-of-date, for today the name St Fergus is known nationally, even internationally. Not the village itself, but the huge gas terminal that has mushroomed on its doorstep.

St Fergus is the most important terminal of its kind in the United Kingdom, handling as much as 67 million cubic metres of gas a day, which is the equivalent in energy terms of a train carrying 1300 tons of coal across the coastline every 20 minutes, night and day. It removes water and other impurities from the gas, monitors and controls its flow, and sends it out through an onshore distribution grid.

Work began at St Fergus in 1974 and the first gas flowed through the system in 1977. The terminal is set against a picturesque line of sand dunes and the aim was that it would blend in as far as possible with the surrounding countryside. The coastal dunes, disturbed by pipeline installation, were carefully restored with the help of environmentalists from Aberdeen University, in the same way that the landscape was protected at Cruden Bay, where oil comes ashore from the Forties field and vanishes into a Spaghetti Junction of underground pipelines on its way to the refinery at Grangemouth on the Firth of Forth.

But you cannot bury an installation spread over nearly 500 acres of land. The gas flares beckon from a long way off, and when you approach it the terminal dominates the flat Buchan landscape. It is even more obtrusive in the dark. I was travelling along the Peterhead-St Fergus road at five o'clock one black winter morning when the whole sky suddenly erupted in a blaze of light. It was startling, leaving me with a sense of shock, as if I had come on some science fiction city in the middle of nowhere. I was heading for Crimond to meet up with Jim Dunbar, warden of the RSPB reserve at the Loch of Strathbeg, to watch the dawn flight of greylag and pinkfeet geese.

The Loch of Strathbeg is the largest coastal dune lake in Britain and the original plan was to bring a pipeline through it to a terminal at the disused military airfield at Crimond, but there was so much opposition that the route was changed to St Fergus. Strathbeg is a vital staging post for wildfowl and it is only when you see thousands of geese rise at dawn with a great whoosh of wings that its importance comes home to you. 'A terrific roar, isn't it', said Jim. 'Coming in, it's the same thing. You can hear the wind ripping through them.'

I met Strathbeg's warden at Crimond Church, which has a large fish on top of its weather vane. There is an inscription on the clock face which says 'The Hour's Coming', but the impact of this sobering message is lessened by the fact that in Crimond the hour is a little late in coming or, at any rate, appears to be. The clock has a 61-minute hour, for the clockmaker unwittingly stuck an extra minute on the last five-minute section, so that it actually shows six minutes.

This is a fascinating area to explore. The Loch of Strathbeg was at one time open to the sea, but about 1720 a great sandstorm choked up the channel, turning it into an inland loch. The sandstorm also finally put an end to the royal burgh of Rattray, which the shifting sands had already all but obliterated by the mid-seventeenth century. Archaeologists from Aberdeen have been searching for Old Rattray, digging history out of the bare Buchan soil. Beyond the dunes is Rattray Head and the jagged reefs which gave rise to a couplet warning mariners of the dangers off the Buchan coast:

> Keep Mormond Hill a handspike high
> And Rattray Briggs ye'll ne'er come nigh.

My wanderings put me on the trail of another 'lost' village. The Fishtown of Corskelly was abandoned and replaced by St Combs at the end of the eighteenth century. It stood at one time halfway between Corsekelly Farm and a building, now turned into two cottages, called Boatlea. Sandy Davidson, the

Fish, fish, fish . . . the harvest of the sea comes ashore, ice-wrapped, at Peterhead fish market. Outside the market, fish lorries from far afield crowd the quays to load the catches.

Corsekelly farmer, dismisses suggestions that the village met the same fate as Old Rattray. He believes that the sea simply receded, leaving Corsekelly high and dry. When the field on which the Fishtown stood was ploughed for the first time in the 1950s, foundation stones were found on the site. It was also while ploughing that Mr Davidson came across shingle bars where there had once been tidemarks. Aberdeen court records show a dispute over land – 'a pleucht (plough) of the landis of Corskellie' – as far back as 1553.

St Combs, Inverallochy, Cairnbulg . . . the villages mark out the miles to Kinnaird Head and Fraserburgh, which the poet George Bruce, who was of Broch fisher stock, once described as 'the outermost edge of Buchan'. Fraserburgh has had more than one name. The parish was originally called Philorth, and the village on which the burgh was founded was called Faithlie – 'auld Faithlie toon, whaur trees are scrunts (stunted) for miles aroon' – but most people know it as the Broch. There are some who think it a slang word, but it is nothing of the sort, for Broch is old Scots for burgh.

Fraserburgh, which received a grant of £1m from the EEC

for a new slip and dredging port, is an important harbour for both fish and general cargo. When the North and South Harbours were deepened in 1887, it was said that the Broch was equipped to compete on equal terms with places like Aberdeen. A century later, it was chalking up in one year a total of nearly a quarter of a million tons handled from 365 ships. It has a busy, confident look about it. As J.C. Milne said of the sands and bents around the auld Faithlie toon, it wears 'a croon o' gowd and siller'.

It boasts the most unusual lighthouse on this or any other coast, for Kinnaird Head lighthouse is also a castle. Sir Alexander Fraser built the castle of Kinnaird Head in 1570, and in 1786 it was converted into the first lighthouse in Scotland. The central tower, with its 6ft. thick walls, is all that remains of the original building, but even with a lighthouse stuck on top it is still unmistakeably a castle. There were originally five floors, but only four remain, the fifth being removed to make way for the lantern chamber of the lighthouse.

Standing on the tip of Kinnaird's Head, the lighthouse marks the point where the Buchan coastline turns west along the Moray Firth, following the rocky Phingask shore to Sandhaven and Rosehearty. Rosehearty is one of the oldest seaports in Scotland and at one time strongly rivalled Fraserburgh as a herring fishing port. In the early years of the nineteenth century a fleet of forty-four fishing boats operated from the port. The herring fishing declined in Rosehearty towards the end of the nineteenth century, and when steam drifters look over there was a general move of both fishermen and fish curers to the Broch.

Here, as elsewhere on the Buchan coast, there is no shortage of ruined castles. There are two almost on each other's doorsteps a short distance south of the Sandhaven-Rosehearty road. One is the Castle of Pitsligo, the other the Castle of Pittullie. Both originally belonged to the Frasers of Philorth, the Pitsligo castle passing from the Frasers to the Forbeses of Druminnor in the fifteenth century. Alexander Forbes, the 4th and last Lord Pitsligo, hid in the Cave of Cowshaven, west of Rosehearty, when a fugitive after the 1745 Rebellion.

Further west is the Castle of Dundarg, a spectacular ruin on a clifftop north-east of New Aberdour. A private house now stands on the old site of Dun Dearg, the Red Fort, which is thought to go back to Pictish times. If you travel to Aberdour by Peathill, inland from Pitsligo and Pittullie, you pass a curious turret standing on a hillock, just off the road. It is, in fact, a decorative nineteenth-century dovecot, and when I passed it on my way to Aberdour workmen were laying out the ground around it as a picnic site.

Here, as you travel towards the Aberdeenshire-Banffshire border, the scenery begins to show a subtle change. The countryside is less bleak, less bare, and suddenly you find yourself among towering cliffs and undulating valleys, with whins and broom splashing the landscape with brilliant yellow. Roads lurch down towards the shore, where tiny communities huddle against the sea. Between Aberdour Bay and Gamrie Bay there are four villages on or near the coast, two in Aberdeenshire, the others in Banffshire, but all in Buchan, or, as the authorities will now have it, that peculiar hybrid known as the district of Banff-Buchan.

New Aberdour was founded in 1798, replacing the old kirkton down on the shore. There is a well on the east side of Aberdour beach known as St Drostan's Well. It is supposed to mark the spot where the Pictish saint landed when he brought Christianity to Buchan. There is also a memorial to Jane Whyte, the Grace Darling of Aberdour, who in October, 1844, helped to save the lives of fifteen members of the crew of the steamer *William Hope* when it was driven ashore in a gale. She plunged into the mountainous seas to get to a lifeline which the crew were trying to throw ashore. The memorial is on the gable of what was her cottage on the seashore.

The waves sweep on to the shore at Aberdour Bay and the pebbles shift and fall back, rumbling gently. There is an old weather rhyme about it:

> Fin the rumble comes fae Pittendrum
> The ill weather's a' t' cum,
> Fin the rumble comes fae Aberdour
> The ill weather's a' ower.

Pittendrum is near Sandhaven. The rumble is the noise of the waves on the pebbly shore, and local folk told me that this piece of weather lore is almost always accurate. There is another cryptic couplet about Cullykhan Bay:

The wide sweep of Aberdour Bay. In this part of Aberdeenshire the bare Buchan landscape gives way to valleys and ravines, with the great cliffs of Troup Head marking the boundary with Banffshire. Down on the shore of Aberdour Bay is St Drostan's Well.

Fin the win cums aff o' Cullykhan
It's neither gude for beast nor man.

The Tor of Troup, a mass of broken hills and wild glens regarded as a botanist's paradise, runs down to Cullykhan Bay, which is just west of Pennan Bay. Pennan, which dates from the seventeenth century, is the most westerly coastal village in Aberdeenshire. It shot to sudden fame when it became the setting for the Bill Forsyth film *Local Hero,* starring Burt Lancaster. The red telephone booth outside the hotel, which became a familiar 'prop' in the film, has settled back into more mundane use.

There is an old kirk on the main Macduff road which has a sign outside it saying, 'Church of Auchmedden – Pennan 1884', and indicating that there are still services there on the last Sunday of every month. This is where you turn off for Pennan, zig-zagging dizzily downhill and hoping that your car brakes are in good order. Suddenly, you are peering down the chimney-pots of red sandstone cottages built around the tiny harbour and its small pier. It is a bird's eye view of an incredibly picturesque corner of Pennan, and I doubt if there is anything to equal it on the Buchan coast.

Peter Anson, who surveyed all the east-coast fishing villages in 1929, had no hesitation in placing Pennan first in the scenic stakes. After a succession of grey villages from Berwickshire to Buchan, he was struck by the fact that at Pennan everything was red – 'red houses, red roads, red cliffs, red beach, red rocks'.

The harbour was built in 1845 and at one time a fleet of forty boats operated from it. A few small inshore fishing boats still sail from the harbour, which was recently strengthened. Like many others on the Buchan coast, the Pennan fishermen of a century ago had a profitable sideline – smuggling. The cliffs at Pennan, boasting names like Hell's Lum, which is 50ft. deep, the Devil's Kitchen and the Piper's Cave, had hiding holes that were made for contraband. The Quayman's Cave, a favourite haunt of smugglers, even had its own landing facilities and a staple in the roof where smugglers hung their lanterns.

It is said that there were once eagles on the cliffs to the east of Pennan. The story is probably true, for the white-tailed or sea eagle was often seen around our coasts last century. At any rate, the *New Statistical Account* believed the tale, for it reported that 'a pair of eagles regularly nested and brought forth their young in the rocks of Pennan'. It also mentioned a prophecy by Thomas the Rhymer that there would be an eagle in the crags as long as there was a Baird in Auchmedden. The Auchmedden estate changed hands, but one eagle returned to the cliffs in 1855 when the land was bought by Robert Baird. The legend came to an end when the local coastguards killed it.

Troup Head looms magnificently on the west side of Pennan, rising almost vertically 365ft. from the sea. To get to the headland you have to follow a farm road running north-east from the school on the outskirts of Gardenstown. The coast curves round from Troup Head to the east side of Gamrie Bay, where the village of Crovie hangs on to the land by its very fingertips. The gable end of almost every house faces on to the sea, the other end thrusting into the cliff face. They are, as a Gamrie schoolmaster, Alexander Whyte, put it nearly a century and a half ago, 'like a brood of young seafowl nestling with their heads under the dam'.

The picturesque village of Pennan on the borders of Aberdeenshire and Banffshire. With its brightly-painted, whitewashed cottages nudging the sea, it is popular with tourists and picnickers. Here it is seen from Cullykhan Bay. Pennan shot to fame when it became the setting for the Bill Forsyth film *Local Hero*.

The native 'seafowl' have fled their nest, for now all the residents are incomers, the majority having bought their cottages as holiday homes. Some, like Helmut Heiss and his wife Eva, come from as far away as Germany to spend their summers at Crovie. Helmut, who is a lecturer in music at Stuttgart, has become infatuated with all things Buchan, even its language. For the past ten years or so he has made a serious study of the Doric and has even given his sons – his 'twa loons', he calls them – Scottish names. One is called Buchan, the other Scotty, and he has named his small daughter Sonsie Dorica after the 'sonsy mistress' in a Charles Murray poem.

Neighbouring Gardenstown, which is linked to Crovie by a path round the shore, is said to be one of the richest fishing villages in Scotland. It is a close-knit community, with a strong family spirit and deeply-held religious beliefs. It was estimated a number of years ago that half the village's population belonged to the Plymouth Brethren, either 'Close' or 'Open'. Outside the Church of Scotland, as if to underline its role in

203

the community, a prominent sign proclaims its creed as 'Evangelical and Reform'. An illustration of how religion impinges on the everyday lives of its fishing folk is the sign at the harbour entrance proclaiming in huge letters, 'God is Love'.

Making my way into the village, I came upon a notice on the door of a large mission hall announcing that it was up for sale. Was this an indication that religious fever was on the wane in Gardenstown? The answer appeared to be 'no', for I was told that there were still six to eight different Brethren sects in the village.

Yet some things have changed. Today, it is highly unlikely that there would be a repeat of the case which came before Banff J.P. Court in 1954, when the Brethren movement was at its strongest. In February of that year two men were accused of committing a breach of the peace by cursing and swearing in the Garden Arms Hotel, Gardenstown. The words they were said to have used were 'damn' and 'bloody'. 'It was blasphemous language, uncommon in a village like Gardenstown, a very respectable village', said Norman Tennant, the hotel proprietor at the time. The charges against the men were found 'Not Proven after a trial'.

Gardenstown, founded in 1720 by Alexander Garden of Troup, drops down to the shore in a series of narrow terraces linked by winding braes. You would expect it to be traffic-free, for it simply isn't made for cars, but they chug up and down the hill as if it was all perfectly normal, squeezing past each other and parking on an impossibly narrow street leading to the Garden Arms Hotel, which was built in 1752. There is a notice pointing out that when you reach the other end of the street there is a turning place only, and no parking space. Trying to turn outside the hotel, I found myself muttering the sort of language that would have landed me in court thirty years ago.

This is where they must have coined the phrase about people living on top of each other. I could understand what Norman Tennant meant when he said, 'In Gardenstown your neighbours are so close at hand that you hardly need to raise your voice'. Some of the houses, like those outside the hotel, are built in tenement fashion, 'high-rise' before their time.

Alexander Whyte, the Gamrie schoolmaster, said that the ground rose so abruptly that a house of three storeys had them all on 'ground' floors. One entrance was at the front, another at the back, and a third at the end.

When Gardenstown was built, the rocks in Gamrie Bay had, as the dominie put it, 'retired a little, leaving room for the village of Gardenstown *and no more*'. I took my leave of the very respectable village of Gardenstown, climbing up what Mr Whyte had called 'a winding footpath like a staircase, on which few can venture, without fear and trembling . . .'

Chapter 12

The Mither Tongue

Although many old place-names still linger on in Buchan, some, like Futret Den, have disappeared. Futret Den, a farm south-west of Fraserburgh, has literally been wiped off the map, almost as if Buchan folk wanted to erase the memory of what happened there more than a century and a half ago. No one knows how the farm got its name, but it must have had something to do with ferrets – futrets. J.C. Milne wrote about a 'work-worn wife in Futtratsprot', but that was a fictional place. Futret Den was only too real.

In 1827, John Lovie, the farmer at Futret Den, was tried for the murder of a servant girl. Margaret Mackessar, who had become pregnant to him. The jury heard how he had discussed abortion with one of his men and had mentioned a 'white kind of poisonous stuff'. It was arsenic. Later, he went to a chemist and bought two packets of arsenic, saying he was troubled with rats. A few days later, Margaret ate her breakfast and began vomiting. By one o'clock, after calling for a drink of water, she was dead. When Lovie was told he exclaimed, 'My God!'

When her body was opened up a large quantity of arsenic was found in her stomach and intestines, and it was established that she was six months gone with the child. Lovie said he had bought some stuff to rub on his cows and heifers, and afterwards had washed the saucer and flung the contents on the dunghill. It was proved that his story was false. He then claimed he had never bought the poison, and that someone must have used his name. The jury retired and came back half an hour later with the astonishing verdict of 'Not Proven'.

The story of John Lovie's trial was told in a rhyme which, despite the verdict, pointed an accusing finger at the Futret Den farmer:

> He pishoned the mother with the child in her womb,
> He sent them both together to death's silent tomb,
> A most horrid murder, against him it stands,
> With the blood o' them both he embrued his hands.

Futret Den, according to one old report, was 'near Percy Horner, not far from Fingask (Phingask)'. There are three Percyhorner farms in the area, all run by the Birnie family. The name comes from *preas,* a small wood, and *horner,* the old Gaelic word for moss or bog, and it is interesting that Bill Birnie, who lives at South Percyhorner, thought that Futret Den was 'the rashie howe' near North Percyhorner. 'Rashie' means covered with rushes, and this is a stretch of ground bordering the road to Fraserburgh. There is, in fact, a suggestion that the North farm *was* Futret Den and that Lord Saltoun, who owned the land, changed the name because he thought it tasteless. It may be that he wanted to rid it of its murky past.

Bill's brother-in-law, Alastair Rannie, whose family have farmed Hillhead of Pittulie for four generations, going back to 1840, remembers Futret Den, but doesn't known how it got its name. He remembers seeing it on a map. Hillhead is only half a mile from Pittendrum, mentioned in the weather rhyme, and Bill looks across his fields to Futret Den. He knew the story of John Lovie, having read it in the *Black Kalendar of Aberdeen,* but he is in a minority, for Futret Den and its tragic story are all but forgotten. It is unlikely that many people know the virulent couplet that went the rounds in Buchan after the Lovie trial.

Malcolm Gillespie, the famous gauger, who built up a formidable reputation for tracking down smugglers, fell foul of the law himself when he forged a number of bills. He was tried on the same day that John Lovie appeared in court, found guilty, and sentenced to death. He was hanged 'looking down Marischal Street' (the usual phrase for describing an execution in Aberdeen), and many people were outraged that Lovie, clearly guilty of murder, had been freed, while Gillespie was sent to the scaffold. Some anonymous rhymer penned the lines:

> It took fourteen idiots and an ass
> To hang Gillespie and let Lovie pass.

These needle-sharp couplets were all the vogue a century ago, flourishing in the days when people used verse to tilt at poverty, humbug, and their betters, and very often at themselves. No one was more skilled at it than the folk of Buchan, whose dry wit put life into a kind of uneasy

perspective. From the farm touns and villages came a
generation of untutored rhymesters who licked the points of
their pencils and hit out at the inequalities of life. If they had
nothing good to say about the farmers, what they said about
farmers' wives was even less complimentary:

> Thin brose and nae breid,
> Oh, God, gin she were deid!

These old jingles are only a step away from the protest
poetry of the bothy ballad era. Gavin Greig and the Rev. James
B. Duncan, the great collectors of North-east ballads, included
in their folksong collection a number of verses which were
never meant to be sung; for instance, the 'brose and breid'
couplet has an affinity with a plaintive two-liner:

> Our feet's cauld, our sheen's thin,
> Gie's a piece an' lat's rin.

Popular rhymes have been virtually ignored in the literature
of the North-east, but a token nod of the head came in 1976
when Grampian Regional Council included a selection in *Poetry
in Northeast Scotland* – 'poetry of a very rudimentary kind', said
the introductory note. They ranged from 'The Wee Folk's
Curse' to the cryptic:

> Towie Barclay of the glen,
> Happy to the maids, but never to the men.

The Gavin Greig of popular rhyme was the Rev. Walter
Gregor, of Pitsligo, who included 'countings-out' in his *Folk-lore
of the North-east of Scotland*. This children's elimination game
took the form of gibberish verse, such as this one from
Fraserburgh:

> Eenrie, twaarie, tickerie, teven,
> Allaby, crockeyry, ten, or elaiven,
> Peen, pan, fusky dam.
> Wheedlum, whadlum, twenty-one.

Some of the old rhymes sniped at neighbouring
communities. Inter-town rivalry is apparent in the names they

thought up for each other . . . the dub-skelpers o' Aul' Deer,
the Maisy Mackers o' Pennan, the Moggan-hose o' Pittulie, and
the Holy Brochers. The following rhyme is interesting in its use
of 'broch' in the name Fraserburgh:

> Aberdeen will be a green
> An Banff a borough's toon,
> But Fraserbroch 'll be a broch
> When a' the brochs is deen.

The old rhymes gradually disappered, but the folksongs
were kept alive, especially in Buchan. Gavin Greig said that
more of our native traditional minstrelsy survived in Buchan
than in any other equal area in Britain. Work is now going
ahead on *The Greig-Duncan Folk Song Collection,* a massively
ambitious project which will bring together in eight volumes
the folksongs collected by Gavin Greig and the Rev. James
Duncan. The late Patrick Shuldham-Shaw, who was first editor
of the collection, estimated that it ran to some 3500 texts and
3300 tunes. He described it as Scotland's biggest and finest
manuscript collection of folksong. The third volume, edited by
Emily B. Lyle and Peter A. Hale, has been published.

Greig said that country life and interests bulked largely in
the folksong of Buchan, but added that there were times when
'very prosaic achievements' became a matter for song. He gave
as an example 'The Buchan Turnpike':

> 'Twas in the year auchteen hun'er an' aucht
> A road thro' Buchan was made straucht,
> When mony a Hielan' lad o' maucht
> Cam' owre the Buchan border.
>
> 'Twixt Peterheid and Banff's aul' toon,
> It twines the knowes an' hollows roon,
> Ye scarce can tell its ups fae doon,
> It's levelled in sic order.

The achievement was not as prosaic as Greig made out, for
the coming of turnpikes brought a revolutionary improvement
in rural transport. The Turnpike Act became law in 1795, and
by 1811 more than 300 miles of turnpike had been laid in
Aberdeenshire. Tolls and toll shares were put up for roup and

'I took a turn at Yokieshill, the teuchest (toughest) place I e'er gaed till'. This is how an old ballad saw the farm of Yokieshill, near Longside. It was one of a number of Aberdeenshire farms immortalised in bothy ballad lore.

toll rates were fixed. On August 15, 1810, as work on the Buchan turnpike speeded up, the *Aberdeen Journal* announced a roup of 'toll duties at the New Pitsligo Bar, on the line of the Turnpike Road from Peterhead towards Banff, passing thro' the village of Pitsligo'. The roup was held in the Pitsligo Arms Inn and the announcement stated: 'The whole line from Peterhead to Banff being now nearly compleated the intercourse on the road will be materially increased, so as to render the above Bar an object worthy the attention of Tollkeepeers'.

There are no toll-bars in sleepy New Pitsligo today, and nothing to remind you of the coming of the turnpike – nothing, that is, except the high road. Dr J.B. Pratt described the whole of the turnpike as 'the high road', but in New Pitsligo there is actually a high road and a low road. 'The village', wrote Dr Pratt, 'is composed of the high and the low streets – the Peterhead and Banff Turnpike being carried through the former.'

Nearly two centuries after completion of the road, 'The

'Buchan Turnpike' holds up a mirror to the past. Only the cold print of official documents recorded the building of the Peterhead-Banff road, but 'The Buchan Turnpike' puts flesh on the bureaucratic bones, telling how 'Hielan' chiels' came to Buchan to work on the road, how they 'bored the steens wi' jumpin' dreels', sweated to push the turnpike 'a bittie forder', and occassionally got themselves into hot water with the locals.

Another rhyme, 'Boyndlie Road', deals with the building of the turnpike road which runs from Fraserburgh to Aberdour and Tyrie and links up with the Buchan road. This is the road that passes Futret Den and goes on through Ardlaw, bringing thoughts of Donald Adie and Sandy Ritchie and all the others who featured in the bothy ballad, 'The Ardlaw Crew'. One of the Ardlaw crew was Maggie Simpson, the kitchen maid, who made the kail. 'I can plainly tell you', said the author, 'she's nae jist very takin',' which meant she wasn't very attractive. Gavin Greig was unhappy about this jibe at poor Maggie and changed the last two lines to read 'she's aften busy bakin'.'

The farm of Mid Ardlaw stands at a junction partly formed by a long straight road coming west from Ford a Fowrie, a farm near the main Fraserburgh-Mintlaw road. It is just over a mile from Fyoordies, as they call it, to Memsie, where the Buchan poet John C. Milne was born. Nearby is the school he went to, half-hidden by the Memsie Cairn. Looking at this huge burial mound, 15ft high and 60ft in circumference, I couldn't help wondering, like Milne, why 'sic a muckle heap o' stanes could ever come to be'. This, at any rate, was the route that Milne took on his way to school, 'rinnin doon te Memsie' on what was known as the Meer or Muir road.

It was in this corner of 'yon braid Buchan lan'' that John Milne found the inspiration for much of his poetry, drawing on memories of his childhood, remembering the 'Tyrie troot and gweed fresh air', the taste of chappit-tatties, stovies and yavel broth (second day's broth), and seeing the gulls, the 'hungry sea-maws', wheeling and crying over the furrows that ran 'straucht and clean fae Tyrie burn te Pickerstane'.

I often wondered if Milne's characters were plucked from real life. Was there really a 'teem (empty), lang-leggit glaiket (foolish) loon' called Jamie Broon, who became an LL.D., or a 'girnie (bad-tempered) gamie' with 'futtrat tails and sic like trock', or a Geordie Grant o' Memsie Cairns, who was always 'sair hudden doon wi' wife and bairns'? In 'O for Friday nicht!' there are lines which read:

> Hing in noo, Jean Calder!
> You tee, Muggsie Wugs!
> Loshtie me, Bill Boddie!
> Fan did ye wash yer lugs?

Bill Boddie was a lecturer at Aberdeen Training College, where J.C. Milne was a lecturer in Methods, and Margaret Milne told me that he was delighted to find himself in a poem by her father. Margaret had more than a passing acquaintance with Muggsie Wugs – that was the pet name her father gave her. Then there was Cadger Lil. John Milne's widow, Mrs Jeannie Milne, now in her nineties, says that Cadger Lil was a fishwife who came round every week with a 'cairtie' when they were living at Pikerstone.

There are still unpublished poems by Milne tucked away in a drawer in the house at Inverurie where Mrs Milne and her daughter now live. He often wrote poems to people instead of letters, or scribbled 'thank you' notes in verse. When Margaret was training to be a teacher he sent her some money and with it a note which said:

> Naething's waur than stark starvation,
> So my Granny used to say,
> Find enclosed a sma' donation
> Jist tae keep the wolf at bay.

On another occasion, when she had just started teaching and was finding life difficult, he dashed off this piece of advice:

> Sursum corda, *
> Haud yer heid heicht,
> Tail up,
> Yer nae deid yet!

Sursum corda – Lift up your heart

Milne, a respected educationist, wrote about 'skweels', dominies, directors and inspectors, and when he took to the hills (he climbed them with the writer Nan Shepherd and his daughter Margaret) he drew sharp word-pictures of the great peaks of the Cairngorms – 'there they were like brithers, Ben Macdhui, Carn Toul, Braeriach – man, a sicht to sair the sowl!' But he never lost his links with his 'Orra Loon' days. When he was given a gift of teuchats' (lapwings') eggs, his letter of thanks was written in verse. It ended:

> Noo fare-ye-weel. There's nae a chiel
> In a' the country toon
> Mair weel-content wi' fut ye've sent
> Than
>   Yours,
>   'The Orra Loon.'

Flora Garry, born three years after John Milne, came from the other side of Mormond Hill, where there are said to be subtle differences in the Buchan dialect. She was born at the Mains of Auchmunziel, where she looked across the raw Buchan landscape to Bennygoak, the Hill of the Cuckoo:

> It was jist a skelp* o the muckle furth,
> A sklyter* o roch grun,
> Fin granfadder's fadder bruke it in
> Fae the hedder and the funn.*
> Granfadder sklatit* barn an byre,
> Brocht water to the closs,
> Pat fail-dykes* ben the bare brae face,
> An a cairt road tull the moss.

skelp – large area; *sklyter* – expanse; *funn* – whin; *sklatit* – slated; *fail-dykes* low turf walls.

You can almost *hear* the Buchan tongue in these lines. The late Dr Cuthbert Graham, in a note to Flora Garry's 'Bennygoak', said that she wrote straight out of childhood memory of life in a Buchan 'ferm toon'. She recreated with fidelity a whole way of life. Certainly, her poetry comes very close to the authentic voice of Buchan. Her use of the words 'hedder' and 'fadder' and 'granfadder' takes us back seventy years to the time when a Lonmay minister, the Rev. James Forrest, was writing about the Buchan dialect in *The Book of Buchan*, giving thought to how 'father' had become 'fadr' and 'close' had become 'closs'. Even then, Buchan words were under the microscope.

Dr Forrest also looked at why *poison* was pronounced puzhin (he obviously hadn't heard about John Lovie's servant being 'pishoned') and whether people still used phrases like 'Fu's a' wi' ye?' The answer to that greeting, incidentally, was 'Oh! we're a' geylies and braulies'. People still use the word 'gey', meaning 'very', but 'braw', meaning 'good' has slipped into disuse.

The Lomnay minister put forward a curious theory on *why* Buchan people speak as they do. He thought that they preferred clearer vowels 'owing to their windswept fields, as well as from their nature'. He added that they would 'consider any great manipulation of the lips as a sign of affectation, and superfluous'. There stands the canny, close-mouthed Buchaner!

In the seven decades since the Rev. Dr Forrest put pen to paper, students of the Buchan dialect have scarcely drawn breath. The Buchan tongue has been dismissed as irrelevant; it has been buried, exhumed, scrutinised and analysed almost to the point of exhaustion. J. Derrick McClure, writing on dialect speech in *The Grampian Book* in 1987, said that Doric and its associated literature were still capable of arousing enormous interest and affection among the middle-aged and elderly, but pointed out that if the interest was not passed on to the younger generation a cultural heritage would be irretrievably lost. The task, he added, was urgent.

Dr Forrest's, 'geylies and braulies' reminded me of 'geets and gibbles'. Dr David Murison, who spent a lifetime editing the *Scottish National Dictionary* before retiring to Fraserburgh, once told the story of how a railway porter at a Buchan station saw a mother with two youngsters trying to board a train and, grabbing her luggage, cried 'Tak' ye the geets an' I'll tak' the gibbles'. The 'geets' were the children, the 'gibbles' the bags. Geets, gibbles, geylies, braulies . . . they have all gone.

Back in the 1920s, a group of Aberdeenshire schoolmasters came up with a piece of research showing that one-third of the Buchan vocabulary had been lost since their young days. David Murison thinks that another third has disappeared in his lifetime. It is not too difficult to work out how long it might be before the final third goes. Nevertheless, he believes that we should fight to preserve the Buchan tongue – by speaking it. Words, he says, are crystallised history.

This century has produced a rich harvest of poets and prose writers in Buchan, building on the heritage of the nineteenth century which gave us *Johnny Gibb of Gushetneuk*. William Alexander's masterpiece is still, like Johnny Gibb's corn, 'gweed, weel-colour't stuff', although I have a sneaking sympathy for John R. Allan's view that some parts of it are tiresome now. Still, it is a dialect classic.

It would be nice to think that the old traditions will be carried into the next century, but the lines are thinning. Gavin Greig, who wrote poetry and prose fiction (his *Logie o' Buchan* has been reprinted in recent years), died in 1914. His epitaph will be the monumental collection of folksongs now being prepared. Patrick Shuldham-Shaw believed it would give the world the opportunity of studying and getting to know the richness of the folksong tradition in the North-east, but whether or not it will be used to teach future generations something about their own culture remains to be seen.

John R. Allan is gone, leaving wistful memories of the big byre at Dungair, the bothies with their kists, Sunday suits, shirts and long woollen drawers hung from nails on the wall, and the sights and sounds of 'that spare but not unlovely land' where he grew up. His *Farmer's Boy* was no less a classic, and his *North-East Lowlands of Scotland* drew a warm and affectionate picture of the North-east neuk, its industry, its pastimes and its people. The past, he said, was as real to him as the present.

W.P. Milne, a Longside man, who became Professor of Mathematics at Leeds University and was president of the Buchan Club for eight years, offered a toothsome taste of Doric in *Eppie Elrick,* published in 1956. The Rev. David Ogston, one of a new generation of North-east writers, took his native tongue a step further in *White Stone Country*, a memory of his Buchan boyhood, written completely in Doric.

John Reid, better known as David Toulmin, has been writing all his life, but it was only in 1972 that his first collection of short stories, *Hard Shining Corn,* was published. Born at Rathen in 1913, he spent most of his working life as a farm servant, and it is into this storehouse of experience that he has dipped for most of his works. He tells me, without great conviction, that his writing days are over. His last book was called *The Clyack Sheaf* – a clyack sheaf is the last bound sheaf, but not the end of the harvest – which hinted at more to come, and when I met him in 1988 he was working on another book. Its title, he said with a smile, was *Yavel Broth* – second day's broth.

One of the chapters in *The Clyack Sheaf* was entitled 'Rear Mirror Look at the Past'. It told how he had motored back some fifty-six years in time to the first farm he worked on in 1927. It drew an amusing picture of young John Reid, only fourteen years old, about to enjoy the pleasures of a clay pipe:

> I began work at Greystones on a Saturday, the day after I left school on my fourteenth birthday, and it was for a whole day because there were no half-day holidays then. My first job was picking sprouts off the tatties in a sod pit behind the steading, on a site now occupied by a huge sprawling implement shed, where I would have been under a roof had it then existed. I had a clay pipe in my pocket and a little tobacco but I was afraid to light up until the farmer did so.
>
> 'Fut wye are ye nae smokin' yer pipe, laddie?' he enquiried.
>
> 'Oh, I wis wytin or ee lichtit your een', I offered as explanation.
>
> 'Weel, laddie ye'll hae a lang time tae wyte, 'cause I dinna smoke. But licht yer pipe man. I dinna mind ye haein' a smoke sae lang as ye hae a lid on yer pipe, an' it's less dangerous aboot the steadin' than smokin' fags.'

There were no clay pipes when I spent my holidays as a youngster at Shevado, on the Brucklay estate near Maud. I always thought of that small Buchan village as a kind of film set for a Wild West movie. It wasn't much of a place, a shanty-town, where cattle bellowed and kicked up dust on the weekly mart day. Jack Webster, a journalist I worked with many years ago on the Aberdeen *Evening Express*, admits that some uncharitable people regard it as the last place on God's earth, but his reply to that is that the good Lord kept the best till last.

If Maud is a Buchan backwater, Jack made it less so when he published *A Grain of Truth*, an autobiography in which he wrote with a nostalgic ardour about his native village. Its sequel, *Another Grain of Truth,* was published in 1988. A great-grandson of Gavin Greig, he recalled the time in 1954 when New Deer staged a diamond jubilee performance of Greig's *Mains's Wooin'*, with Nellie Metcalfe as the chairwoman. Nellie, who had been leading lady at the first performance of *Mains's*

Wooin' sixty years earlier, was the wife of Archie Campbell, the farmer of Auchmunziel, and mother of Flora Garry.

This corner of Buchan comes alive in *A Grain of Truth* . . . the feein' markets, Lizzie Allan's sweetie shoppie, the hairst (harvest) and the meal-and-ale, Aikey Fair, and the memory of wartime evacuees from Glasgow arriving in Maud. 'Goad, wha' a dump!' said one youngster. Jack's book led to two BBC documentary films about his beloved Maud, one dealing with the sale of his family's farm at Honeyneuk, the other recalling his childhood in the village.

One of the characters who strides out larger than life from *A Grain of Truth* is Jack's father, John Webster, the local auctioneer, a man who, according to his son, 'embodied a talent for rural vulgarity'. He was, for instance, apt to say that something hard was 'as hard as Hinnerson's erse'. I never knew, until I read Jack's book, that Henderson was a North-east name for the Devil. John Webster reminded me of the Maud auctioneer in David Ogston's *White Stone Country*, who dominated the auction scene with 'his ain tongue and a timmer (timber) haimmer in his nieve (fist)'. Perhaps they were one and the same person.

Over in Peterhead, there is a confusion of Buchans. Peter Buchan, born in Peterhead in 1790, was a well-known ballad collector, an eccentric and controversial figure, who lived more than a century before Gavin Greig began his work. Greig called him the prince of ballad collectors. Buchan, whose first collection of ballads appeared in 1819, was also a printer and the author of *The Annals of Peterhead*. But it is his 1980s namesake who claims attention today – the Peter Buchan who wrote:

Altho' yer name's nae Buchan, if ye come fae Peterheid,
It's surely mair gin likely ye've a drap o' Buchan bleed,
For the Buchans thro' the centuries, for better or for waur (worse),
Hae mairrit into ither tribes till gweed kens fit ye are.

This Peter Buchan lives at Mount Pleasant (the name he gave to his book of poetry) and he is in no doubt about who or what he is. He lives in a house overlooking Peterhead Harbour and writes mostly about the sea, which sets him a little apart from

Jim Duncan, who was the driving force behind the founding of the Buchan Heritage Society. A former navy lieutenant, he returned to Aberdeenshire in 1976 to discover that the Buchan he had known had all but vanished.

other Buchan poets, who have sought their inspiration from the land. He has said that there is more to Buchan than the 'braid Buchan lan'. 'Buchan athoot the sea is jist like tatties athoot saut!' he declared in the Buchan Heritage Society's magazine, *Heirskip*, which he has edited for the past two years. He is a bit like John Webster, not afraid to call a spade a spade, full of rough humour, steering his audiences through his poems in the unerring way that he guided vessels into Peterhead Harbour when he was assistant traffic controller.

The previous editor of *Heirskip* was Jim Duncan, a former navy lieutenant, who was the driving force behind the setting up of the Heritage Society. Back in 1937, Jim worked on his father's farm at Faddenhill before going off to see the world. When he returned in 1976 he found that the Buchan he had known in his youth had all but vanished. He rediscovered it in the poetry of J.C. Milne and Flora Garry, and in David

Toulmin's *Straw Into Gold,* and he set out to take Buchan's heritage into the future.

I remember Jim telling me of a Buchan schoolmaster who said he couldn't get jobs for his pupils by reading J.C. Milne's poetry to them. This was the sort of attitude he had to overcome, and he succeeded, for today, with its meetings, concerts and annual Buchan Heritage Festival at Strichen, the society is a strong arm in defence of Buchan's culture. Jim Duncan believes, however, that concern for the Buchan language should not be confined to the Doric; there is, he says, the language of music – Buchan fiddle music, to be precise.

He is married to Ivory, the daughter of James Fowlie Dickie, the great Buchan fiddler. Dickie, who was born at Cartlehaugh, Old Deer, in 1886, taught him to play the fiddle as a child. In a sleeve note to a cassette called 'The Dickie Style', Jim recalled Gavin Greig's remark that if any one thing of our Scots heritage was worth preserving for all time, it was our music. Dickie was a close friend of Scott Skinner, who once wrote a letter addressed to 'Mr Dickie, Slater and up-and-coming Scottish violinist, freen of Scott Skinner, New Deer'. In it, he said of Dickie, 'You are one of Nature's gentlemen'.

So the fiddles dirl and dance at Heritage Society concerts, reaffirming a musical tradition that stretches back over the years and embraces names like John Murdoch Henderson, the great collector of Scots Traditional music, William Hardie, the fiddler and composer from Methlick, Charles Sutherland, from Fraserburgh, a pupil of Scott Skinner, and George Wright, who was taught by Peter Milne, of Tarland.

Some won themselves flamboyant titles like the Methlick Wonder, which was how the violinist Charles Hardie was described, or Joseph Sim, the Wonderful Boy of New Byth, who was a powerful athlete as well as a talented fiddler. Sim was related to Francis Jamieson, better known as Fruncie Markiss, a first-class cellist, who lived in an old thatched house with his living quarters at one end and a 'sheltie' and cow at the other. There is a marvellous picture of Fruncie sitting outside his house with his 'cello between his legs, wearing a tammy and tackety boots.

Fruncie had twin talents, for he was an expert on the 'oxter pipes' as well as the cello. Another musician who had two strings to his bow was James Dickie's brother, John, who played the penny whistle as well as the fiddle. His mantle has been taken over by Alex Green, who played Dickie's 'fussel' at the festival in Aberdeen.

Some, like William Christie, of Cuminestown, who published a collection of reels in 1820, were also dancing masters. Jim Duncan has always been anxious to see Buchan 'get back to the dancing again'. He remembers the days of 'Dancie' Craighead, a New Deer postman, who was also a dancing master, charging sixpence a night for his lessons. There were others like 'Dancie' Scott, who featured in a rhyme called 'Dubbieneuk'.

> In the cauld month o' December
> When aneath a roof we jouk (bow),
> Dancie Scott's ta'en up a dancing
> At a place called Dubbieneuk
>
> There came the gardners up frae Florth
> And lads frae Catchiebrae,
> There came a souter frae Hairstane
> An lassies frae Pitblae.

When Jim Duncan lived at Mains of Cairncrake, near Cuminestown (he moved later to Old Meldrum), I went with him on a kind of cultural tour of the area. We stopped at Netherton of Delgaty, where James Cowie, the Cuminestown artist, was born, we travelled along the Idoch valley, and we passed the Barnyards of Delgaty, which looked little like the farm of the bothy ballad, whose horses were 'naething but skin and bone'.

Our travels took us to the home of John M. Henderson and up to the schoolhouse where Gavin Greig taught. We went to the Mains of Auchmunziel, Flora Garry's birthplace, and to the kirkyard where Gavin Greig is buried. Nearby is the grave of James Dickie, with the words carved out on the stone, 'One of Nature's gentlemen'. Up there, on the Hill of Culsh, looking out over the fertile lands of Buchan, I thought that if the Lord came down and had a 'dauner roon' (wander round)', as J.C. Milne has suggested in one of his poems, he would find that some things had remained unchanged.

Further Reading

Alexander, Sir Henry – *The Cairngorms* (Scottish Moutaineering Trust 1968)

Alexander, William – *Johnny Gibb of Gushetneuk* (Douglas 1912)

Allan, John R. – *The North-east Lowlands of Scotland* (Hale 1952)

Clark, Ronald W. – *Balmoral* (Thames and Hudson 1981)

Garry, Flora – *Bennygoak* (Akros 1974)

Gibbon, Lewis Grassic – *A Scots Hairst* (Hutchinson 1967)

Gibson, Colin – *Highland Deerstalker* (Culross 1958)

Graham, Cuthbert – *Portrait of Aberdeen and Deeside* (Hale 1972)

Keith, Alexander – *A Thousand Years of Aberdeen* (Aberdeen University Press 1972)

Milne, John C. – *Poems* (Aberdeen University Press 1963)

Murray, Charles – *Hamewith* (AUP 1979)

Pratt, John B. – *Buchan* (Heritage Press 1978)

Toulmin, David – *The Clyack Sheaf* (AUP 1986)

Tranter, Nigel – *The Queen's Scotland* (Hodder and Stoughton 1972)

Victoria, Queen – *Leaves from the Journal of Our Life in the Highlands* (Smith, Elder 1870)

Webster, Jack – *A Grain of Truth* (Paul Harris 1981)

Whittle, Tyler – *Victoria and Albert at Home* (Routledge and Kegan Paul 1981)

Wyness, Fenton – *City by the Grey North Sea: Aberdeen* (A.P. Reid 1965)

Wyness, Fenton – *Royal Valley: The Story of the Aberdeenshire Dee* (Reid 1968)

Index